UNLEVEL PLAYING FIELDS
UNDERSTANDING WAGE INEQUALITY
AND DISCRIMINATION
FOURTH EDITION

UNLEVEL PLAYING FIELDS

UNDERSTANDING WAGE INEQUALITY AND DISCRIMINATION

FOURTH EDITION

Randy Albelda

Robert Drago

Economic Affairs Bureau, Inc.
Publisher of *Dollars & Sense*
Boston, Massachusetts

UNLEVEL PLAYING FIELDS:
UNDERSTANDING WAGE INEQUALITY AND DISCRIMINATION
FOURTH EDITION

Randy Albelda and Robert Drago

ISBN: 978-1-939402-05-9

Economic Affairs Bureau, Inc., publishes *Dollars & Sense* magazine, which explains the workings of the U.S. and global economies and provides progressive perspectives on current economic affairs. It is edited and produced by a collective of economists, journalists, and activists who are committed to social justice and economic democracy.

Economic Affairs Bureau, Inc., also publishes the following books: *Real World Macro*, *Real World Micro*, *The Wealth Inequality Reader*, *Current Economic Issues*, *Real World Globalization*, *Labor and the Global Economy*, *Real World Labor*, *Real World Latin America*, *Real World Banking and Finance*, *Introduction to Political Economy*, *The Economics of the Environment*, *Striking a Balance*, and *The Economic Crisis Reader*.

For subscription or ordering information, contact:

Dollars & Sense
One Milk Street, 5th floor
Boston, MA 02109

Phone: (617) 447-2177
Fax: (617) 447-2179
E-mail: dollars@dollarsandsense.org
Website: www.dollarsandsense.org

Cover design by Chris Sturr
Layout by Chris Sturr
Cover photo by Immanuel Giel (public domain; available at Wikimedia Commons).

For Rick Edwards

CONTENTS

LIST OF TABLES AND FIGURES

TABLES

FIGURES

PREFACE

Labor markets in the United States have experienced dramatic shifts since the 1950s. One of the most striking shifts has been the entrance of white women into the paid labor force. In 1954, 33.3% of all white women were in the labor force, a figure that rose to 58.0% by 2011. An equally striking change occurred for black workers (both men and women), but of a different nature: the type of work performed. Since the 1950s, the percentage of black men and women working in agriculture and private households has radically changed. In 1950, 41% of all black women were working in the homes of white Americans as domestics; today, less than 1% are. In 1950, 25% of all black men worked in agriculture. Today, less than 1% do.[1] White men have seen noteworthy changes in their jobs and job prospects as well. In addition to the integration of women and blacks into the manufacturing and non-domestic service sectors, white men have seen the striking disappearance of many blue-collar manufacturing jobs, jobs which were traditionally available to white men who had not attended college.

These changes have caused the experiences of working women and black men to look increasingly similar to those of white male workers. One might expect these similar experiences to bring about more equality among workers, and perhaps even a shared appreciation of race and gender differences. However, wage differences between white men and everyone else persist, unemployment rates of blacks are twice that of whites, women are still concentrated in low-paying "female" jobs, and minorities and women argue there is a "glass ceiling" at the upper rungs of the job ladder. This new competition in the face of declining economic opportunities has resulted in a backlash against labor market policies such as affirmative action, which attempt to integrate women and blacks into managerial positions.

What exactly is going on? Is the playing field for jobs and wages level or not? Do white men really have an advantage in the labor market: getting jobs more easily, getting better pay, and getting promotions? Are women and people of color not as well qualified or motivated as their white male competitors? Should they stop "whining" and playing the race or gender "card" when they can't get ahead? In short, do women and blacks face labor market discrimination? If the answer is yes, what can be done about it? If the answer is no, what explains the large and persistent wage, unemployment, and job differences?

Answering these questions is not easy. Because most people define themselves as either men or women, discussions of gender issues involve most everyone. The same can be said about race. While most of the U.S. population is white, no one is untouched by the historic

ntemporary color lines in this country. No one is a neutral spectator. To complicate
s further, social scientists offer conflicting answers to these questions depending on their
of the world. Answers to these questions, however, are crucially important. They shape
nment and corporate policies, and they shape the way that we think about people—in
homes, in our neighborhoods, in our workplaces, and in our country.

Recently, governmental, corporate, and university policies regarding race and gender have
ome a flashpoint in our society, particularly given the 2008 election of America's first black
:sident, and debates over these policies are often implicitly or explicitly shaped by the discipline
economics. While economists have produced some very good books on the topic for use by
:nior undergraduates both inside and outside the field of economics, they have been surprisingly
quiet in terms of books that work for the average undergraduate, who has no prior knowledge of
economics or how economists treat discrimination. That's why we wrote this book.

This book fills a large gap, but it is incomplete. The text deals narrowly with women and
blacks, with some added content on Hispanics in this edition. But there are other sources
of difference that we hope teachers will also focus on as they explore this arena. The book is
short enough to allow teachers to supplement it with additional texts, student presentations,
articles, movies, guest speakers, and so forth. As the reader will quickly see, history in general
and groups other than heterosexual black and white Americans are largely, though not entirely,
neglected. There is much wonderful work by scholars like Teresa Amott, Lee Badgett, Nancy
Folbre, Eugene Genovese, Claudia Goldin, Alice Kessler-Harris, Patrick Mason, and Julie
Matthaei (all of whom are cited later in this book) that fills these gaps, and we hope that people
will read further on the topic.

No book is ever published without the help and support of friends, family, and colleagues.
This book is no exception. We wish to thank our professors and fellow graduate students at
the economics department, University of Massachusetts-Amherst, where we learned much
of what we know about neoclassical economics and political economy. They can take a fair
amount of the praise—or blame—for setting us on the road that ultimately led to *Unlevel
Playing Fields*. In addition, we are grateful to the hundreds of students at the University of
Wisconsin-Milwaukee who struggled through early drafts of the book. Their insights and
opinions improved the final product enormously, and we hope their education was not
damaged too severely by our learning process. We appreciate the small grant for research
support from the University of Massachusetts-Boston, and many thanks to the following
people for their advice (although not always taken) at various stages: Jeanne Alexander,
Margo Anderson, Lee Badgett, Bob Cherry, Bisi Oliana Dean, Eva Drago, Sophia Drago,
Rick Edwards, Nancy Folbre, Herbert Gintis, Daniel Hamermesh, John Heywood, Mary
King, June Lapidus, Meg Lewis, Tiffany Manuel, Elaine McCrate, Richard Perlman, Peter
Philips, Charles Sackrey, Ronnie Steinberg, Mary Stevenson, Lucille Sutton, Andres Torres,
Frank Wilson, and Jan Yoder.

Without *Dollars & Sense*, this book would have died after its first edition. We appreciate
the staff's willingness to continue printing the book and facilitating each update. In particular,
Tami Friedman, Chris Sturr, Linda Pinkow, and Alejandro Reuss have been instrumental
in various editions. We also thank *Dollars & Sense* interns Aaron Markiewitz, Hannah
Nussbaum, Aarth Saraph, and Ana Villar for their work on this fourth edition.

Randy Albelda and Robert Drago

ENDNOTE

[1] Labor force participation data are from "Economic Report of the President," Washington, D.C.: Government Printing Office, 2001. Figure on black women's employment in 1950 comes from Randy Albelda, "'Nice Work If You Can Get It: Segmentation of White and Black Women Workers in the Post WWII Period," *Review of Radical Political Economics* 17(3), 1985. Figure on black men's employment in 1950 is from Michael Reich, *Racial Economic Inequality: A Political Economic Analysis*, Princeton, NJ: Princeton University Press, 1981. Data on black men's employment in 2009 are from U.S. Bureau of Labor Statistics, "Employment and Earnings," October 2009. Data on black women's employment in private households from the September 2009 CPS, accessed with the U.S. Census data ferrett, November 6, 2009. Data on white women's labor-force participation in 2011 from "Women in the Labor Force: A Databook," Bureau of Labor Statistics (BLS), Report 1040, February 2013 (bls.gov).

ABOUT THE AUTHORS

RANDY ALBELDA is Professor of Economics and Senior Research Associate at the Center for Social Policy at the University of Massachusetts at Boston. She has served as a Vice President of the International Association for Feminist Economics (IAFFE) and is a *Dollars & Sense* Associate. Her research and teaching focus on poverty, women's economic status, welfare reform, income inequality, and state and local finance. In addition to many articles and book chapters, she is the author of *Economics and Feminism: Disturbances in the Field* (Twayne Publishers, 1997), co-author of *Glass Ceilings and Bottomless Pits: Women's Work, Women's Poverty* (with Chris Tilly, South End Press, 1997), and co-editor of *The Dilemmas of Lone Motherhood: Essays from Feminist Economics* (Susan Himmelweit and Jane Humphries, Routledge, 2005). She is an active participant in legislative and educational efforts to improve government assistance and employment policies that affect low-income women and their families. Albelda received her Ph.D. in economics from the University of Massachusetts at Amherst in 1983.

ROBERT DRAGO was Professor of Labor Studies and Women's Studies at the Pennsylvania State University, held a Research Professorship at the University of Melbourne (Australia), and was Professor of Economics at the University of Wisconsin at Milwaukee. He holds a Ph.D. in Economics from the University of Massachusetts at Amherst, and has been a Senior Fulbright Research Scholar and a National Science Foundation Fellow. He is also the author of *Striking a Balance: Work, Family, Life* (*Dollars & Sense*, 2007).

PART ONE

INTRODUCTION TO WAGE INEQUALITY

1

TWO VIEWS ON INEQUALITY AND DISCRIMINATION

A GLIMPSE AT DISCRIMINATION

Julie lives in a section of New York City called Harlem. She is 20 years old, shares a tiny apartment with her two young children, and completed high school with a "B" average. Like most residents of Harlem, Julie is black. She receives a monthly stipend called Temporary Cash Assistance (New York City's welfare program using Temporary Assistance to Needy Families—TANF—funds) that she uses for rent and bills; she buys milk and cereal for her children with coupons from the Women, Infants, and Children (WIC) program; and she uses Food Stamps to buy the rest of her groceries.[1] Her family receives medical coverage through the Medicaid program. Still, putting it all together, Julie's family is officially below the U.S. government's poverty line.

To receive help from the government, and particularly TANF payments, Julie is required to look for, and ultimately hold down, a job. TANF payments are time-limited, so she cannot depend permanently on government help, regardless of how poor her family is. Fortunately, her mother volunteers to care for her children if Julie finds a job, and Julie decides to apply for a job at a burger joint around the corner called Burger Hut. Surely, Julie thinks, they will give her a chance.

While this story is fictitious, we know the likely ending because of research undertaken by anthropologists Katherine Newman and Chauncy Lennon (1995) on job applicants for fast-food restaurants in Harlem. Julie will probably be turned down for the job.

Two things work in Julie's favor, however. Julie has a high school degree, as do most employees at the Burger Hut in Harlem. Julie also has an advantage in that she is older than many applicants. This factor alone doubles her chance of getting the job compared with an 18-year-old's.

So, why is Julie likely to be turned down? First, she lives in Harlem, and local fast-food employers do not like to hire people from that area. Maybe their friends will come in to hang out or get free food. If Julie lived three miles from Burger Hut, her chances of getting the job would more than triple, but then she would have an expensive commute and couldn't get to her children immediately in an emergency. Second, because so many employees commute to the store from elsewhere, Julie doesn't know anyone working at the store. Her chances would almost triple if she knew a current Burger Hut employee. Third, while few whites will apply for the job, and although most of Burger Hut's customers are black, Julie suffers because of her skin color. Indeed, a foreign-born applicant would be almost three times more likely to get the job, even though Julie undoubtedly would communicate more effectively with the customers. Fourth, Burger Hut tends not to hire welfare recipients, and this cuts in half Julie's chance of getting the job. Finally, even if we ignore all the specifics regarding Julie, jobs at Burger Hut are hard to land; there are far more applicants than openings, a situation that has only gotten worse in recent years as the economy has entered a recession.

Having lost out at Burger Hut, Julie may be frustrated and confused. Part of her says that it was her own fault for not getting the job. If only she had prepared better for the questions they asked, applied at a different time of day, or been an "A" student, maybe it would have worked out. Even if Burger Hut doesn't want to hire a young black woman from Harlem, she'll show them. She'll find a job with someone else. Besides, with so many people applying for so many jobs, she is likely to get one eventually if she just keeps trying. Further, she *must* get a job, because the government will not support single mothers like her for much longer.

Another part of Julie says that she is not alone in her frustration. She lost the job not because of anything she did but because of who she is, the color of her skin, and where she was born. This part of her is angry. Why should some white guy from the suburbs make money by owning Burger Hut, selling to a black clientele, and discriminating against people like her? And even if she had gotten the job, why should she need a high school degree to flip burgers or punch pictures of hamburgers on a cash register just to get the legal minimum wage?

Julie is also very worried. She loves her children and works hard to be a responsible mother, but the job she is likely to get won't pay much, probably won't have health insurance, and will keep her away from her children for long hours. She knows that she can't rely on her mother to take care of her children all the time but also that she won't make enough to afford child care. This part of Julie recalls Martin Luther King's "dream" of equality and tells her that to change things, she needs to be part of an organized movement telling employers, the government, and white America that she and others like her will not put up with such inequalities, unfairness, and injustice anymore.

TWO VIEWS FROM ECONOMICS

Julie's situation highlights important issues that confront workers in our society. Economists use two main approaches to understand her situation. These approaches are termed *neoclassical economics* and *political economy*. Both views admit that Julie's individual actions count and that Julie is operating on an unlevel playing field that works against her. Both approaches provide explanations for why women and blacks earn less than white men, and both explanations are consistent with their general approach to economic phenomena. Beyond these commonalities, however, the emphases of neoclassical economics and political economy diverge. The former views competitive markets, individual initiative, and government policies that leave the market alone as being sufficient to level the playing field. The latter views Julie as being caught in a web of oppressive class, race, and gender relations that can be changed only by fighting alongside others who are committed to her cause.

We can introduce these two views by casting our glance backward in time to two founders of economics: Adam Smith, an 18th-century Scottish scholar; and Karl Marx, the 19th-century German scholar and social activist. Smith argued that competitive markets caused people to serve the common good—increasing the wealth of the nation—by acting in their own self-interest. As he put it in what is probably the most famous single line of *The Wealth of Nations,* an individual functioning in a market economy is "led by an invisible hand to promote an end which was no part of his intention" (Smith, 1910; 400). If the market works, then there is no obvious role for the government except to print money and defend the country militarily. Those who followed in Smith's footsteps—called *neoclassical economists*—extended this argument to suggest that the market will take care of discrimination and will ultimately help to provide opportunities for Julie so long as she is willing to work hard and persist.

On the other end of the political spectrum, we find Karl Marx. Marx believed that capitalism—a profit-driven, market economy where some people own businesses while others work for them—serves the interests of the few at the expense of the many. Marx's most well-known line appears in the *Communist Manifesto,* which he coauthored with Frederick Engels. It concerned the need for collective action against capitalists: "working men of all countries, unite!" By extension, economists following in Marx's footsteps argued that the end of capitalism was required to alleviate the problems of discrimination. This is the origin of the voice calling Julie to band together with others against oppression.

Most economists fall somewhere in between these two extreme views (indeed, many economists would be offended if you called them by either label).[2] There are several reasons for relatively few economists fitting our "neoclassical" and "political economy" molds. As economics has developed, economists have discovered greater complexity in the world than is suggested by these two views. Some economists respond by using neoclassical tools but challenging key assumptions, and by arguing that people are concerned with fairness, that they cannot accurately forecast the future, or that markets usually are not competitive. Other economists believe that a detailed examination of history is more important than using the tools of either neoclassical or political economy. Nonetheless, we present these two views alone, because they provide logical and compelling frameworks for gaining an initial understanding of economic approaches.

This book looks at how the two economic approaches understand wage discrimination. *Discrimination* is defined as adverse treatment based on one or more defining characteristic of an individual, such as race, ethnicity, gender, sexuality, or religion. *Labor market discrimination* means adverse treatment in hiring, firing, and treatment in a job. Labor market discrimination could mean not being able to get a job, limited job opportunities, or being paid less than others based solely on characteristics that have nothing to do with a person's ability or effort.

Discrimination: Adverse treatment of people based on group identity

Neoclassical economists focus on how individuals discriminate and how that discrimination is translated into labor market outcomes. Political economists focus on how institutions in society (e.g., firms, unions, schools, government) have rules and regulations that are discriminatory, even if the individuals in those institutions do not personally discriminate.

Economists have often noted that women and blacks face very different labor market situations than whites and men do. Typically, women and black writers have called attention to the role of gender and race discrimination as a cause of these differences, but their work has rarely been widely or well received.[3] Only relatively recently have a substantial number of neoclassical and political economists extended their work to include a more thorough investigation of women's domestic work and blacks' exclusion in wage labor.

Discrimination entered the economic lexicon in reference to blacks, and particularly black men, during the 1940s and 1950s. In this area, economists were led by the pioneering works of neoclassical economist Gary Becker (1957) and political economist Gunnar Myrdal (1972), both of whom eventually won the Nobel Prize. Their research forms the bedrock upon which the theories of discrimination presented here were built.

The neoclassical view looks at discrimination from the standpoint of supply and demand within markets, while the perspective of political economy emphasizes the interplay of economic, social, and political forces. To simplify, Becker argued that individuals of one type may object to associating with individuals of another type, which can result in discrimination by employers, employees, and/or customers. Neoclassical economists put an individual's likes and dislikes, loves and hates, and so forth under the heading "tastes." While you might think of taste as concerning goods—as in, "I have a taste for tofu"—the meaning is here broadened to include such things as having a "taste" for discrimination. Discrimination then is like tofu in that it is something you are willing to pay for—if you have the "taste." Becker was presenting an alternative to Myrdal's theory, in which prejudice creates discrimination and discrimination in turn reinforces prejudice. According to Myrdal, discrimination is a vicious cycle between white perceptions and black behaviors that results from economic exploitation, social hierarchy, and political repression.

When women made their initial entrance as a proper subject for economic study, the issue of discrimination was far from central to the debate. After all, if you work in the home, how could you experience discrimination? Becker's and Myrdal's theories of discrimination rest on the notion that whites do not "like" blacks. This idea might be right as far as it goes, but it simply doesn't wash when we ask about discrimination against women. How many men would admit to "disliking" their mother, wife, sisters, or daughters? In her trailblazing work on women's wages, economist Barbara Bergmann (1971) noted this problem and argued that a theory of social roles, socialization, or appropriate social behavior was needed to understand discrimination against women. Similar arguments have been extended to blacks. Instead of thinking about discrimination in terms of an irrational prejudice, many economists now emphasize the incentives that encourage discrimination both inside and outside of the marketplace.

Indeed, until the 1960s, women hardly appeared in economists' models. Part of the reason for this historical absence of research on the topic is hinted at in the fact that both the Smith and Marx quotations cited earlier refer only to "men." This was not a fluke of language; when Smith or Marx wrote about the economy, they pictured men going about the business of buying, selling, and working. When women make their rare appearances in these works, it often is as a homemaker or sexual object. So, it is not surprising that when women did begin to appear explicitly in much of the economics literature during the last few decades, it was largely in the role of homemaker.

Until recently, Julie's situation would have been ignored by most economists, but the fact that over half of all U.S. women of working age are currently employed means that theories based on women as homemakers and men as breadwinners are flawed. In response, research and writing on women in the workplace have grown explosively during the last two decades, and you will see much of that literature cited in later chapters.

While both neoclassical and political economists have made great strides toward understanding discrimination against black men and white women, there remains a kind of uncomfortable gap regarding black women. A large segment of black women have worked for wages since shortly after the end of the Civil War, suggesting this group might be thought of as similar to black men. On the other hand, the situation of black women in terms of occupations and wages is fairly close to that of white women, suggesting that we should analyze the group as women. Discrimination against black women is not a simple mix of the particular barriers that face black men and white women, and this implies that the story of "Julie" is one that we cannot fully explain even today.

The study of discrimination contains many such conundrums and complexities. Because we are not here to advance novel theories, we have taken what exists at present on the neoclassical and political economy sides of the fence and tried to present it as clearly and simply as possible. The references at the end of each chapter suggest further readings that explore some of the problems beyond the scope of this book.

WHAT'S AT STAKE HERE

This book explains why blacks[4] and women earn less than white men; however, our focus on blacks and women relative to white men clearly restricts our view and understanding of the world. Where are Native Americans and Asians, Mexicans, and Persians—or gays and lesbians? Haven't they experienced discrimination? For many members of these groups, the answer is "yes," but we largely ignore those groups for two reasons. First, the economic literature on white–black relations and on gender is far more developed than for these other groups. Second, we believe that theories of discrimination built to explain white–black and female–male differences do not provide good explanations for discrimination in other contexts. For example, a gay male may experience little overt discrimination at work if he "pretends" to have a girlfriend or a wife, which is a situation with little relevance to the experience of heterosexuals, whether male or female, black or white. We have purposefully kept this book short so that in relevant courses it can be supplemented with material on other groups that have experienced discrimination. Stated differently, we hope to give readers a good idea of how economists view discrimination against women and blacks, but we urge readers to extend their horizons beyond these two groups.[5]

Turning to the two groups of interest, we believe there are sound political and moral reasons to examine discrimination against blacks and women. Blacks were brought to this country in chains and enslaved, segregated and disenfranchised by the system of U.S. apartheid called "Jim Crow," systematically terrorized by lynchings and mob violence, and isolated as sharecroppers in the South and in ghettos in the North. Arguably, the black poor of today are more segregated from society at large than any other minority group (Massey and Denton, 1993). Black Americans have not simply given up in the face of such violence, oppression, deprivation, and discrimination, however. The civil rights struggle of blacks over the course of the 20th century made it impossible for the rest of the country to ignore the contradiction between racism and democracy that Myrdal emphasized. The election of Barack Obama to President of the United States helped America realize that truth; nonetheless, we have not achieved racial equality.

Women also bring a crucial historical perspective to the question of inequality, although one that is quite different from that of blacks. Women also were disenfranchised and considered to be the property (although they could not be sold) of their owners (i.e., their husbands) until the 20th century. Often, they were the victims of violence in the home and on the street—as they are today in shocking numbers. Their lives were limited by deeply rooted gender roles that created a sexual division of labor inside the home and the workplace. However, in contrast to the social segregation that is characteristic of race relations, gender relations are defined by the integration, and often the intimacy, of men and women within most households. This curious and combustible mixture of oppression and love makes it clear that discrimination and inequality are not a simple issue of "us-against-them." Instead, they have more to do with the systems in which all of us live and work—the market system, production system, and the reproduction system. These systems may work with us and allow us to express our individual preferences and abilities, or they may work against us and limit our opportunities.

Thus, the issues of race and gender inequality are at heart issues of morality, of democracy, of family, and of opportunity. They are deeply embedded in our social soul. They also are political issues, in part because slavery, Jim Crow, and disenfranchisement existed by governmental decree and in part because the political struggles of women and blacks changed that history. Debates over inequality and discrimination are also debates over the proper role of government and its relation to the market. For this reason, the differing interpretations of inequality and discrimination offered by neoclassical economists and political economists are at the same time differing interpretations of the meaning of life in the United States, and that is the larger theme of this book.

PLAN OF THE BOOK

The introductory section (of which this is part) concludes in Chapter 2 with a look at the numbers that are relevant to discrimination. For each of the four groups we address—black women, white women, black men, and white men—the chapter details historical trends in terms of differences in wages, unemployment, and occupations. The data in Chapter 2 urge us to look for reasons why blacks and women suffer economically.

The following section contains three chapters explaining the neoclassical view of discrimination. Chapter 3 outlines the basics of neoclassical economics—utility maximizing individuals, supply and demand, competition, efficiency, and a look behind the scenes at the division of labor. An appendix is provided for those who want to know the source of these ideas. Chapter 4 takes the neoclassical vision into the labor market, looking at the supply and demand for labor, reasons other than discrimination for wage differences, and unemployment. Chapter 5 goes to the heart of the matter, with the neoclassical view of discrimination. We present Becker's "taste for discrimination" as well as the "statistical" theory of discrimination, and then we address the role of competitive markets in ending discrimination, measures of wage discrimination, why discrimination persists, and what the government might do to alleviate its ill effects.

The third section discusses the political economy approach. We begin as before with the basics, as captured in the "Four Cs" of political economy—context, collective behavior, conflicting interests, and change—then apply these to relations of class, race, and gender. These in turn are connected to various forms of oppression—exploitation, exclusion, and domination—that keep some people in power at the expense of others. The role of the marketplace and why oppression might end are discussed at the end of Chapter 6; again, an appendix is provided for those who want a look back to the origins of this theory. Chapter 7 takes the political economy view into the labor market and the workplace; starting with the notion of wages reflecting a customary standard of living, it explores the roles of the labor theory of value, work in the home, and government services in explaining wage levels. The chapter then turns to the impact of the business cycle on wages and looks at how capitalists get people to work hard. The chapter concludes with political economy's model of why wages differ among workers. Chapter 8 presents the political economy view of discrimination, starting with the role of context and the notion of "institutional discrimination" (which often is unconscious). We then look at the economic incentives for firms and workers to discriminate, how the economy perpetuates discrimination through "positive feedback," and why firms abandon discriminatory practices only slowly—if at all. The chapter looks at how discriminatory outcomes and attitudes change both over the business cycle and in the long run. It concludes with a discussion of government policies to reduce wage discrimination.

For those who are wondering where the authors fall along the "neoclassical" and "political economy" divide, we consider ourselves to be political economists. The reasons for our position are explained best, we believe, in Chapters 6 through 8. We do not accept neoclassical economics' emphasis on individual tastes and preferences as a guiding principle for economic behavior and outcomes, nor do we have much faith in the ability of markets to correct glaring inequalities. Nonetheless, we have worked hard to present a positive and clear exposition of the neoclassical view.

This book does not provide a critique of either neoclassical economics or political economy. We wrote this book because when we teach this material, there is an absence of texts that clearly and simply describe the general elements of *both* views, explaining how the economy in general, labor markets, and discrimination operate. This approach is not meant to downplay the importance of critical thinking. Rather, we encourage teachers and students to use what follows as a springboard for analyzing the shortcomings of each theory. We also encourage readers to supplement this book with other materials that focus on specific groups who face labor market discrimination.

DISCUSSION QUESTIONS

1. If you were in Julie's position and were turned down for the job at Burger Hut, what would you do?

2. Referring to Julie's story, do you think the ending might have been different if the government abolished the minimum wage? Are there reasons why Julie might have found it easier to get a job if the minimum wage was *increased*?

3. Economic historians have found evidence of discriminatory wages for women and blacks dating back at least 100 years, and often earlier. Why do you think it took U.S. economists so long to begin studying this phenomenon seriously?

4. Myrdal called his famous book on racism *An American Dilemma* to highlight the conflict between U.S. ideals and the denial of civil and economic rights to blacks a half-century ago. Do you think that a similar dilemma exists today? What evidence can you cite to support your opinion?

5. Why do you think that neoclassical economists tend to run the political gamut from conservatism to liberalism, while political economists tend to run the political gamut from liberalism to radicalism?

6. Have you ever observed an incident of discrimination? Describe the incident, and explain why you think it occurred.

7. How do you respond to people when you hear them make racist or sexist remarks?

SUGGESTED READINGS

Amott, Teresa L. and Julie A. Matthaei. 1991. *Race, Gender & Work*. Boston: South End Press.

Ash, Michael, and M.V. Lee Badgett. 2006. "Separate and Unequal: The Effect of Unequal Access to Employment-Based Health Insurance on Same-sex and Unmarried Different-Sex Couples." *Contemporary Economic Policy* 24.4 (20).

Becker, Gary. 1957. *The Economics of Discrimination*. Chicago: University of Chicago Press.

Bergmann, Barbara. 1971. "The Effect on White Incomes of Discrimination in Employment." *Journal of Political Economy* 79 (March- April).

Blandford, John M. 2003. "The Nexus of Sexual Orientation and Gender in the Determination of Earnings." *Industrial and Labor Relations Review* 56(4).

DuBois, W.E.B. 1939. *Black Folk, Then and Now: An Essay in the History and Sociology of the Negro Race.* New York: H. Holt & Co.

Edgeworth, F.Y. 1922. "Equal Pay to Men and Women for Equal Work." *Economic Journal* 32(128).

Engels, Frederick. 1948 (originally 1884). *The Origins of the Family, Private Property and the State.* Moscow: Progress Publishers.

Gilman, Charlotte Perkins. 1898. *Women and Economics.* Boston: Small, Maynard & Co.

Marx, Karl and Frederick Engels. 1972 (originally 1848). "Manifesto of the Communist Party." In *The Marx- Engels Reader.* Robert C. Tucker, ed. New York: W.W. Norton & Co.

Massey, Douglas and Nancy Denton. 1993. *American Apartheid: Segregation and the Making of the Underclass.* Cambridge, MA: Harvard University Press.

Myrdal, Gunnar. 1972 (originally 1944). *An American Dilemma: The Negro Problem and Modern Democracy.* Two volumes. New York: Harper and Row.

Newman, Katherine and Chauncy Lennon. 1995. "Finding Work in the Inner City: How Hard is it Now? How Hard will it be for AFDC Recipients?" Mimeo. Department of Anthropology, Columbia University.

Smith, Adam. 1910 (originally 1776). *The Wealth of Nations.* New York: E.P. Dutton.

Whitehead, John and Cobie Kwasi Harris (editors). 1999. *Readings in Black Political Economy.* Dubuque IA: Kendall/Hunt Publishing.

ENDNOTES

[1] The Food Stamp Program changed names in 2008 and is now called SNAP—Supplemental Nutrition Assistance Program.

[2] For example, only 5% of graduate students in six of the top economics programs disagree with the statement that "Neoclassical economics is relevant for the economic problems of today." Nonetheless, the *laissez faire* policy conclusions associated with neoclassical economics do not necessarily follow, since fewer than 20% of these same students disagree that "The income distribution in developed nations should be more equal." Source: David Colander, "The Making of an Economist Redux," *Journal of Economic Perspectives* 19(1), 2005.

[3] At the turn of the 20th century, W.E.B. DuBois, a black economist who received his Ph.D. from Harvard, wrote extensively on the labor market conditions of black workers. Charlotte Perkins Gilman wrote on women's unequal and unfair status, as did Karl Marx's colleague, Frederick Engels. See books by DuBois [1939], Gilman [1898], and Engels [1884], or Francis Edgeworth's [1922] paper in the list of suggested readings at the end of this chapter.

[4] We use the term "black" rather than "African-American" throughout the book. Both terms are commonly used in the literature (both by neoclassical and political economists) but "black" is simpler to write or speak. Our apologies to anyone who is offended by the term (as would be true, for example, in Australia, where "black" is considered a racial slur against Aboriginal people).

[5] To look at discrimination against other ethnic groups in the United States, a good place to start is Teresa Amott and Julie Matthaei [1991]. On sexual orientation, see Michael Ash and Lee Badgett [2006] or John Blandford [2003].

2

LABOR MARKET INEQUALITY BY THE NUMBERS

INTRODUCTION: LIES, DAMN LIES, AND STATISTICS

Julie's predicament in Chapter 1 gave us a glimpse of a few of the problems that people face in U.S. labor markets. To broaden our view, we need to look at some numbers on overall inequality. For many economists, numbers are the central tools used to describe, think about, and explore a society. However, there are diverse ways to look at numbers describing inequality, so disagreements among economists about the extent and causes of, as well as cures for, labor market inequality abound. Economists continue to debate the best way to measure inequality and interpret its trends.

These debates are not merely academic. The issue of wage growth occasionally finds its way into the discourse of U.S. presidential campaigns. One candidate typically argues that Americans are better off now because per-capita income, the average amount of income each person gets each year, adjusted for the overall level of prices, has risen steadily over the last 30 years. The other candidate often argues that most workers are not much better off now than they were 30 years ago; the evidence given here is the lackluster change in average inflation-adjusted wages since the mid-1970s. Typically, one candidate wants to emphasize people's continued prosperity as a reason for the electorate to stick with a particular set of policies while the other candidate is trying to convince the American people that they need new leadership to move the country toward a path of high-wage growth.

Whose facts are right? Both are! Because more and more people are working in the second decade of the 2000s than in the 1970s (as a percentage of the population) and the economy has grown, there is more income generated per person, which by definition means per-capita income has risen. The increase in the percentage of the population working stems almost entirely from more women working outside the home and the coming of age of the post-World War II baby boomers. However, average real wages (measured in terms of what you can buy with them) were lower in 2011 than they were in the 1970s: a typical person made more per week in terms of purchasing power in 1970s than in the second decade of the 21st century.

This chapter looks more carefully at the extent of employment inequality in recent years by looking at three labor market areas: wages, unemployment, and the distribution of jobs by occupation and industry. We also take a look at wealth inequality, as it also has an impact on labor market outcomes. You may ask, if social scientists cannot agree on the extent of inequality, does it make sense to argue there is a set of "facts" about labor market inequality? The answer is yes—for two reasons. First, it is crucial to see what the numbers are, as well as what they do and don't say when it comes to differences by race and gender, so you can become a more critical consumer of these numbers. Second, believe it or not, there is almost universal agreement among economists on some points: 1) white men, on average, make more than anyone else;[1] 2) average real wages, especially for men, fell from the 1970s through the mid 1990s and have risen slightly since then; 3) white unemployment rates (for men and women) are much lower than black unemployment rates; and 4) men and women typically work in different jobs. Familiarity with these facts brings you up to speed with what economists and policy makers already know and debate.

You may be wondering why we present data on unemployment, occupational and industry distribution of jobs, and family wealth in a book about wage inequality. The answer is simple. The ability to get a particular type of job is a crucial factor in determining anyone's wage. Because lower wages for women and blacks can result from being in different kinds of jobs than white men, the occupational and industry distribution of jobs is important. Investment in quality education, even at very early ages, is an increasingly important factor in determining the type of job one can and will get, so patterns of family wealth (and with it the ability to purchase education) also matters. We present this data here because throughout the book we will refer to the definitions, trends, and statistics on wages, unemployment, job distribution, and wealth distribution provided in this chapter.

WAGES: THE BASICS OF WAGE INEQUALITY

Most adults have income because they have a job that provides a paycheck for the work they perform. The Census Bureau refers to this form of income as earnings. Technically, there are three kinds of earnings: wages (usually an amount paid per hour worked), salaries (paid as lump sum regardless of hours worked), and self-employment income.[2] Earnings are not the only form of income most people have, although they usually are the most important. Other types of income include interest, dividends, rent, government assistance, alimony, and things like lottery winnings and profits on things you sell on eBay. Together, non-earnings income accounts for 25% of all income generated in the United States every year.

While wages are the primary source of income, not all people in the United States work for wages—nor does society necessarily expect them to. People who gain their income from property—in the form of profit, interest, dividends, capital gains, rent, etc.—do not, of course, have to work for wages. Additionally, in the United States, and many other countries, children are not expected to earn wages. We do, however, expect them to be supported by their parents or other family members. Furthermore, we typically expect people to retire from paid work when they are about 65 years of age, and we typically do not expect severely disabled persons to work. However, society's expectations about who should work for wages, and how to support those who do not, have changed considerably over time. One hundred years ago, it was not uncommon or unexpected to see children in poor families working. Until the passage of the Social Security Act in 1935, every adult male was supposed to work until he died (or be supported by his adult children). And, until fairly recently, we as a society did not expect women with children to do paid work. Now, as debates around government assistance to low-income families make clear, we are a society that expects every non-elderly, able-bodied adult to earn a wage and not to receive public assistance.

Earnings: Income from employment, including hourly wages, salaries, and money from self-employment

The Minimum Wage

Perhaps the most important distinction for understanding wages is the difference between *real* and *nominal* wages. Nominal wages are the actual amount that people get paid at any given point in time, while real wages correct for inflation. For example, suppose you receive $10 an hour for a job without any raises for a period of 10 years. Your nominal wage is always $10 because that is what you receive. But wait—if there is inflation during this period, meaning a general rise in prices, then the amount your paycheck will buy falls over time. Suppose that inflation during the period is 10% per year. In that case, your wage will purchase 10% less by the end of the first year, an additional 10% less by the end of the second year, and so forth. At the end of the ten years, your "real wage" will have fallen and you will only be able to purchase $3.87 worth of the ten dollars in goods you could purchase at the beginning, so inflation acts like a negative interest rate on the value of your pay. Real wages, then, are adjusted by some measure of the change in prices from year to year. The most common index of price changes currently used is the Consumer Price Index (CPI) for urban dwellers. That is the index we use for all the data presented in this chapter.

Nominal wage: the actual hourly wage at any given point in time

Real wage: the hourly wage corrected for inflation, reflecting purchasing power

To see this difference in action, consider the federal minimum hourly wage. As shown in Figure 2.1, in 1938, the government started with a minimum wage of only 25 cents. That does not sound like much, but if we apply the Consumer Price Index (CPI) with 2008 dollars as the base to correct for inflation, the real value of the minimum wage in 1938 was over $3.82 in 2008 dollars. In 1950, the government raised the minimum wage to 75 cents an hour. While this was triple the nominal wage of 1938, it is $6.70 in 2008 dollars, after adjusting for inflation, or less than twice the inflation-adjusted (real) value of the 1938 rate. The real minimum wage hit its highest level in 1968 ($9.90 in 2008 dollars) and then got eroded by inflation through to the 1990s. Since then, it has hovered around $6.00 in real dollars, about where it was in the early 1950s.

The Rise and Fall of Real Wages

Documenting wage inequality can be a tricky business. First, each researcher must decide which workers' wages to compare. Two of the thorniest choices are: 1) whether to compare wages of all workers, regardless of how many hours a week or weeks per year they work, or instead to only compare workers who work comparable hours; and 2) whether to compare wages received for the entire year or those received for an hour's worth of work. These choices matter because some workers (e.g., teens, college students, mothers) are more likely to work fewer hours or fewer weeks per year than other workers. Because women, for example, are much more likely to work fewer hours than men, comparing all women workers with all men workers would show substantial wage differences; however, their hourly wages may not differ as greatly.

A second difficulty that researchers face is the availability of data. Economists typically rely on nationally collected data from government-sponsored wage surveys, which provide extensive information on a random sample of all workers. We look at wage data from two surveys in this section. Each survey has certain data limitations and forces researchers to make decisions about which workers to compare. Still, the picture emerging from both is consistent on one front: workers (particularly men) have faced declining wages over the last several decades.

One of the two most widely used surveys is the Current Employment Statistics (CES), which is undertaken by the U.S. Labor Department's Bureau of Labor Statistics (BLS). The sample size is large: about 400,000 worksites are surveyed monthly. Employers are asked how much they pay workers on an hourly and weekly basis.[3] Data from this survey have the advantage of comparing wages earned per hour worked, which avoids the problem of variations in total hours worked per year. However, these data exclude about 20% of all workers, mainly supervisors in private service-providing industries and the self-employed. Figure 2.2 depicts average weekly earnings from 1959 through 2011 for all private-sector workers using data from the CES and adjusting for inflation.

From 1959 until 1973, average real earnings for all workers in the CES climbed steadily. From the mid-1970s through the mid-1990s average weekly earnings fell. Since 1997, real wages have begun to rise, but have only reached their early 1980s level. In 2011, at $653.16 a week, average weekly earnings were lower in purchasing power than they were from 1969 to 1979.

There are some specific benefits of looking at CES data. First, they are not self-reported but rather come directly from payroll information. The advantage of employer-reported information is that it avoids the problem of people either over-reporting or (as is more likely) underreporting their income. Both rich and poor people might have an incentive to underreport to a government agency collecting data (some rich people might fear the Internal Revenue Service (IRS), while some low-income people might fear losing government aid). Further, the data give a truer measure of all workers' wages when they actually do work, because the data are weekly rather than annual.

FIGURE 2.1
NOMINAL AND REAL VALUE OF THE MINIMUM WAGE, 1938-2012 (IN 2012 DOLLARS)

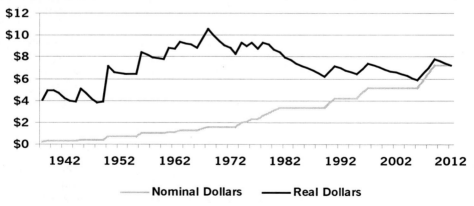

Note: Corrected for inflation using CPI-U.
Sources: U.S. Department of Labor, Wage and Hour Division, "History of the Federal Minimum Wage Under the Fair Labor Standards Act," retrieved February 2013 (www.dol.gov/whd/minwage/chart.htm); U.S. Bureau of Labor Statistics, Consumer Price Index History Table, retrieved February 2013 (ftp.bls.gov/pub/special.requests/cpi/cpiai.txt).

There are drawbacks to the CES as well. First, the survey collects information only on nonsupervisory workers (except in manufacturing, mining, and construction). This is a problem, because over the last several decades, the number of supervisory and self-employed workers has increased as a percentage of all workers and there are good reasons to believe that supervisors' wages have also increased over that time. Therefore, the trends depicted in Figure 2.1 might be overstated. Second, the wage data don't necessarily tell you how well off a particular worker might be, just how much he or she made on a weekly basis. For example, how much you get from earnings over the year depends on whether you had a job the week that the survey was taken, whether you work full- or part-time, and whether you have more than one job. The CES only provides a snapshot from the employer's view.

The second commonly used source of data on earnings comes from the BLS and the U.S. Census Bureau Household Data, collected in the Annual Social and Economic Supplement of the Current Population Survey (CPS). Each March, about 50,000 U.S. households (0.05% of all households, or one out of every 2,000) are interviewed at length about income sources and work experiences from the previous year. Income information from that survey is published by the Commerce Department.[4]

The advantage of the CPS data is that they include annual income, including earnings from work. Further, CPS data include all workers. However, this data source also has disadvantages. Because the data are self-reported, they likely suffer from underreporting by earners at both the low and the high ends of the wage scale. Further, the data are "top-coded" so people earning millions appear like people earning considerably less (whatever the level of the top code is for that year). Hence, data from the CPS often are considered to be inaccurate at the two ends of the income scale. Second, because they are annual data based on each person's memory of the previous year, the data are not considered to be as reliable a source for hourly earnings information as the BLS data,[5] making comparisons of annual earnings less meaningful unless they first are adjusted for hours and weeks worked. Finally, income data are reported separately for men and women. While this is extremely useful for examining differences by gender, it makes the overall picture of the "average worker" unclear.

Figure 2.3 depicts the median annual earnings from the CPS for men and women who are black or white. The median earnings is the exact midpoint, with half of the workers making

FIGURE 2.2
AVERAGE WEEKLY EARNINGS, 1959-2011 (IN 2011 DOLLARS)

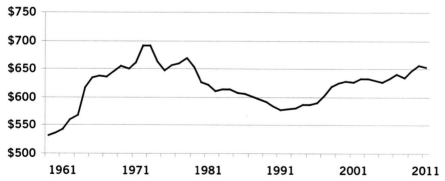

Note: Corrected for inflation using CPI-U-RS.
Source: Economic Report of the President, 2000 Table B-45 and 2012 Tables B-47 and B-60 (www.gpoaccess.gov/eop/download.html); Bureau of the Census, Appendix A from P-60-243 (census.gov/hhes/www/income/data/incpovhlth/2011/CPI-U-RS-Index-2011.pdf).

more than that amount and half making less. White men earn the most, and have for a long time. However, their earnings have been stagnant for a long time as well. Black men experienced a substantial rise in their earnings during the 1990s. Even so, they currently earn about 80% as much as white men. Black and white women continue to have the lowest earnings. Both groups experienced significant increases in their earnings but continue to make around two-thirds of what white men do.

Figure 2.4 depicts the median annual earnings of male workers who worked year-round (50 or more weeks a year) and full-time (35 hours or more a week). Looking at those who work year-round and full-time adjusts for hours worked. It is this wage ratio that is most often mentioned in media reports. Because women (especially white women) are more likely to work part-time, and because those who work year-round and full-time make more than workers who do not, wage levels for all groups are higher and, once adjusted for hours per week and weeks per year, the wage gaps with white men narrow. White women workers who work full-time, year round consistently make more than comparable black women, and have recently caught up to black men.

The same data for Hispanics can be found in Figure 2.5. As explained in Box 2.1, "Hispanic" is a separate and overlapping category, including mainly white, but also some black Americans. Hispanic men (all workers and those who worked year-round and full-time) found their wages falling until around 1990, when all male Hispanic workers saw median earnings rise back to just around the level where they started in 1974. Those men now earn incomes that are lower than those of black males. The pattern for Hispanic women is similar to that for white or black women, with steady increases over time. However, Hispanic women now earn less than white or black women (around 30 % less for year-round, full-time workers and 23 % less for all women workers).

There are two key points to take from this analysis. First, although equality across the dividing lines of race and gender has decreased, it remains the case that white men rule when it

FIGURE 2.3
MEDIAN ANNUAL EARNINGS FOR BLACK AND WHITE,
MALE AND FEMALE WORKERS, 1967-2011 (IN 2011 DOLLARS)

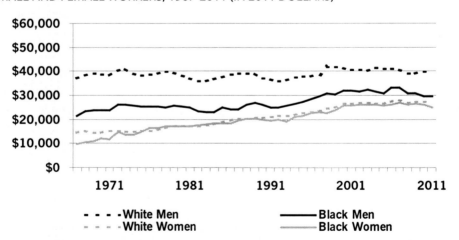

Source: U.S. Census Bureau, Historical Income Tables - People, Table 41 (census.gov/hhes/www/income/data/historical/people/2011/P41W_2011.xls and census.gov/hhes/www/income/data/historical/people/2011/P41B_2011.xls), retrieved February 2013. Corrected for inflation using CPI-U-RS.

Note: For 2001-2011, data are for "White Alone" and for "Black Alone." For prior years, data are for "White" and "Black" (which include men and women of mixed race).

FIGURE 2.4

MEDIAN ANNUAL EARNINGS FOR YEAR-ROUND, FULL-TIME WHITE AND BLACK, MALE AND FEMALE WORKERS, 1967-2011 (IN 2011 DOLLARS)

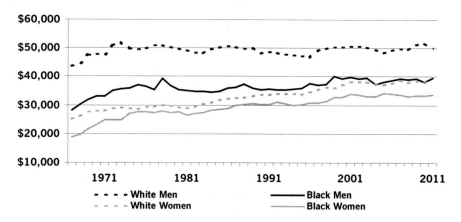

Source: U.S. Census Bureau, Historical Income Tables - People, Table 41W_2011 and Table 41B_2011, (census.gov/hhes/www/income/data/historical/people/2011/P41W_2011.xls and census.gov/hhes/www/income/data/historical/people/2011/P41B_2011.xls), retrieved February 2013. Corrected for inflation using CPI-U-RS.

Note: For 2001-2011, data are for "White Alone" and for "Black Alone." For prior years, data are for "White" and "Black" (which include men and women of mixed race).

FIGURE 2.5

MEDIAN ANNUAL EARNINGS FOR ALL AND YEAR-ROUND, FULL-TIME HISPANIC MALE AND FEMALE WORKERS, 1974-2011 (IN 2011 DOLLARS)

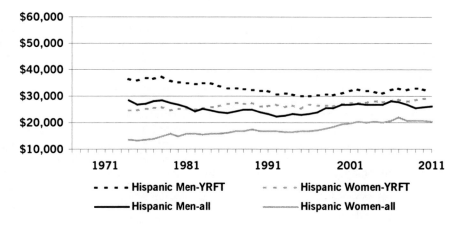

Source: U.S. Census Bureau, Historical Income Tables - People, Table 41h_2011 (census.gov/hhes/www/income/data/historical/people/2011/P41H_2011.xls), retrieved February 2013. Corrected for inflation using CPI-U-RS.

Note: For 2001-2011, data are for "White Alone" and for "Black Alone." For prior years, data are for "White" and "Black" (which include men and women of mixed race).

comes to earnings or wages. Second, race and gender effects are not additive. If they were, we would expect that, since black men and white women earn less than white men, black women should earn even less than black men or white women. The fact that black women earn almost the same amount as white women shows that difference and discrimination are complex, and anything but additive.

The Increase in Wage Inequality

Over the same period that real earnings for men have declined, the distribution of earnings has become more unequal. The gap between low- and high-wage workers has grown, and the gap between wages and profits also has grown. The old saying that "the rich get richer while the poor get poorer" has become ever more true. A large fraction of Americans have seen their economic fortunes fall faster than the trends in overall earnings would suggest.

Table 2.1 shows the earnings that wage earners at the 20th, 40th, 50th (median), 60th, and 80th percentiles earned for five different years that correspond to peak years (for earnings) over the last several business cycles. The 20th percentile includes the lowest-earning fifth of all workers, the 40th percentile includes the lowest-earning 40% of all workers, and so on. The wages of workers at the low end of the distribution grew much more slowly than the wages of workers at the high end. For example, the highest-paid worker among the bottom 20% of wage earners in 1973 made

---

BOX 2.1
RACE ISN'T JUST BLACK AND WHITE

During the 1990s, the U.S. Census Bureau received complaints from individuals who believed that the race and ethnicity categories used in the census administered every ten years were too confining. So, starting with the 2000 census, the government allowed people to enter multiple race categories. Some people took advantage of the option. Out of over 281 million people in the U.S. population, almost 7 million (2.4%) reported two or more races.

At that time, 75.1% of the population self-reported as white only, 12.3% as black only, 0.9% as American Indian or Alaska Native, 3.6% as Asian, 0.1% as Native Hawaiian and other Pacific Islander only, and 5.5% as some other race only. Looked at this way, 87.4% of the population reported being exclusively black or white.

In addition, four large cross-over groups accounted for over half of the 7 million reporting multiple race categories: white and American Indian or Alaska Native, white and Asian, white and black, and black and American Indian or Alaska Native.

To complicate things, the Census Bureau approaches Hispanic, Latino, or Latina background not as a racial characteristic but as a matter of ethnicity. Hispanics can come from any race or a variety of races. In 2000, 12.5% of the population reported Hispanic background, with most (58%) reporting Mexican origin. Looking at the overlap between the Hispanic and race categories, it turns out that the vast majority (93.7%) of Hispanics classify themselves as white alone. This implies that the non-Hispanic, white-only population represents 63.4% of the total population.

By 2011, births to white non-Hispanics represented only a minority of births, suggesting this group will become a minority of the U.S. population in future decades.

Sources: U.S. Bureau of the Census, Census 2000 Briefs, Overview of Race and Hispanic Origin C2KBR/01-01 March 2001, and The Hispanic Population C2KBR/01-3 May 2001; Projections from U.S. Bureau of the Census, Population; U.S. Bureau of the Census, "Most Children Younger Than Age 1 are Minorities," press release, May 17, 2012.

$8.78 per hour (measured in 2007 dollars). In 1989, after adjusting for inflation, the highest-paid worker in that group made only $8.37. The long economic expansion of the 1990s helped low-wage workers, and by 2000 wages at the 20th percentile grew to $10.15 an hour (in 2011 dollars). During the early 2000s and into the recession, low-wage workers saw only a slight decrease to $9.86 an hour. In the longer term, workers at the bottom 20% of all wage earners saw their real wages stagnate since 1973, when they were $9.75. Workers at the top 80th percentile of wage earners saw their wages increase by 22.4% between 1973 and 2011, from $23.53 an hour to $28.80. The top-earning 80% of workers made $13.78 more per hour than the best-paid workers in the bottom 20% of earners in 1973; by 2011, this gap had grown to $18.94. In short, the workers in the bottom deciles of all workers—those with the most need—had the smallest gains.

Growing Family Income and Wealth Gaps

As wages grew more unequal, it is not surprising that family income grew more unequal too, since earnings comprise a large component of income. However, other trends have increased family income inequality as well. The growth in single-adult households, especially among those with children, coupled with the increased participation of women in the labor market, has meant that two-adult families often have two earners, leaving those with one adult further behind. If we lined up all the households in the United States in the order of their incomes (from those with the least to those with the most), we would see that those households at the 20th percentile saw their real household incomes increase from $20,211 in 1979 (in 2011 dollars) to $20,262 in 2011, a 0.25% increase. The incomes for the households at the 80th percentile saw an inflation-adjusted increase from $83,730 in 1979 to $101,582 in 2011—a 21.3% increase. Those at the top 5% saw an even larger increase of 37.5% over the same time period.[6]

The ratio of median income for white families to that of black and Hispanic families over time has changed very little, despite some increases in median earnings of black men and women. Black families have a median income that has risen slightly compared to white families (59% in 1980 and 64% in 2011), while the median family income of Hispanics compared to that of whites has fallen slightly since, from 68% in 1976 to 64% in 2011.[7]

TABLE 2.1
HOURLY WAGES FOR WAGE WORKERS (IN 2011 DOLLARS)

Year	Percentile				
	20th	40th	50th	60th	80th
1973	$9.75	$13.47	$15.45	$17.72	$23.53
1979	$9.73	$13.34	$15.21	$17.64	$24.29
1989	$9.08	$13.01	$15.12	$17.66	$25.12
2000	$10.15	$13.71	$15.99	$18.92	$27.25
2007	$10.25	$14.04	$16.40	$19.46	$28.50
2011	$9.86	$13.88	$16.07	$19.03	$28.80
Change 1973-2011	1.1%	3.0%	4.0%	7.4%	22.4%

Note: Corrected for inflation.

Source: Lawrence Mishel, Josh Bivens, Elise Gould and Heidi Shierholz, The State of Working America, 12th Edition (Ithaca, NY: Cornell University Press, 2012), Table 2.5 (stateofworkingamerica.org/chart/swa-wages-table-4-4-hourly-wages-workers/).

TABLE 2.2

MEDIAN FAMILY INCOME AND MEDIAN NET WORTH BY RACE AND ETHNICITY, 2007

	Non-Hispanic White	Non-Hispanic Black	Hispanic	Non-Hispanic Black as a % of Non-Hispanic White	Hispanic as a % of White
Income	50,000	30,000	35,000	60.0%	70.0%
Net Worth	143,600	9,300	9,100	6.5%	6.3%

Source: Edward N. Wolff, "Recent Trends in Household Wealth in the United States: Rising Debt and the Middle-Class Squeeze—an Update to 2007," Levy Economics Institute of Bard College, Working Paper No. 589, March 2010, Table 10. Household Income and Wealth by Race, 1983–2007, Table 11. Family Income and Wealth for Non-Hispanic Whites and Hispanics, 1983–2007.

In addition to growing income inequality, inequality also grew between those with assets (wealth) and those without. In 1983, the richest 20% of all households owned 81.3% of all the wealth (household assets minus their debts); by 2004, their share of the nation's wealth grew to 84.7%. Conversely, the poorest 40% held 1.2% of all the wealth in 1983; by 2004 that fell to 0.7%.[8] The causes of this increase in inequality are debated, but the consequences are clear: low-wage workers gained very little, while the rich made out quite well.

Although black and Hispanic median family income is about 64% of that of white families, this difference pales compared to differences in median wealth. Table 2.2 depicts median family income and median family wealth for non-Hispanic white, non-Hispanic black, and Hispanic families in 2007. The median net worth of non-Hispanic black families and Hispanic families is just over 6% than that of non-Hispanic white families.[9]

The combination of very slow-growing wages for workers in the bottom 60% of all earners since the early 1970s and the increase in income from ownership (e.g., stock dividends) in the 1980s and 1990s has resulted in a dramatic redistribution of all income in the United States. In 1973, the poorest 40% of U.S. families got 17.4% of all the income, compared with the 15.5% of all income received by the richest 5% of families. By 2010, there was a distinct reversal of fortune: the poorest 40% received 13.3% of total income, while the richest 5% garnered 20.0%.[10]

UNEMPLOYMENT TRENDS SINCE THE 1950s: PERSISTENT INEQUALITIES

If you don't work at a job, you won't have any earnings; it's that simple. Therefore, the ability to get a job, if you want one, is going to be an important factor in your overall economic well-being. In the United States, there are two important facts about unemployment. First, it gyrates wildly with the ups and downs of the economy. Second, whites (both men and women) face far less unemployment than other racial and ethnic groups. We will discuss each of these phenomena, but first, it is useful to get a look at how unemployment is defined.

Measuring Unemployment and Employment

The BLS is the government agency that tracks unemployment. Every month, as part of the CPS survey, 50,000 households are asked questions on the employment status of household members over the age of 16. Based on this, analysts at the BLS decide whether household members are employed, unemployed, or out of the work force altogether. The first Friday of every month, the Labor Department announces the results of the previous month's survey.

The BLS considers you employed if during the week of the survey:
- You worked at all for pay
- You worked 15 or more hours without pay in a family business
- You did not work because you were on vacation, involved in a labor dispute, ill, on parental leave, or you were prevented from working because of bad weather or other personal reasons

Being employed is pretty easy to determine, but how does the BLS decide if you are unemployed? Being without a job is not necessarily being unemployed. The BLS classifies someone as unemployed only if the person was jobless during the interview week, available to work, and made some specific effort to find a job in the preceding month. Anyone who is not working for pay because of a long-term disability, or who is home taking care of children, in school full-time, or just discouraged from looking for work, is considered to be out of the labor force altogether, and he or she is not classified as unemployed. Box 2.2 defines some of the key terms economists use in discussions on employment and unemployment.

Before turning to more facts about unemployment, it is worthwhile to think about why unemployment rates are important and what they do and don't tell us about labor markets and the economy. Politicians and economists typically look to unemployment rates as a crucial indicator of how the economy is working. When unemployment rates are low, they indicate that the economy is generating a high demand for workers, which is assumed to be a sign of a healthy, or at least a growing, economy. Conversely, high unemployment rates are one indication of a sluggish economy. However, there are reasons to be cautious about looking at unemployment rates as an indicator of economic health.

The BLS is criticized for both overestimating and underestimating unemployment rates. People who work informally and in the underground economy usually are not counted as employed. If they were, unemployment rates would be lower than they are. People who are working "under the table" or who are engaged in illegal activities would be reluctant to give that information to the BLS (or the IRS!). Further, some of those who are not working may exaggerate their job search efforts. For these reasons, the official measures may overstate unemployment.

The BLS also underestimates unemployment rates for two reasons. First, there are people who would like to work and have been looking for a while but can't find work. If they give up even temporarily and don't actively look for work that month, the BLS classifies them as being out of the labor force. Economists refer to this as being a "discouraged worker." In 2008, there were just under half a million (462,000) discouraged workers, a figure that rose to 909,000 by 2012. Second, the BLS counts workers as being employed regardless of whether they are working part-time or full-time. People who can only find part-time work but want full-time work and are working at a job in which they are overqualified probably consider themselves at the very least to be "underemployed." In 2008, there were 5.9 million workers who were working part-time involuntarily.

If you are both unemployed and looking for work, or if you are employed or self-employed, then you are in the labor force (see Box 2.2). Other individuals are not looking for work. Figure 2.6 provides information on labor force participation for men and women according to whether they are white or black or Hispanic (recalling that Hispanics overlap with both the white and black categories). As the figure shows, there has been increasing equality across race and gender groups over time. The Hispanic, white, and black men at the top of the figure all showed decreases in labor force participation, with black men giving up on employment more often than the others. The Hispanic, white, and black women all increased their labor force participation.

BOX 2.2

SOME LABOR MARKET TERMS

Measures of employment and unemployment not only provide a wealth of information for labor economists, they also provide the tools necessary to understand some common labor market terms:

The **labor force** is defined as the sum of the number of people employed and the number of people unemployed (16 years old and over) at any given point in time:

$$Labor\ Force\ (LF) = \#\ of\ Employed + \#\ of\ Unemployed \qquad (2.1)$$

The **labor force participation rate** is the percentage of the entire noninstitutional population 16 years and older that is either employed or unemployed:

$$LF\ participation\ rate = \frac{\#\ in\ LF \times 100}{\#\ in\ Noninstitutional\ Population} \qquad (2.2)$$

The **employment-to-population ratio** is given as the percentage of the noninstitutional population 16 years and older that is employed:

$$Employment/Population\ ratio = \frac{\#\ Employed \times 100}{\#\ in\ Noninstitutional\ Population} \qquad (2.3)$$

Finally, the **unemployment rate** is defined as the percentage of the labor force that is unemployed:

$$Unemployment\ rate = \frac{\#\ Unemployed \times 100}{\#\ in\ LF} \qquad (2.4)$$

Table 2.3 gives the labor force, employment, and unemployment statistics for all black and white workers (men and women) for 2008. In that year, the United States was experiencing a recession (which got worse in terms of unemployment in 2009) and had 154.3 million people in jobs and 8.9 million people "pounding the pavement"—wanting to work but unable to find a job. You can see from the table that there are large differences in labor force participation rates between men and women and in unemployment rates between blacks and whites.

TABLE 2.3:

LABOR FORCE, EMPLOYMENT, AND UNEMPLOYMENT STATISTICS FOR CIVILIAN POPULATION 16 YEARS AND OLDER, 2012*

Category	Total	White Men	White Women	Black Men	Black Women	Hispanic Men	Hispanic Women
Civilian, Non-Institutional Population	243,284	94,266	98,938	13,508	16,400	18,434	18,324
Labor Force	154,975	66,921	56,763	8,594	9,805	14,026	10,365
Employed	142,469	61,990	52,779	7,302	8,553	12,643	9,235
Unemployed	12,506	4,931	3,985	1,292	1,252	1,383	1,130
LF Participation Rate	63.7	71.0	57.4	63.6	59.8	76.1	56.6
Employment-Population Ratio	58.6	65.8	53.3	54.1	52.2	68.6	50.4
Unemployment Rate	8.1	7.4	7.0	15.0	12.8	9.9	10.9

*Numbers in thousands

Source: U.S. Dept. of Labor, Bureau of Labor Statistics, CPS Tables Annual Averages Table 3 and 4 (www.bls.gov/cps/tables.htm#charem, retrieved February 2013).

FIGURE 2.6

LABOR FORCE PARTICIPATION RATES FOR WHITE, BLACK, AND HISPANIC
MEN AND WOMEN, 1973-2012

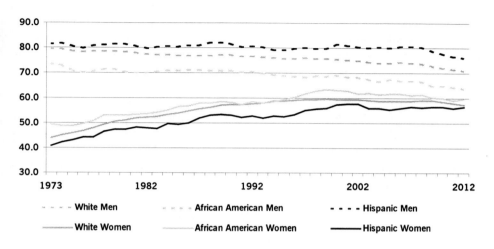

Source: Bureau of Labor Statistics, created from Labor Force Statistics from the Current Population Survey (http://www.bls.gov/cps/data.htm).

Unemployment and the Business Cycle

The periodic ups and downs of economic activity in market economies are referred to as business cycles. The downswings are called recessions (with the lowest point being the *trough*), and the upswings are called expansions (with the highest point being the *peak*). No one really knows exactly why a bust turns into a boom, or vice versa, although there are lots of theories. However, everyone knows that it will happen—like the sun rising and setting every day. Unlike the position of the sun in the sky, however, business cycle movements are virtually impossible to predict with accuracy. It is even harder to figure out exactly when the economy is—or was—in a recession. To deal with this problem, there is a group of economists who officially pronounce when a recession or expansion is over. The Commerce Department has charged the National Bureau of Economic Research (NBER), a private research organization, with calling the business cycle play-by-play. The NBER's Business Cycle Dating Committee consists of seven economists who judge the beginning, middle, and end of a business cycle. The committee looks at a variety of economic indicators—including unemployment rates—but really has no hard and fast rules to decide the precise dates of peaks and troughs. The NBER defines a recession as a recurring period of decline in total output, income, employment, and trade, usually lasting from six months to one year, and marked by widespread contractions in many sectors of the economy.

Business cycles: Periods of three or more years during which the economy busts or has a recession and then booms or has a recovery

Table 2.4 lists the eleven business cycles the NBER has tracked from 1945 to 2012. Until the mid-1970s, the entire business cycle (peak-to-peak or trough-to-trough) lasted anywhere from three to five years. Since that time, however, the length of business cycles has been far less predictable. There have been some very short business cycles and some very long ones, one lasting most of the 1960s, another most of the 1980s, the third lasting for almost all of the 1990s and into 2001, and the one that began in 2007 and ended in June 2009.

When the economy expands, there is increased demand for workers. As a result, unemployment falls. At this point, wages should rise, because as firms need new workers, they are willing to pay a little more for them if they are hard to find. Figure 2.7 gives unemployment rates from 1947 to 2012 and it shows that peak business cycle years (just before a recession begins) are associated with lower unemployment rates. The spikes represent recessions, with small spikes in 1958, 1961, and 1972, and larger spikes in 1975, 1982, 1992, 2002, and 2009. These spikes represent millions of workers losing their jobs, and millions of others unable to find work.

Figure 2.7 also illustrates an important trend. Besides moving with business cycles, unemployment rates show a secular or long-run trend as well. Over the entire post-World War II period, unemployment rates have crept upward. The trend line in Figure 2.7 shows this upward creep, the unemployment rate moved from a 4% average in the late 1940s to a 6.3% average since 2000.

The Race Gap

Unemployment is not spread evenly across the economy, and one striking and persistent difference is by race. Generally, black workers are twice as likely to be unemployed as white workers, with Hispanic workers having unemployment rates that fall in between those of whites and blacks. Figure 2.8 depicts Hispanic, black, and white unemployment rates from 1947 to 2012 (there are only data from 1973 for Hispanics). Table 2.5 further breaks down unemployment rates by

TABLE 2.4
NBER BUSINESS CYCLE PEAKS AND TROUGHS 1945-2009

Peak Month	Year	Trough Month	Year
November	1948	October	1949
July	1953	May	1954
August	1957	April	1958
April	1960	February	1961
December	1969	November	1970
November	1973	March	1975
January	1980	July	1980
July	1981	November	1982
July	1990	March	1991
March	2001	November	2001
December	2007	June	2009

Source: National Bureau of Economic Research, Inc., 1050 Massachusetts Ave., Cambridge, MA 02138, retrieved from http://www.nber.org/cycles. html (October 2009). A complete list of NBER Working Papers and Reprints can be accessed on the Internet: www.nber.org.

FIGURE 2.7
ANNUAL UNEMPLOYMENT RATE, 1947-2012

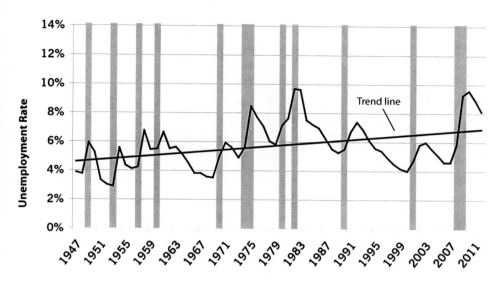

Source: *Economics Report of the President*, 1995 and 2012. Shaded areas correspond to recessions. Data are seasonally adjusted.

FIGURE 2.8
WHITE, BLACK, AND HISPANIC ANNUAL UNEMPLOYMENT RATES, 1947-2012

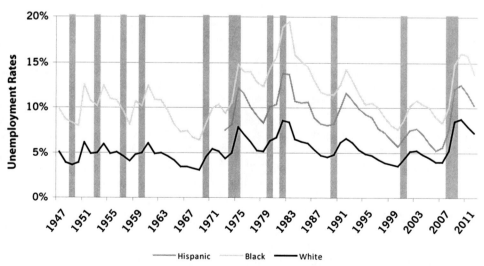

Source: *Economics Report of the President*, 1995 and 2012. Shaded areas correspond to recessions. Data are seasonally adjusted.

*Includes Black and others through 1971, otherwise Black only.

TABLE 2.5

UNEMPLOYMENT RATES AND RATIOS BY GENDER, RACE, AND AGE
IN TROUGH AND PEAK YEARS OF BUSINESS CYCLE

Year	Men			Women			16-19 year olds		
	White	Black*	Ratio	White	Black*	Ratio	White	Black*	Ratio
Trough Years									
1954	4.8%	10.3%	2.1	5.5%	9.2%	1.7	12.1%	16.6%	1.4
1958	6.1%	13.7%	2.2	6.2%	10.8%	1.7	14.4%	27.4%	1.9
1961	5.7%	12.8%	2.2	6.5%	11.9%	1.8	15.3%	27.7%	1.8
1970	4.0%	7.9%	2.0	5.4%	9.3%	1.7	13.5%	29.0%	2.1
1975	7.2%	14.8%	2.1	8.6%	14.8%	1.7	17.9%	39.4%	2.2
1980	6.1%	14.5%	2.4	6.5%	14.0%	2.2	15.5%	38.5%	2.5
1982	8.8%	20.1%	2.3	8.3%	17.6%	2.1	20.4%	48.1%	2.4
1991	6.5%	13.0%	2.0	5.6%	12.0%	2.1	16.5%	36.2%	2.2
2001	4.2%	9.3%	2.2	4.1%	8.1%	2.1	12.7%	29.0%	2.3
2009	9.4%	17.5%	1.9	7.3%	12.4%	1.7	21.8%	39.5%	1.8
Peak Years									
1957	3.6%	8.3%	2.3	4.30%	7.3%	1.7	10.60%	19.1%	1.8
1960	4.8%	10.7%	2.2	5.30%	9.4%	1.8	13.50%	24.3%	1.8
1969	2.5%	5.3%	2.1	4.20%	7.8%	1.9	10.70%	24.1%	2.3
1973	3.8%	8.0%	2.1	5.30%	11.1%	2.1	12.60%	31.5%	2.5
1980	6.1%	14.5%	2.4	6.50%	14.0%	2.2	15.50%	38.5%	2.5
1981	6.5%	15.7%	2.4	6.90%	15.6%	2.3	17.30%	41.4%	2.4
1990	4.9%	11.9%	2.4	4.70%	10.9%	2.3	13.50%	30.9%	2.3
2001	4.2%	9.3%	2.2	4.10%	8.1%	2.0	12.70%	29.0%	2.3
2007	4.2%	9.1%	2.2	4.00%	7.5%	1.9	13.90%	29.4%	2.1

*For the years 1954–1970, data are for blacks and others; after 1970 data are for blacks only.
Source: Economic Report of the President, 2012 and Bureau of Labor Statistics Annual Averages.

gender and age and includes the black (and other)/white unemployment ratio for men, women, and youth in peak and trough years of the business cycles between 1954 and 2009.

The figure, however, hides some important facts. First, even though black men are more likely to be unemployed than black women, those who are employed earn more than black women (see Figures 2.3 and 2.4). Second, the steady decline in labor force participation rates for black men, shown in Figure 2.6. Over the last 20 years, many men have simply given up on finding jobs in the labor market, but black men have been particularly hard-hit—and if you are not in the labor force, you do not count as unemployed.

The Great Recession of the late 2000s hit black workers exceptionally hard. In 2010, the unemployment rate for black men had risen to 18.4%—almost one out of every five black men was without a job and actively seeking employment. This is a level not seen in since the early 1980s. The rate for black women peaked in 2011 at 14.1%, compared to a high of 7.7% for white women in 2010.[11]

The race gap has important economic implications in the United States. First, it means that one of the harshest aspects of a market system—unemployment—is not shared equally among whites and blacks. Second, because of residential segregation, the impact of high black unemployment rates is deeply felt on a community-wide basis in black communities. To the degree that government policies can affect unemployment rates, there are political implications to the racial disparity in unemployment rates as well. If whites, with their large electoral majority, do not perceive unemployment as being a major problem in this country, they may be more likely to vote in officials who are willing to accept higher average rates of unemployment.

Gender Differences

Women and men are equally susceptible to the business cycle in that unemployment rates move in the same direction for both; up in recessions, and down in recoveries. However, there has been a recent important change in the relationship between men's and women's unemployment rates, as shown in Figure 2.9. Until the 1980s, women's unemployment rates always exceeded men's for both blacks and whites, but since that time, women's unemployment rates have often been lower than men's, especially in economic downturns. One possible explanation for this is that women are more likely than men to fall back on their spouses' wages if they become unemployed. As a result, women are more likely than men to leave the labor force and become discouraged workers, so it appears that they are out of the labor force, when in fact they are "unemployed" in the everyday sense of the word. Another important explanation has to do with the specific ways in which the economy has changed since the mid-1970s and the fact that many jobs are sex-segregated. Over time, jobs in industries that are more likely to hire women have experienced tremendous growth while industries that tend to hire men have experienced steady declines in employment. Furthermore, the last several recessions have hit hardest the industries that are most likely to hire men and been less harsh in the industries in which women predominate. Now, we turn to the distribution of jobs, which also has important implications for wage differences.

FIGURE 2.9
MEN'S AND WOMEN'S ANNUAL UNEMPLOYMENT RATES, 1947-2012

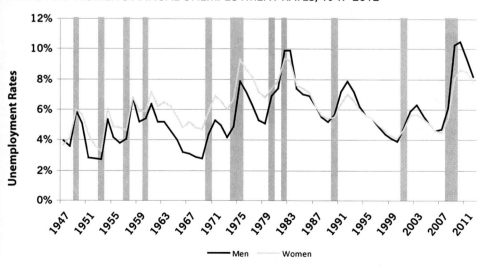

Source: *Economics Report of the President*, 1995 and 2012. Shaded areas correspond to recessions. Data are seasonally adjusted.

THE DISTRIBUTION OF JOBS: NICE WORK IF YOU CAN GET IT

Everybody knows that some jobs pay better than others. For example, doctors make more money than orderlies in the same hospital. This makes sense, because doctors have to train for many years while orderlies don't necessarily need a high-school diploma. In other cases, however, it is hard to understand why one job pays better than another. For example, median hourly earnings of truck drivers were $18.37 in 2012, while median hourly earnings for bank tellers were $11.99. These jobs are very different and require different skills, but in terms of the education and training needed to be good in either field, the jobs are comparable. A more vexing comparison is that between child-care workers and animal trainers. Median hourly earnings for child-care workers were $9.38, while median hourly earnings for animal trainers were $12.15![12]

Industry Differences

Social scientists who are interested in understanding wage differences and trends watch both the occupation and the industry in which workers are employed. Industrial employment figures tell us the total number of people who are employed, categorized by the type of good or service they produce. There are several broad industrial sectors. One that receives a lot of attention because it is shrinking and has traditionally paid high wages is the manufacturing sector, which includes the automobile and steel industries. A particularly fast-growing sector is the service industry, which includes health care, education, personal services, and entertainment. Table 2.6 provides employment by industry for 1980, 1990, 2000, and 2010.

TABLE 2.6
EMPLOYMENT BY INDUSTRY 1980, 1990, 2000, AND 2010*

	1980		1990		2000		2010	
	Number	Percent	Number	Percent	Number	Percent	Number	Percent
TOTAL	99,303	100.0%	118,793	100.0%	136,891	100.0%	139,064	100.0%
Agriculture	3,364	3.4%	3,223	2.7%	2,464	1.8%	2,206	1.6%
Mining	979	1.0%	724	0.6%	475	0.3%	731	0.5%
Construction	6,215	6.3%	7,764	6.5%	9,931	7.3%	9,077	6.5%
Manufacturing	21,942	22.1%	21,346	18.0%	19,644	14.4%	14,081	10.1%
Transportation and Communications	6,525	6.6%	8,168	6.9%	11,439	8.4%	10,283	7.4%
Wholesale Trade	3,920	3.9%	4,669	3.9%	4,216	3.1%	3,805	2.7%
Retail Trade	16,270	16.4%	19,953	16.8%	15,763	11.5%	15,934	11.5%
Finance, Insurance, and Real Estate	5,993	6.0%	8,051	6.8%	9,374	6.8%	9,350	6.7%
Services	28,752	29.0%	39,267	33.1%	57,473	42.0%	66,614	47.9%
Public Administration	5,342	5.4%	5,627	4.7%	6,113	4.5%	6,983	5.0%

Source: U.S. Census Bureau, Statistical Abstract 1994 (Table 641) and 2012 (Table 620).
*Numbers in thousands.

In 2002, the Census Bureau implemented major changes to the way it classifies jobs by industry, limiting the ability to make good comparisons. Still, the data in Table 2.6 reveal an important trend—an increasingly smaller percentage of the workforce is employed in manufacturing. This shift is often referred to as "deindustrialization," a term made popular by economists Bennett Harrison and Barry Bluestone in their 1982 book *The Deindustrialization of America*. In 1980, 22.1% of employed persons worked in the manufacturing sector, but by 2010, only 10.1% did so.

Deindustrialization: The long-term decline in employment in blue-collar jobs in manufacturing industries

Table 2.7 depicts the composition of employment by industry for women, blacks, and Hispanics in 2012. That year, women represented 47.0% of all persons employed. If they were equally distributed in jobs across all industry sectors, we would expect to see 47.0% of those employed in the construction industry or the service industry to be female. This is not the case. Instead, we find that women were only 9.0% of all persons employed in the construction industry, but just under 75% of those in education and health services. Women are overrepresented in retail trade, financial activities, and all services except professional and business services.

Similarly, in 2012, around one out of every ten workers was black, one out of every seven workers was Hispanic, and one out of every 20 workers was Asian, yet these workers were not evenly

TABLE 2.7
COMPOSITION OF INDUSTRIAL EMPLOYMENT BY GENDER, RACE, AND ETHNICITY, 2012

	Total (in 1,000s)	Percent of total			
		Women	Black	Hispanic	Asian
Total, 16 years and over	142,469	47.0	11.1	15.4	5.4
Industry:					
Agriculture, forestry, fishing, & hunting	2,186	25.6	2.8	22.5	1.5
Mining	957	13.2	4.7	17.5	1.4
Construction	8,964	9.0	5.6	24.4	1.9
Manufacturing	14,686	29.0	8.7	15.3	6.2
Wholesale trade	3,694	28.6	7.1	16.8	5.0
Retail trade	16,182	48.3	11.4	15.2	5.1
Transportation and utilities	7,271	23.2	15.9	16.2	3.9
Information	2,971	38.2	11.1	10.2	6.2
Financial activities	9,590	53.3	9.6	11.7	5.8
All Services					
Professional and business services	16,539	41.1	9.6	15.2	6.9
Education and health services	32,350	74.5	14.3	11.4	5.3
Leisure and hospitality	13,193	50.8	11.3	21.9	6.6
All other services	7,168	52.0	9.8	18.0	7.7
Public administration	6,717	45.4	15.7	11.1	4.1

Source: Bureau of Labor Statistics, Labor Force Statistics from the Current Population Survey, Table 18 (www.bls.gov/cps/tables.htm).

distributed among industry sectors. Blacks were overrepresented in the areas of transportation and utilities, education and health services, and public administration. They were underrepresented in agriculture, mining, construction, and wholesale trade. Hispanics were overrepresented in agriculture, mining, construction, and leisure and hospitality services. They are underrepresented in financial activities, information, education, and health services, and public administration. Asian workers were overrepresented in manufacturing, information, and all services except education and health services. They were very underrepresented in agriculture, mining, and construction.

The industrial distribution of jobs seems to matter in terms of wages paid. Average hourly earnings in 2012 were $23.95 in construction and $19.08 in manufacturing, while they were $11.63 in the leisure and hospitality sector. Because wages depend in part on the level of technology workers use, certain industries with high levels of technology will probably have higher wages than labor-intensive, low-technology industries. Further, if workers in some industries are more likely than others to be represented by unions, it might help them to bargain successfully for higher wages.

Occupational Differences

We tend to have an image of the kinds of jobs that people do in different industries. For example, in the mining industry we think of people actually extracting minerals from the ground, and the retail trade industry conjures up a sales clerk. However, the industrial

TABLE 2.8

EMPLOYMENT BY OCCUPATION FOR MEN, WOMEN, WHITES, BLACKS, HISPANICS, AND ASIANS, 2012

	All	Men	Women	White	Black	His-panic	Asian	Median Weekly Earnings
Total, 16 yrs. & over (thousands)	142,469	75,555	66,914	114,769	15,856	21,878	7,705	$768
Percent	100%	100%	100%	100%	100%	100%	100%	
Mgt., prof., and related	37.9	34.7	41.6	38.7	29.5	20.6	48.5	$1,108
Service	17.9	14.7	21.4	16.6	25.5	26.3	18.4	$485
Sales and related	10.8	10.5	11.3	10.9	10.3	9.6	10.6	$689
Office and admin. support	12.4	6.3	19.4	12.3	14.4	11.7	9.7	$643
Farming, fishing, and forestry	0.7	1.0	0.3	0.8	0.3	2.0	0.2	$435
Construction and extraction	4.9	9.0	0.03	5.4	2.7	9.3	1.4	$740
Installation, maintenance, and repair	3.4	6.2	0.02	3.6	2.6	3.7	1.9	$808
Prod., trans., and material moving	11.7	17.6	5.5	11.7	14.8	16.9	9.3	$624

Source: Bureau of Labor Statistics, Labor Force Statistics from the Current Population Survey, Tables 10 and 39 (http://www.bls.gov/cps/tables.htm).

distribution of jobs includes everyone who works in that industry, regardless of the work they do there. For example, a clerical worker or nurse at General Motors will be included in the manufacturing sector, while the machine repair technician or plumber who is employed by a hospital complex will be included in the service industry.

Occupational distributions classify jobs by the type of work performed, regardless of the industry. So, for example, managers are listed in the managerial occupation category whether they manage a McDonald's, supervise a farm equipment factory, or work as a chief executive officer (CEO) in a hospital. The Census Bureau revised how it classifies occupations in the early 1980s and again in 2002, making meaningful comparisons over time difficult. However, reflecting the deindustrialization trends just discussed, there has been a decrease in the share of workers in "blue collar" occupations (Production, Installation, Maintenance and Repair). There has also been a decline in office administration's share of jobs, but a rise in managerial and professional jobs.

Table 2.8 shows the occupational distribution for all male, female, white, black, and Hispanic workers in 2012, and the median weekly earnings in those occupations for year-round, full-time workers. More than one out of every three workers was in a managerial or professional occupation, with one out of every six workers in a service-related occupation. Nine percent of jobs combined are in farming, fishing, and forestry; construction and extraction; and installation, maintenance and repair occupations. The rest of workers are almost evenly divided among the following three broad occupational categories: sales, office and administrative work, and production, transportation and material moving. The table reveals some of the key differences in the gender and racial distribution of jobs. Men's and women's distribution in "white collar" jobs (managerial and professional occupations) is both high and similar to one another. This is good news for women, since this is the highest-paying occupational category. However, one out of every five women works in services, which is a low-paying occupation. The percentages of white, black, Hispanic, and Asian workers in sales and related occupations are similar. But for most other occupations, the distribution of white workers differs substantially from that of black, Hispanic, and Asian workers. Black and Hispanic workers tend to be underrepresented in the high-paying professional and managerial occupations, while Asians are overrepresented. Black and Hispanic workers are overrepresented in the lower-paying service and production, transportation, and material-moving occupations.

FIGURE 2.10
OCCUPATIONAL COMPOSITION BY GENDER, 2012

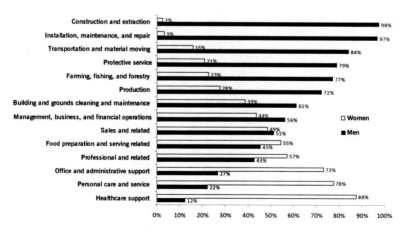

Source: Bureau of Labor Statistics, Household Data, Table 9, Employed persons by occupation, sex and age (bls.gov/cps/cpsaat09.htm).

Figure 2.10 provides a different way of looking at occupational distribution; it shows how employed men and women were distributed within each occupational category in 2012. In 2012, women held 44% of all jobs, but there are only four of the fourteen occupational categories in which women's representation is close to that. For three of the major occupational categories, women hold 70% or more of the jobs in those occupations. For six major occupational categories, men hold 70% or more of the jobs.

Occupational Segregation

The CPS provides data on occupational and industrial categories that are much more detailed than those presented in the previous tables and figures. For example, there are just over 500 detailed occupations included in the CPS data, and Tables 2.9 and 2.10 present a closer look at the ten detailed occupations that account for the greatest share of women's and men's employment, respectively. For women, the top ten occupations employ 31.1% of all women. There is a distinct bunching of women into a small number of occupations. Four of those occupations are over 85% female, and another is 80.9% female. Social scientists refer to the crowding of a large number of women or men into a small number of occupations as "occupational segregation."

TABLE 2.9
TOP 10 DETAILED OCCUPATIONS FOR ALL FULL-TIME EMPLOYED WOMEN, 2012

	Total number of women*	Percent of all women employed	Percent women of all employed in occupation	Median weekly earnings	Total men and women in occupation*
Secretaries and administrative assistants	2,146	4.7%	95.3%	$669	2,251
Healthcare support occupations	2,060	4.5%	87.7%	$482	2,350
Elementary and middle school teachers	1,971	4.3%	80.9%	$942	2,435
Registered nurses	1,946	4.3%	89.4%	$1,097	2,176
Nursing, psychiatric, and home health aides	1,285	2.8%	88.1%	$451	1,458
Customer service representatives	1,033	2.3%	67.3%	$608	1,535
First-line supervisors of retail sales workers	977	2.1%	42.6%	$711	2,295
Cashiers	941	2.1%	69.8%	$376	1,348
Managers, all other	902	2.0%	38.1%	$1,258	2,367
Accountants and auditors	886	1.9%	60.2%	$1,110	1,471
Top ten	14,147	31.1%	71.9%		19,686
Total women employed	45,462	100.0%	44.2%	$768	

Source: Bureau of Labor Statistics, Labor Force Statistics from the Current Population Survey, Table 39 (www.bls.gov/cps/tables.htm). *In thousands.

Occupational segregation: When groups are disproportionately overrepresented in some types of jobs and underrepresented in others

A clearer picture of occupational segregation emerges if we look at more detailed occupations rather than just at broad occupational categories.[13] For example, men and women are equally represented overall in professional, technical, and sales occupations, yet a closer look reveals distinct women's and men's jobs within these categories. Consider nursing and teaching, which together account for one out of every three women employed in the professional occupational category. As Table 2.9 indicates, these two occupations are highly segregated by sex.

Occupational segregation is important because of the striking differences in pay that are associated with men's and women's jobs. As Tables 2.9 and 2.10 show, average weekly earnings for full-time workers in the ten top occupations for men are significantly higher than for the ten top occupations for women. This is not the only source of pay differentials, however. Large pay gaps also exist within many detailed occupational categories. Consider the figures on "management-related occupations" shown in Table 2.11.

Management-related occupations are narrowly defined occupational categories, a subsubset of all managerial occupations. The people in these positions are likely to have similar amounts of education, and these jobs do not require any attributes linked to sex differences or physical strength. Nonetheless, female financial managers make 70% of the weekly wage of male financial managers. Female education administrators make two-thirds of their male

TABLE 2.10
TOP 10 DETAILED OCCUPATIONS FOR ALL FULL-TIME EMPLOYED MEN, 2012

	Total number of men*	Percent of all men employed	Percent men of all employed in occupation	Median weekly earnings	Total men and women in occupation*
Driver/sales workers and truck drivers	2,613	4.4%	95.7%	$709	3,416
Managers, all other	1,477	2.5%	62.6%	$1,359	2,533
First-line supervisors/ managers of retail sales workers	1,382	2.3%	56.8%	$781	2,367
Laborers and freight, stock, and material movers	1,194	2.0%	85.8%	$508	2,295
Construction laborers	1,180	2.0%	97.5%	$558	1,842
Retail salespersons	1,148	1.9%	57.5%	$623	1,514
Janitors and building cleaners	1,096	1.8%	72.6%	$493	1,322
Carpenters	975	1.6%	98.9%	$655	937
Sales representatives, wholesale and manu.	844	1.4%	73.8%	$1,064	1,240
Cooks	832	1.4%	63.4%	$404	1,005
Total top ten	12,741	21.4%	74.6%		18,471
Total men employed	59,439	100.0%	55.7%	$798	102,749

Source: Bureau of Labor Statistics, Labor Force Statistics from the Current Population Survey, Table 39 (www.bls.gov/cps/tables.htm). *In thousands.

TABLE 2.11

Median Earnings of Full-Time Workers by Sex in Management-Related Occupations, 2012

Occupations	Male	Female	Female/Male
Education administrators	$1,566	$1,052	0.67
Financial managers	$1,405	$988	0.70
Social and community service managers	$1,151	$883	0.77
Food service managers	$744	$601	0.81
All management-related occupations	$1,428	$1,036	0.73

Source: Bureau of Labor Statistics, Labor Force Statistics from the Current Population Survey, Table 39 (www.bls.gov/cps/tables.htm).

counterparts' weekly wage. Overall, women in management-related occupations (of which we list only two) make 73 cents for each dollar made by men in management-related occupations.

The Possibility of Discrimination

Differences in job distributions and wage disparities between men and women in similar occupations suggest the possibility that discrimination is occurring. If women's and men's wages were equal, there would be little reason to believe that discrimination was at work. However, as we will see in the remaining chapters, social scientists offer many possible explanations for such differences, and discrimination is only one.

SUMMARY AND CONCLUSIONS

A lot of facts and statistics have been presented in this chapter, but concluding that discrimination exists from the data presented here would be hasty. Even so, the evidence does point to large and persistent labor market inequities based on race and gender. The rest of this book examines two very different approaches to why white men fare better in labor markets than women and blacks. As you begin to consider the explanations for inequality, here are several main points to keep in mind:

- Real wages rose steadily from World War II until the early 1970s. After that, wages fell through the early 1980s, stagnated through the mid 1990s and have risen only slightly since then.
- Over the same period, inequality has increased. Low-wage workers have seen the smallest gains in their wages.
- Black men still earn only about 80% of the wages of white men.
- The wage gap between black and white women fell over the 1960s and 1970s to less than 10%. Since then, it has risen slightly.
- The male-female wage gap has fallen steadily since the early 1970s; however, female earnings are still only a little more than three-fourths of male earnings.
- Overall unemployment trended up slightly over many decades, then rose sharply during 2008 and remains high by historical standards. Black unemployment rates have consistently been over twice as high as white unemployment rates. In contrast, female unemployment rates have usually been lower than male rates since the early 1980s.

- Blacks, Hispanics, and women are much more likely than white men to work in low-wage industries and occupations. Nonetheless, race and gender wage gaps result from differences within as well as between occupations.
- Race and gender wage gaps persist even when age, education, and labor force commitment are comparable.

As you consider these trends, it is important to bear in mind that some inequality is not necessarily bad for the economy. If working harder or more intelligently pays off, inequality will result in economic growth with widely dispersed benefits. Further, some degree of inequality is inevitable in a world where individuals have distinct tastes and talents—nor would one expect groups to be automatically equal, as cultural, social, and even biological differences can have economic effects. In other words, it is quite possible to look at the numbers in this chapter without getting upset.

On the other hand, it is possible to look at these same numbers and get very upset. As Robert Frank and Philip Cook argue in their book *The Winner-Take-All Society*, too much inequality can reduce opportunity and hope—and we certainly have a lot of inequality. While groups will never automatically be equal, it is disturbing that today's losers are the same groups that lost yesterday, yesteryear, well into the last century, and often beyond. It is hard to believe that the racism and sexism that have run through U.S. history have disappeared without a trace. If inequality results from past or present discrimination, then our society is unjust. That would be a bitter pill to swallow.

Each of these interpretations is backed up by a substantial body of theory and evidence. We will explore both interpretations and related debates in detail in the chapters that follow.

DISCUSSION QUESTIONS

1. If discrimination is not responsible for inequality, how might differences in wages, unemployment rates, and occupational distributions by race and gender be explained?

2. If we were to equalize wages between blacks and whites as well as between men and women, does this mean that white men's wages must fall further?

3. If discrimination has declined, why has the black–white unemployment gap widened?

4. If discrimination has not declined, why did the black-white wage gap among women decline until the 1980s?

5. If discrimination exists now but is reduced in the future, would inequality necessarily remain?

6. Using Figures 2.3 and 2.4, explain what has happened to the wage ratios between black and white men and women over the last several decades. Given what you already know about the labor force history of women and blacks, what might explain the wage ratio trends?

7. What reasons might explain the high unemployment rates for persons 16 to 19 years of age (see Table 2.4)?

8. Why do you think unemployment rates for blacks are so high?

9. Explain why unemployment rates rise during economic contraction and fall during expansions.

10. Between 1980 and 2010, the number of persons who were employed rose by 40%. Which industries experienced relative, but not absolute, declines in employment?

SUGGESTED READINGS

Council of Economic Advisors. 2000 and 2009. "Economic Report of the President," www. gpoaccess.gov/eop/.

Economic Report of the President. 2013. Washington, DC: Government Printing Office.

Frank, Robert H., and Philip J. Cook. 1995. *The Winner-Take-All Society.* New York: Free Press.

Harrison, Bennett, and Barry Bluestone. 1982. *The Deindustrialization of America.* New York: Basic Books.

Mishel, Lawrence, Jared Bernstein, and Heidi Shierholz. 2009. *The State of Working America, 2008-09.* Ithaca, NY: Cornell University Press.

Mishel, Lawrence, Josh Bivens, Elise Gould, and Heidi Shierholz. 2012. *The State of Working America,* 12th edition. Ithaca, NY: Cornell University Press.

U.S. Census Bureau. Historical Income Tables: Households, retrieved from www.census.gov/ hhes/www/income/data/historical/household/ (July 2013).

Wolff, Edward. 2010. "Recent Trends in Household Wealth in the United States: Rising Debt and the Middle-Class Squeeze—an Update to 2007." *Working Paper* No. 589. Levy Economics Institute of Bard College, Annandale-on-Hudson, NY.

ENDNOTES

[1] These differences persist even after adjusting for the age, education, and experience of individual workers. Studies that make those adjustments are explored in Chapter 5.

[2] In much of this book, we use the term "wage" to refer to both wages and salaries. Because self-employment income is a relatively small portion of earnings, the trends in earnings and wages are similar.

[3] Each year the annual results of the Establishment Data survey are published in the January issue of the Bureau of Labor Statistics, *Employment and Earnings.* Monthly tables from *Employment and Earnings* can be found at http://www.bls.gov/web/empsit.supp.toc.htm#header1.

[4] The income data collected from the March CPS are available annually from the U.S. Census Bureau's website on income (www.census.gov/hhes/www/income.html).

[5] A subset of people are asked about their weekly and hourly earnings, however.

[6] U.S. Bureau of the Census, Historical Income Tables: Households, Table H-1. Income Limits for Each Fifth and Top 5 Percent (census.gov).

[7] U.S. Bureau of the Census, Historical Income Tables: Households, Table H-9. Race of Head of Household by Median and Mean Income (census.gov).

[8] Mishel, Bernstein, and Shierholz, *The State of Working America, 2008-09*, Table 5.2.

[9] Edward N. Wolff, "Recent Trends in Household Wealth in the United States: Rising Debt and the Middle-Class Squeeze—an Update to 2007," Levy Economics Institute of Bard College, Working Paper No. 589, March 2010.

[10] Mishel, Bivens, Gould, and Shierholz, *The State of Working America*, 12th edition (2012), Share of aggregate family income received by quintile and top 5% of families, 1947-2010 (stateofworkingamerica.org).

[11] *Economic Report of the President* (2013), Table B–43. Civilian unemployment rate by demographic characteristic, 1972–2012.

[12] May 2012 National Occupational Employment and Wage Estimates, Bureau of Labor Statistics retrieved from www.bls.gov/oes/current/oes_nat.htm (July 2013).

[13] There are similar, although not as pronounced, differences to be found by looking at detailed industrial breakdowns. For example, while women are 29% of all workers in manufacturing, 53% of those employed in textile manufacturing are female, while only 13% of those who work in steel and iron foundries are women (see U.S. Department of Labor, Bureau of Labor Statistics, *Labor Force Statistics from the Current Population Survey*, Table 18, retrieved from www.bls.gov/cps/tables.htm (July 2012).

THE NEOCLASSICAL APPROACH

3

THE BASICS OF NEOCLASSICAL ECONOMICS

CENTRAL IDEAS: MARKETS AND COMPETITION

Most economists share a core set of ideas known as the neoclassical approach. This chapter provides a broad look at the neoclassical approach, its central concepts, how the model works, what it implies for government policies, and finally, a look behind the scenes to understand why markets exist. We start with this general overview as it helps to explain how most economists approach, explain, and make government-policy recommendations on virtually any issue, including discrimination.

When political economists think about the economy, they focus first on work and production. When neoclassical economists approach the economy, they focus on how goods and services are exchanged. This latter approach takes us to the question of markets.

For example, suppose an economist is wandering the streets of downtown New York City, and someone asks her how the city ended up with so many skyscrapers. If she is a political economist, she would attribute the skyscrapers to the millions of hours of work that went into the structures, but if she is a neoclassical economist, she would argue that the skyscrapers result from the workings of supply and demand.

When you purchase a car, lemon, or artichoke, you engage in a market exchange. In each case, we can identify the price paid, the quantity of the good purchased, and the two sides of the market—those who supply the good and receive money, and those who demand the good and spend money. The goods and services that are exchanged in markets are called commodities. To be a commodity, a thing or activity must be owned and be exchanged in the market.

Markets themselves may be beneficial for society if there is competition. The version of competition described in neoclassical economics is unlike that found in sports or scholarships, where there always are winners and losers. Instead, it centers on the notion that competition prevents individuals from exercising control over the market. "Perfect competition" means that no one has power in the sense that no one can influence the market price.

Perfect competition: Where no single buyer or seller controls the market price

How can we tell if a market is competitive? One check is whether there are many buyers and sellers. If you can only buy electricity from one company, then there is not competition in the electricity market. Another check is whether the goods or services sold in the market are similar. The beer market may have lots of buyers and sellers, but if many consumers are convinced that "Bud is King," competition is imperfect. A final check is whether buyers and sellers know about all the happenings in the market. There are lots of car dealerships in the world, but if people only check out the prices at one before buying, competition will again be imperfect.

While it is harder to see in practice, the surest sign of a competitive market is that neither buyers nor sellers control the price; a market-dictated price emerges instead. Consumers may try to reduce prices and producers to raise prices, but competition stops them cold. Producers charging higher prices will be unable to sell anything, and consumers looking for discounts will be unable to find any. The idea that the market, rather than individuals or corporations, controls what happens in an economy explains the quip that it doesn't take any neoclassical economists to change a light bulb, because if it needed changing, the market would have done it already. This is an example of what neoclassical economists call the "invisible hand," by which markets create harmony among individuals with conflicting interests. This idea was developed by the father of neoclassical economics, Adam Smith, in *The Wealth of Nations*, originally published in 1776. This chapter begins with the concepts of markets and competition, because competitive markets are viewed favorably by neoclassical economists, and this view strongly flavors the neoclassical approach to economic phenomena, including discrimination. Why is competition viewed as desirable? You have seen one part of the answer already: no individual or company can control a competitive market. Another part is the belief that prices in competitive markets reflect the value that society places on each good or service. For example, if consumers desire more bread, they will switch their purchases from some other product, and the new, and usually higher, price will reflect both the greater cost to society for producing more bread and the consumers' greater desire for the good. Related to this, competition is also an incentive mechanism: if people come to value horseshoes more than penknives, they will translate those preferences into new buying patterns, and producers will have an incentive to produce more horseshoes. A final part of the argument is that competitive markets are efficient, but this is getting ahead of our story.

By highlighting the role of markets and competition, neoclassical economics provides a strong vision of how market economies function and a powerful rationale for endorsing competitive markets over other mechanisms to govern the economy. When we come to the question of discrimination, neoclassical economists argue that market competition can even help to solve this problem (Box 3.1). To understand how we get there, we start by gathering up the neoclassical tools that will be needed in later chapters to analyze labor markets and discrimination.

Conditions for Perfect Competition:
- ✔ *Many buyers*
- ✔ *Many sellers*
- ✔ *Homogeneous products*
- ✔ *Perfect information*

BOX 3.1
DISCRIMINATION AND BARRIERS TO COMPETITION

In the neoclassical view, competition ensures that equally productive workers receive the same wages. If black or female workers are paid less than equivalent whites or males, this might result from discrimination (see Chapter 5). Such unfair (and inefficient) wage differences may emerge because competition is blocked by racist or sexist governmental policies or labor unions.

Robert Higgs shows that black economic progress after slavery was hindered by racist behavior (including the use of extreme violence) by government, unions, and communities in the southern United States. Blacks who were able to acquire skills and migrate north, however, escaped these barriers and often improved their circumstances. While blacks still faced much discrimination in the northern United States, discriminatory laws and practices were less severe, so markets operated more freely. As a result of greater competition, Higgs concludes, blacks who moved north were better off.

Similarly, Herbert Hill argues that trade unions prevent competition from occurring (i.e., an employer only has one source of labor) and often have been a major source of employment discrimination and job segregation. During the early part of the 20th century, the American Federation of Labor (AFL) consistently excluded blacks and organized strikes against employers who attempted to hire them. The Congress of Industrial Organizations (CIO, founded in 1935) improved matters, because it had a policy of solidarity among black and white workers. Nonetheless, after the 1955 merger that created the AFL-CIO, the trade union movement was largely absent from the civil rights struggles of the 1950s and 1960s, and since then often has opposed policies such as affirmative action.

Organizations such as unions or government can become means by which the white majority insulates itself from competition from blacks. In the neoclassical view, if competition had been allowed to operate freely, historical patterns of race and gender inequality might have been reduced dramatically.

Sources: Robert Higgs, "Black Progress and the Persistence of Racial Economic Inequalities, 1865-1940," and Herbert Hill, "Black Labor and Affirmative Action: An Historical Perspective," both in Steven Shulman and William Darity, Jr., eds., *The Question of Discrimination: Racial Inequality in the U.S. Labor Market* (Middetown, Conn.: Wesleyan University Press, 1989).

HOW PEOPLE ACT: RATIONALITY, SCARCITY, AND OPPORTUNITY COST

The neoclassical vision of markets outlined earlier stems from assumptions about how people act. The key assumption is that economic behavior is undertaken by a rational individual. This individual has a set of likes and dislikes, which the theory takes as given. These likes and dislikes are called exogenous preferences, implying that people know what they want (i.e., the preferences part) and that those wants come from outside the economy (i.e., the exogenous part). The individual tries his or her best to fulfill those preferences using all available information and searching out all possible courses of action to maximize the benefit to her or himself, which neoclassical economists call the individual's "utility."

Rationality: Using all available information to make decisions that maximize individual utility

Rational individuals need not be hedonistic, seeking to accumulate wealth and live the high life. Some might place a relatively high value on maintaining a healthy lifestyle, others on money, and still others on the enjoyment of music, sleep, work, or fine foods. Individuals do not, however, in the models used by neoclassical economists, feel positively or negatively about the utility of others.

The utility-maximizing individual must make consumption decisions because resources are scarce. Scarcity means that society cannot provide each individual with all the goods, services, or time that they desire. On the one hand, scarcity implies a finite quantity of resources and, on the other, that we desire more resources than are available.

Utility: The way an individual measures the relative pains, pleasures, costs, and benefits of some action

Scarcity is a truism. If you take $20 to the grocery store, then buying more bread means buying less ice cream. If you are reading this book, then you cannot be performing yoga at the same time (go ahead and try it). For neoclassical economists, the fact that you probably would like more money than you currently have and that there are other things you would also like to be doing while reading this implies the problem of scarcity.

Scarcity: The clash of limited human and physical resources with unlimited individual wants

Assuming that we always desire more than we have, any activity we select necessarily implies giving up something else. The utility given up when selecting a particular activity (e.g., through buying one good instead of another) is called the opportunity cost of that activity. This utility may be represented by the dollars that could have been spent on an alternative purchase. For example, consider the opportunity cost of attending college. Look at the direct costs of tuition and books and the psychological costs of going to class and taking tests (we assume you can put a monetary value on these), then compare this to the opportunity cost—the indirect costs of college include the wages you would have received from a job you would have held and the enjoyment, if any, that would have gone along with that job (you also have to account for the fact that as a college graduate, you would earn more later in life, but that is a story for the next chapter). If you translate all this into monetary terms, or think of it in terms of utility, then you go to college only if the opportunity cost is sufficiently low.

Opportunity cost: The next most valued alternative to what you do or choose, what is "foregone" when you make a choice

The possibility of rational individuals confronting scarcity by using the notion of opportunity costs is important for several reasons. First, because individuals make decisions based on their own desires, opportunity costs diverge across individuals. Faced with the same dollar costs of going to college, some people choose to attend and others to avoid college. In the neoclassical view, we all are distinct, so it is not surprising if we make different decisions.

Second, although individuals have different preferences, the use of opportunity cost by rational individuals to make decisions implies that many economic actions are predictable. If wages for jobs held by high-school graduates rise, then the opportunity cost of attending college also rises, so at least some people should drop out of college or never enroll. The notion of rational individuals applying the concept of opportunity cost means that neoclassical economists can make predictions about the behavior of individuals who may have very different wants and desires.

Third, if rational individuals use opportunity costs to make decisions, we can view people as utility maximizers. In other words, we each calculate how to make ourselves better off. You might ask why neoclassical economists do not just assume that money is the yardstick we use to calculate opportunity costs. The problem is that money would not allow each of us to differ in what we like, and it would imply that economists can compare how well-off various individuals are according to income. Neoclassical economists reject this possibility, because they assume we each have our own preferences. Even for identical twins, one might prefer blue clothing over green, while the other enjoys green clothing and detests blue. More directly, if two people purchase the same make of automobile, does this mean that they enjoy it equally? Such an occurrence would be entirely accidental, so neoclassical economists assume that each of us has our own measuring stick for pain and pleasure.

The notion of opportunity costs may be applied to almost any decision, but it usually is applied to decisions about buying and selling. We now turn to these matters.

WELCOME TO THE MARKET: DEMAND AND SUPPLY

This section examines a market for a specific good, looking first at demand, then at supply, and finally at equilibrium. Throughout, we assume there is competition, so that no one controls the price of the good.

Demand

Suppose you are thinking about purchasing a package of chewing gum. As a rational individual, you say, "Aha, I'll calculate the opportunity cost, then decide." Your alternatives may include purchasing candy instead, putting the money in a savings account, or perhaps working a few minutes less each day instead of earning money for gum. It does not matter which alternative is relevant, only that you think about the most-valued one. If the relevant alternative is purchasing candy, you compare the costs and resulting enjoyment from consuming gum and candy.

If the price of gum or candy is one dollar, you decide to buy candy—but what if the price of gum were only 50 cents? Then, you would be more likely to buy the gum. If the price of gum drops to 25 cents, you would be even more likely to purchase gum and forget the candy.

This inverse relation between change in price and change in the quantity demanded is called the law of demand. This law helps to explain why markets are predictable. Also, notice that differences in people's preferences have not disappeared here, because the price you pay to buy a product does not signal its utility for you. Certainly, if you paid 25 cents for the gum, it is worth at least 25 cents, but maybe it is worth more to you, maybe even one dollar a pack.

Law of demand: As the price of a good rises, desired purchases decline

Demand can, and does, change for a variety of reasons. In the gum market, if incomes rise as more people quit smoking or it is discovered that chewing gum leads to healthy teeth, demand would increase. In these cases, the law of demand is not involved: at any price, people want to buy more. It is only when the price of the good in question changes and people respond that we see the law of demand at work.

For our purposes, the most important reason for changes in demand is the availability of substitute goods. In the case of candy and gum, these are substitutes, and what we did not point out earlier is obvious: when the price of gum fell, consumers bought less candy. When two goods are substitutes, a fall in the price of one leads consumers to switch to that good and away from the other.

> **Determinants of Demand:**
> ✔ Consumer preferences
> ✔ Income of consumers
> ✔ Population
> ✔ Availability of substitutes

Why do we care about the notion of substitutes? Because in a crucial market— the labor market—employees of different races and genders may be viewed as substitutes by employers. To get somewhat ahead of our story, if equivalent black workers are much cheaper than white workers, then it would seem that rational employers would have a strong incentive to substitute blacks for whites.

Substitute goods: Where buying more of one good usually means buying less of the other

Supply

Go back to the gum example, and consider the supply side. Unlike consumers, producers of gum do not worry about whether they enjoy chewing it, whether it is healthy, or whether used gum damages the environment or is a social nuisance. All the producers worry about is profits. Firms try to maximize profits, which is parallel to consumers who try to maximize utility. Consumers can deal with all the messy calculations involved in figuring out how much enjoyment they get out of gum or candy; firms keep their eye on the bottom line.

Profits: The difference between sales revenues and costs for a firm

When firms make a determination to supply some good or service to the market, they will typically obey the law of supply, which means that firms will produce more at higher prices and less at lower prices, all in an effort to maximize profits. Why would firms wish to sell more at higher prices? The short answer is that the more money a firm receives for producing a particular good, the higher the opportunity cost for producing something else (or for going out of business). Firms simply weigh these opportunity costs and move their efforts where profits are the highest. For example, suppose you are producing bagels and bags. If the market price (i.e., the selling price) of bagels rises, then your profits go up if you switch at least some of your efforts away from bags and to bagels. Investors do much the same thing. As the price at which a good can be sold goes up, investment funds move toward producing more of that good.

> **Determinants of Supply:**
> ✔ Technology
> ✔ Income of consumers
> ✔ Costs of capital, labor, or other inputs
> ✔ Alternative market opportunities

Law of supply: As the price of a good rises, desired sales also rise

Alternatively, the law of supply may hold because average costs increase as production increases. For example, suppose that an automobile factory runs a single shift during the day and can produce 450 cars at an average cost of $20,000 per car. The only way to produce more cars is to pay workers overtime or hire another shift at higher wages (because people usually receive higher wages for working evenings or nights). Either way, the average cost of producing a car is bound to rise, perhaps to $22,000 per car. Once the plant is producing all the cars that its capacity will allow, efforts to produce even more cars will increase the average cost of a car even more dramatically. The bottom line here is that because car producers find average costs going up as they produce more, they will only be willing to sell more cars if the market price rises. The law of supply holds in this case.

Like demand, supply can change such that firms will wish to sell more (or less) at any given price. As technology improves, this reduces a firm's costs and directly increases its profits. At the same time, new, lower-cost technologies give firms an incentive to produce and sell more goods. If wages or the price of other inputs fall, the firm similarly will wish to sell more at the going price. For a variety of reasons, some industries may have a large number of potential producers, where firms would find it easy to shift from one product to another. When this is the case, such as with producers of pants and blouses, supply is affected, because small changes in price can draw in or out a large number of producers. By extension, many firms keep an eye on a wide variety of potential markets, looking for the most profitable one.

The supply of goods to the market is based on profit maximization by firms. As the earlier examples suggest, firms have strong incentives to seek low-cost production methods and to provide goods that consumers will purchase. These incentives later turn out to help make competitive markets efficient.

Equilibrium

We now arrive at the combination of supply and demand in the market. Supply and demand are connected by the concept of market equilibrium. Equilibrium in a market is the price at which quantity supplied (the quantity suppliers are able and willing to offer for sale at a particular price) and quantity demanded (the quantity buyers are able and willing to buy at a particular price) are equal, subject to constraints such as scarce resources. At this price, everything that is produced is purchased, so no goods are left unsold and no desired purchases go unmade (the market, in the language of neoclassical economics, "clears"). At all other prices, the quantity supplied and the quantity demanded will be unequal.

Equilibrium: A situation with no tendency to change

The notion of a "market-clearing" equilibrium has long fascinated economists, because it implies that under competition, everyone is doing exactly what they wish to do. No one is forced to sell or buy, and no one who is willing and able to buy or sell is left out. Most remarkably, all this interaction occurs in a setting where individuals neither know nor care about who they are dealing with. If you want to buy Peruvian perfume, you don't need to know who produced it or whether they enjoy or detest the product. You only know they are willing to provide the product at the price you pay, so they must be better off producing perfume as opposed to doing something else. Similarly, the producer neither knows nor cares who you are.

Rarely do we see equilibrium in the real world, because the conditions that determine supply and demand frequently change. Consumer desires, incomes, population, technology and prices of inputs all are subject to change, so why is equilibrium important if it is a moving target? It is important because it tells us where the economy is going and something about what the economy will look like in the future (though we are unlikely to be able to predict a future equilibrium with any certainty, since changes in all these factors will continue to happen).

Suppose we are in disequilibrium, with sellers' inventories of chewing gum stacking up on the shelves. Supply and demand theory tells us this is a situation of excess supply. Further, we can predict that price will fall, desired sales will decrease, and desired purchases will increase as we move toward equilibrium (Box 3.2). In parallel fashion, if stands cannot keep gum in stock, there is excess demand, and we would expect the price to rise, desired sales will increase, and desired purchases will decrease as we move toward equilibrium.

BOX 3.2
GETTING TO EQUILIBRIUM: THE CASE OF ARTICHOKES

If we rarely see a situation in which equilibrium occurs, then where are we? We are heading toward equilibrium.

The artichoke market is described by Figure 3.1. Consumers purchase artichokes to eat and will purchase other vegetables when the price of artichokes rises, so it makes sense that the law of demand holds in this market. As the price of artichokes rises, consumers purchase fewer artichokes. As the price of artichokes falls, such as when they are in season, consumers purchase more. Figure 3.1 shows the law of demand with the quantity demanded increasing from 1,000 to 2,000 artichokes as the price of artichokes falls from $2.00 to $1.50. The quantity demanded continues rising to 3000 artichokes as the price falls to $1.00.

The law of supply also is likely to hold in the artichoke market, because as the price rises, farmers growing other foodstuffs will find artichokes increasingly attractive. The opportunity cost of growing tomatoes instead of artichokes goes up. Figure 3.1 shows a demonstration of the law of supply with the quantity falling from 3,000 to 2,000 artichokes as the price falls from $2.00 to $1.50, and falling again to 1000 artichokes as the price falls to $1.00.

The equilibrium price and quantity can be found where supply and demand cross—at $1.50 per artichoke. However, how do we get there if we are not there al-

FIGURE 3.1
EQUILIBRIUM IN THE ARTICHOKE MARKET

ready? If the price is too high, such as $2.00, there will be excess supply. Farmers will grow and send 3,000 artichokes to market, but consumers will only wish to purchase 1,000 artichokes. Indeed, the only way to dump all 3,000 artichokes is to sell them at $1.00 each, but farmers won't get caught napping again. Next season, they will produce less, until the equilibrium price of $1.50 is achieved.

Similarly, if the price is too low, such as $1.00, then consumers will want to buy 3,000 artichokes but only find 1,000 in the stores. Now the price goes up until it hits $1.50, where the amount that farmers wish to produce equals the amount that consumers will purchase.

BOX 3.3
CHANGING EQUILIBRIUM: ARTICHOKES AGAIN?

Much of the reason we rarely see equilibrium occurring is that supply or demand, or both, frequently change. The laws of supply and demand help us to predict how prices and quantities will respond to such changes.

Return to the artichoke market example. Suppose that the latest craze in cooking is braised artichokes, as shown around the country on the television series, "The Baltimore Chef" (name changed to protect the innocent). Soon, everyone is trying braised artichokes, or stated differently, demand for artichokes increases. Figure 3.2 shows such an increase in demand. Consumers who purchase artichokes wish to buy more than 2,000, sold at $1.50 each. This results in excess demand (4,000 artichokes is the quantity demanded, 2,000 the quantity supplied, and 2,000 the excess demand). The price will be bid up until the excess demand disappears and equilibrium is achieved—here, at a price of $2.00 per artichoke, with 3,000 being bought and sold. Therefore, supply and demand allow

FIGURE 3.2
CHANGE IN DEMAND FOR ARTICHOKES

us to predict that after "The Baltimore Chef" makes braised artichokes popular, more artichokes will be sold and at a higher price.

On the supply side, researchers develop a "super-artichoke seed" that doubles the yield of artichokes per acre of land employed and at a lower cost per artichoke. The laws of supply and demand allow us to predict what will happen.

The speed at which a market approaches equilibrium depends on the specific market. In the market for chewing gum, it would be relatively easy for the quantity supplied to fall or rise to meet demand in a short period of time. Firms producing gum would put on or remove an extra shift. In a market such as that for nurses, however, disequilibrium could exist for a long period, because if there is an excess demand, it takes years to train more nurses. If there is an excess supply, nurses may find precious few comparable jobs available (given their skills), so many will stay on for decades, even if wages fall. Regardless of the speed at which equilibrium is approached, the point remains that the market will tend to balance supply and demand.

The main reason that we frequently are out of equilibrium is located in changes in demand and supply (Box 3.3). A change in any of the "givens," such as technology or tastes, will alter the relationship between supply and demand. Suppose consumers change their preferences and desire less of the product. This change will disrupt equilibrium, because sellers cannot sell all that they have produced. Then, we return to our story of disequilibrium (starting here with excess supply).

A drop in supply does the opposite. Suppose that an opportunity for especially high profits opens up in the chocolate market. Some chewing gum producers will close up shop or switch to chocolate production as investors move their capital out of the old market and into the new. In the gum market, we will find excess demand as fewer firms are willing to produce gum at the old equilibrium price. Now we are back at disequilibrium, although here with excess demand, so the price should rise as gum chewers entice producers back into the chewing gum market.

We have just argued that the forces of supply and demand drive a market toward equilibrium. Stepping back for a moment, however, we see that the real forces at work are those behind supply and demand—rational consumers and profit-maximizing firms. Rational consumers constantly seek out cheaper and higher-quality products. They place dollars behind that search, and they reward firms for reducing costs, improving quality, and generally giving consumers what they want. The firm, on the other hand, does not care what consumers want, but it does care about profits, which are a reward for keeping down costs and satisfying consumers. This reward system keeps firms and consumers moving toward equilibrium regardless of changes in the economy.

A variety of conclusions follow from these neoclassical stories. First, although we may have different wants and needs, may look and act differently from each other, and cannot pretend to even know how each other feels, competitive markets can generate an equilibrium where each of us does precisely what we wish to do. Second, although we are so diverse, our behavior in the market is largely predictable. While equilibrium does not often occur per se, economists can predict what will happen to prices and quantities sold in particular markets in the future by looking at changes in supply and demand or at disequilibrium situations. Third, competitive markets tend to eliminate overproduction and underproduction automatically. When consumers wanted "beanie babies," the dolls were produced in abundance, but thanks to markets, few are produced today. Finally, the movements of consumers and investors in and out of different markets make the market system work. Competition depends on mobility, and anything that obstructs mobility—such as legal restrictions or trade unions (Box 3.1)—will mean that some people are not being allowed to do as they wish. As a result, we all suffer. To see why, we turn to the neoclassical understanding of efficiency.

EFFICIENCY, EQUITY, AND THE GOVERNMENT

The neoclassical economic view favoring markets over government intervention stems from the claim that competitive markets are efficient and, at least in a weak sense, equitable. Here, we look at the ideas of efficiency and equity to reach the government policy conclusions.

Efficiency

Neoclassical economists use the concept of efficiency as defined by the turn-of-the-20th-century Italian sociologist, Vilfredo Pareto. According to Pareto, a situation or event is efficient if no one can be made better off unless someone else is made worse off. This implies, for example, that it may be inefficient to use outdated technology. If we know how to produce automobiles on an assembly line using one-quarter of the labor it would take to assemble cars in someone's garage, it would be inefficient to build in the garage. Theoretically, the worker who builds in his garage could make more money producing on an assembly line (after paying for capital), and consumers would pay less for cars. Everyone would be better off, so efficiency can be improved. More directly, if you trade a popsicle for an ice-cream cone held by a friend, this must be an efficient outcome: if you were not both better off, the trade would not have occurred.

> ### Efficiency: Situations where one person cannot be made better off without harming someone else

The last example explains why competitive markets are viewed so favorably by neoclassical economists. No rational individual would engage in a trade that would not leave him or her at least as well off as before the trade. You would not work for someone, buy a product from someone, or rent out a house or apartment unless you gained in the process. The person or corporation on the other side of the market must similarly gain. This is the sense in which there is no power held by anyone in a competitive market.

This neoclassical understanding of efficiency fits neatly with the notion that we cannot know the preferences and pains of others. All we know is that—with scarcity—more is better, and that—because of rationality—people will strive to increase their utility. A market trade therefore is efficient—it improves the well-being of the participants (and we assume it does not affect the well-being of anyone else)—even though we do not know why each participant engaged in the transaction.

In actual economies, it is difficult to think of changes that are efficient in the sense used here. If an automobile manufacturer introduces a new technology that uses fewer workers, the economy may be able to produce the same amount of cars using fewer resources. The laid-off workers will produce something else, but they may experience a pay cut in the process and so be worse off. Or, consider a government policy such as increasing taxes to fund an improved educational system. We might end up able to produce more as a result, but in the meantime, someone is paying higher taxes and so may be worse off.

Economists respond to these problems in various ways, but largely, they look at potential, rather than actual, efficiency improvements. In theory, the new automobile technology allows us to produce more, so the laid-off automobile workers could still receive their old wages and everyone would benefit. Similarly, the government could ask those who receive education to pay back the previous generation for their earlier funding of education, and everyone would gain. Stated differently, if some change in the economy results in our producing more goods and services with fewer resources, then this change represents a potential improvement in efficiency. Often, potential improvements in efficiency are the most that we can hope for in the real world.[1]

Equity

When economists think of fairness or equality, they use the term equity. Historically, economists have thought of equity as meaning equal outcomes (Blaug, 1997). If you want to achieve an equitable distribution of a pie between two people, you divide it in half (you can ensure that the division is fair if one person cuts and the other chooses first). In the entire economy, equity may mean that everyone has an equal amount of wealth and receives the same income. The lower incomes and poorer housing that are experienced by the average black as opposed to the average white American are then "inequitable."

Equity: Either equal opportunities or equal outcomes

No one claims that competitive markets provide equity in this sense. To see why, try a "thought experiment" in which we assume that everyone starts out with the same amount of money when they are born and that we allow competition to rule the marketplace. Some people, however, may be better at mathematics, some may excel in literature, and others may not do well at anything. When these people enter the job market, the laws of supply and demand will take hold. Those who produce more of the goods that people desire and will pay for in turn will receive higher incomes; those who produce less will receive less.

Just as you are ready to give up on the idea of having equity in a market economy, an idea dawns on you: tax the rich, and give the money to the poor. That way, the market still works, and we can have equity. Not so fast, however. You've accidentally stepped on the law of supply here, and the market will no longer be efficient. For example, someone who would have become a doctor now may deduce that they can earn the same money holding down an easier job having better hours.

This is just one example of what Arthur Okun (1975) called the "trade-off" between equity and efficiency. The trade-off emerges from the fact that as money, wealth, education, or any other economic resource is shifted from the rich to the poor, everyone has less reason to work hard and try to get ahead. This is particularly troubling for entrepreneurs and innovators. Such individuals take big risks, knowing that they likely will come out losers but hoping for the big score, to develop the next iPad, a cleaner fuel source, a better microwave popcorn, or a cure for breast cancer. If they know that winning just means the government will take more from them, the incentive to innovate will be reduced, and we may all suffer as a result (i.e., efficiency falls).

There is a more limited sense in which the notion of equity fits into a competitive economy: equity as equal opportunity. The market may not make each of us rich, but in the neoclassical view, it provides each and every one of us with the opportunity to try to start the next Apple Computers, to become a doctor, or to become a seamstress. Theoretically, the market is blind to who we are, what we like, and who we know, so each of us has an equal chance to contribute to the economy and be rewarded accordingly.

Laissez-Faire Policies

The major government policy conclusion for many neoclassical economists is that the government should "leave it alone," or as the French saying puts it, to engage in *laissez-faire* economic policies.

Laissez-faire: Government policies that do not interfere with markets

The chief reason for supporting laissez-faire policies follows from our discussion of the trade-off between equity and efficiency: government interference to create equity usually distorts the market and causes inefficiency. From the definition of efficiency, it follows that we could make at least one person better off without making anyone else worse off if the government stopped interfering. Neoclassical economists agree that certain types of markets warrant government intervention, but before turning to those cases, let's look at the rationale for laissez-faire policies.

A classic example of inefficient government interference is the imposition of tariffs or quotas on foreign goods. Tariffs are taxes on imports that make the products of domestic firms relatively cheaper. Quotas limit the amount of foreign imports and so also make domestic firms' products more attractive (or at least more available). Such policies are inefficient and may even be inequitable, so neoclassical economists argue that tariffs and quotas should be avoided.

In the early 1980s, the big three U.S. auto producers (GM, Ford, and Chrysler) were losing sales to Japanese producers, so they lobbied for—and got—a quota on Japanese imports. The result? Consumers paid more for cars. How much more? The equivalent of $160,000 per year per U.S. worker whose job was "saved" by the quota.[2] The affected U.S. auto workers may have preferred a one-time cash payment of $160,000 as a bribe to leave the industry, and U.S. consumers would have saved the money in remaining years. A laissez-faire policy of no quotas, even with such a bribe, would have made many people better off without harming anyone; such a policy would be efficient without damaging our sense of equity.

You might wonder why, if an efficient policy was available, the U.S. government did not use it. Nobel Prize-winner in economics James Buchanan offers insight into this question. Buchanan argues that government officials should themselves be viewed as rational utility maximizers. This means they act just like everyone else in the economy but with one crucial difference: there is no market-dictated, competitive price for government actions. Government officials therefore are able to improve their position regardless of whether their actions harm others. Periodic elections place a limit on the scope for officials to act in their own interests, but in Buchanan's view, elections do not provide anywhere near the strict discipline of the market. In fact, they may even lead directly to inefficient outcomes. Under Buchanan's approach, it is not surprising that the government acted inefficiently and imposed quotas on Japanese automobiles; campaign donations from the big three U.S. auto producers and votes from United Auto Workers union members ensured that a more efficient policy—free trade—simply was not in the cards.

For some neoclassical economists like Buchanan or another famous Nobel Prize-winner, Milton Friedman, the cry for laissez-faire economic policies is often the first and last word, whether the topic is foreign competition, poverty, discrimination, or even illicit drug use. Many neoclassical economists, however, are more liberal (in the modern sense), so they tend to make four exceptions to this rule. The first concerns Okun's trade-off between equity and efficiency. If we value both equity and efficiency, then we would defend limited government intervention in the market, such as a graduated income tax (i.e., increasing tax rates for higher incomes) or food programs for the poorest members of society in the name of equity, while mainly permitting markets to function in the name of efficiency. The second exception is imperfect competition, markets where there is power on either the supply or the demand side. In these cases, markets are inefficient, and government regulation might help. For example, if one type of computer software dominates 90% of the market, then prices will be high (i.e., above the competitive price), so the government might regulate and reduce prices to improve efficiency. The third is externalities, or aspects of goods and services that affect people who do not buy the product. Cigarette smoke in a public elevator, a boombox on a neighbor's front porch, or the smell of flowers in an office are examples of products with externalities. Government regulations such as restrictions on permissible sound levels may improve efficiency in the presence of externalities.[3] The fourth exception concerns public goods, which are goods that everyone can enjoy regardless of who purchased them.[4] For example, if you plant a tree in your yard (assuming you have a yard), everyone can enjoy the resulting reduction in carbon in the atmosphere. By related logic, child care and education may have public-goods aspects insofar as we all benefit from having a well-educated and healthy populace.

Public goods: Goods or services the free market underproduces because everyone benefits regardless of who pays

If there is a rule for neoclassical economists who step away from laissez-faire, it is that government policies should strive to create "market-like" conditions. If we cannot have a competitive market, at least we can come close. This approach, which is recommended by notable economists such as Alan Blinder and Nobel Prize-winner Robert Solow, explains why economists, and the Obama administration, believe that the problem of pollution can be solved in part by selling "carbon credits," which firms could buy and sell, a system (also referred to as "cap and trade") which became law in California as of 2012.[5] Firms who find it very costly to reduce carbon emissions will purchase the rights, while companies who can easily or cheaply cut back on those emissions will sell those rights. Therefore, we will end up with pollution being reduced by the lowest-cost avenue, and by making this process like a market, efficiency is improved. Similarly, if education is underprovided by the market because it is a public good, neoclassical economists might recommend voucher systems to maintain competition between schools for students while providing public funding (Sandstrom and Bergstrom, 2004).

BEHIND THE MARKET: THE DIVISION OF LABOR AND COMPARATIVE ADVANTAGE

Why do markets exist? This seemingly innocuous question is not easy to answer. We know that competitive markets may be efficient and that government intervention may be harmful, but where do markets come from in the first place? The answer lies in the division of labor, whereby people specialize in various tasks. The reason for specialization and the division of labor in turn can be found in the concept of comparative advantage. We introduce these concepts here as they underpin the neoclassical explanation for why women typically earn less than men and bear the brunt of child-rearing tasks. To understand discrimination, you need to understand these concepts.

Adam Smith begins *The Wealth of Nations* by arguing that a major distinction between a rich and a poor society lies in the division of labor. In the rich society, everyone is doing something different; some people are carpenters, others selling food, still others cooking, cleaning, etc. In the poor society, individual people or families struggle to do everything needed to survive, including carpentry, cooking, growing food, etc. The division of labor allows people to learn particular tasks, hone their skills, and develop improvements in how jobs are performed. In modern terminology, Smith was arguing that the division of labor is efficient, and he believed the market promoted the division.

Division of labor: Jobs are attached to particular products, and for a single product, there are various specialized jobs

In a famous passage from *The Wealth of Nations*, Smith used the process of pin-making to describe how productivity improves with the division of labor, but we can see the process in any workplace. Some people learn how to handle paperwork, others to handle and develop relationships with customers, others to transport the product or supplies, and still others to work on producing the firm's good or service. Without this division of labor, no one person could know all the relevant jobs well enough to perform them efficiently.

The division of labor results in specialization. As jobs and tasks are divided, each of us becomes a specialist in his or her own area of expertise. We become more proficient and more knowledgeable. If you are thinking this may lead to drudgery, tedium, and repetitive work, you are right, and Smith agreed that specialization was not always pleasurable. Nonetheless, if we abandoned the division of labor, it would mean that the next time you are sick, your doctor would know as much about treating you as about building a car or farming. The actors that you see in the movies would have the expertise of your local community theater, and your lawyer would know as much about the law as you do. And Smith believed that this is precisely what would happen if we abandoned our market economy.

There is another reason why the division of labor is efficient. It allows an economy to use the law of comparative advantage. This notion was developed by David Ricardo to account for the fact that nations often produce different commodities, which then are exchanged. The United States may produce wheat while Mexico produces tomatoes, and wheat flows south while tomatoes flow north. Ricardo asked himself why this occurred. One answer is that Mexico receives more sunshine and tomatoes grow well in high sunlight, so we have an efficient division of labor across national borders.

Comparative advantage: When a person, community, or nation can produce a good or service for exchange relatively more cheaply than another

We still have to explain why Mexico does not just grow both tomatoes *and* wheat. This is where comparative advantage really comes in. The law of comparative advantage implies that relatively poor resources should be applied to tasks where the relative cost of using superior resources is higher. If wheat can be grown just about anywhere but tomatoes only with high levels of sunlight, then even if Mexico can produce wheat more cheaply, it is efficient for them to specialize in tomatoes while the United States specializes in wheat.

Consider an example closer to home. Suppose that on average, men are taller than women. This gives men an advantage in cleaning windows, which often stretch above head level. If we found a married couple with a man avoiding windows and a woman cleaning them, the law of comparative advantage may help to explain why. Ask what the man and woman would have to give up to clean the windows (i.e., the opportunity cost). If the man would have to give up $100 from paid employment to clean while the woman would only lose $50 for the same time, then it may be efficient for the woman to clean the windows. Implicitly, the couple has contracted for the man to bring in money in exchange for work by the woman at home; in that contract, the couple is using the law of comparative advantage.

Like the couple deciding about who cleans windows, competitive markets should also follow the law of comparative advantage. Your doctor might have become a very productive bus driver, but the market rewards her more for going into the field where her comparative advantage is found. Many people can drive buses, but few have the aptitude to be a good doctor.

SUMMING UP

The neoclassical approach focuses on markets and competition. To understand how these phenomena operate, we consider how individuals make decisions. Rational individuals face the problem of scarcity and respond by weighing the costs and benefits of alternative actions; they measure the opportunity cost of actions. Stated differently, by making decisions based on opportunity costs and preferences, individuals maximize their personal utility. We cannot touch, taste, or measure the utility that others receive, but rationality and scarcity imply that we can think of people as maximizing utility.

We all may have different preferences and opportunity costs, but we are also predictable. As the costs of performing some activity rise, fewer people will want to engage in it. This predictability leads to the laws of supply and demand, so we know, for example, that when the price of gasoline rises, people will drive less and service stations will want to sell more.

Competitive markets head us toward equilibrium. In a competitive market equilibrium, everyone who is willing and able to sell or buy at the going price can do so. While we may not see equilibrium, there are powerful market forces pushing us in that direction, because only at that point is everyone who would benefit from trade able to do so. Equilibrium in competitive markets therefore is efficient: no one can be made better off unless someone else suffers.

Many neoclassical economists favor laissez-faire government policies, letting the market work efficiently to the benefit of all participants. Nonetheless, markets sometimes are imperfect, and even where competition rules, markets may lead to severe income inequality. For these reasons, other neoclassical economists believe there may be a positive role for government intervention.

Why are markets needed at all? The initial answer—that efficiency improves as the division of labor increases—helps to explain why we might find individuals doing very different jobs. More importantly, when people specialize in different jobs or tasks, the market will reward them for using their comparative advantage. It is what you are relatively good at, not just what you are absolutely good at, that you should focus on.

The next chapter takes these arguments into the workplace in search of an explanation for why some people earn more than others.

DISCUSSION QUESTIONS

1. What markets for goods or services best fit the idea of competition, and why? Are there numerous substitute goods or services in this market?

2. Could you use supply and demand to explain why, as incomes rise, people typically have fewer children? Could you also use supply and demand as an explanation if, instead, people had more children as incomes rose?

3. Do the notions of opportunity cost and utility maximization explain decisions you made on a recent shopping trip? If so, can you identify decisions that would have been "irrational"?

4. Do the notions of opportunity cost and utility maximization help to explain people's religious beliefs, choice of marriage partners, or choice of friends?

5. What is the opportunity cost of having a child? Is it the same for men as for women? Why, or why not? How can the notion of opportunity cost help to explain the steady decline in fertility of women over the last 150 years?

6. If a market was competitive but not in equilibrium, would it be efficient? If the market was not competitive but was in equilibrium, would it be efficient?

7. Can you explain why a neoclassical economist might or might not support a government program such as WIC (Women, Infants, and Children), which improves average nutrition by providing free milk, bread, and other necessities for poor children?

8. What's different about the market for child care as opposed to others (e.g., the chewing gum market)? Is child care a public good?

SUGGESTED READINGS

Blaug, Mark. 1997. *Economic Theory in Retrospect*, 5th ed. New York: Cambridge University Press.

Blinder, Alan. 1987. *Hard Heads, Soft Hearts: Tough-Minded Economics for a Just Society.* Reading, MA: Addison-Wesley.

Buchanan, James. 1975. *The Limits of Liberty.* Chicago: University of Chicago Press. Friedman, Milton. 1962. *Capitalism and Freedom.* Chicago: University of Chicago Press. Okun, Arthur. 1975. *Equity vs. Efficiency: The Big Tradeoff.* Washington, D.C.: Brookings Institution.

Ricardo, David. 1973 [originally 1817]. *The Principles of Political Economy and Taxation.* London: J.M. Dent.

Sandstrom, F. Michael and Fredrik Bergstrom. 2004. "School Vouchers in Practice: Competition Will Not Hurt You." *Journal of Public Economics* 89, 351-380.

Smith, Adam. 1976 [originally 1776]. *An Inquiry into the Nature and Causes of the Wealth of Nations.* Oxford: Clarendon Press.

Solow, Robert. 1994. "How Race and Gender Issues Arise in Economics." In *Race and Gender in the American Economy.* Susan F. Feiner, ed. Englewood Cliffs, NJ: Prentice-Hall.

APPENDIX:
A Closer Look: The Roots of Neoclassical Economics

Adam Smith and *The Wealth of Nations*

The founder of neoclassical economics, Adam Smith, was born in 1723 in the Scottish town of Kirkcaldy. While Smith was growing up, the town was a booming seaport, with local mining for export, manufacturing of nails and other products, and markets for both locally produced agricultural products and goods from abroad. The 18th century yielded the advent of large-scale industry and the emergence of democratic political theories. While few of Smith's observations were completely original, his ultimate achievement in *The Wealth of Nations* was to integrate these events and phenomena into a coherent vision for understanding the economy.

Smith's exposure to markets and manufacturing led him to believe that the division of labor was a crucial step toward improving standards of living. Production could be increased if firms specialized in the creation of particular goods and the labor within firms were divided into specialized tasks. The market stimulated this development, because specialization increased productivity and the lowest-cost producers wound up in the strongest market positions. Markets were able to expand the variety of goods available to consumers and have those goods produced in the most efficient manner possible.

Smith argued that competition benefited society, because it stimulated economic growth. As improvements in technology increased productivity, more goods would be produced, and the economy would grow. More growth meant higher standards of living. As workers and owners produced more, wages and profits would rise, because competition would ensure that additional output was rewarded with additional income. Owners would raise wages in an attempt to hire more workers and produce more goods. Profits would also rise as markets expanded and more goods were sold. On the other hand, if economic growth slowed, the reverse process would occur: prices, profits, and wages would fall. Competition thus regulated prices, production, and incomes without any need for conscious direction over the economic system as a whole. For this reason, Smith characterized competition as an "invisible hand" that guides the economy toward a better world.

David Ricardo and Comparative Advantage

Smith's defense of competition was elaborated in the early 1800s by David Ricardo, an English financier and politician. Ricardo tried to persuade the English government to shed its practice of restricting trade in foreign-grown corn through tariffs. His defense of free trade rested largely on the concept of comparative advantage, the notion that some countries find it relatively cheaper to produce a particular good while others must be relatively better at producing other goods. "Relatively cheaper" in this context means that less is given up in terms of the alternative uses of productive resources (i.e., land, labor, capital). For example, assume that both the United States and France produce wheat and wine and that France is better at making wine while both are equally good at making wheat. To produce more wheat, the United States must give up less wine in comparison to France (because it cannot produce as much wine with the additional resources it has diverted from wheat production). To produce more wine, France must give up less wheat in comparison to the United States (because it needs to divert fewer resources from wheat production to wine production as a result of its greater productivity in wine production). The United States has a comparative advantage in wheat and France a comparative advantage in wine. Instead of both countries producing both goods, it would be better for each to specialize and trade. It is cheaper for France to produce only wine and trade for wheat and for the United States to produce only wheat and trade for wine than for each to produce both goods. In other words, specialization benefits both trading parties.

The Marginalists

Comparative advantage is a story about production. To be complete, a theory of market exchange also must explain purchasing or demand. This task was accomplished by the so-called marginalist revolution of the mid-19th century (Blaug, 1997). Marginalists such as Stanley Jevons, John Bates Clark, Alfred Marshall, and Leon Walras believed that economic decisions could best be understood in terms of small, step-by-step changes ("at the margin"), which allowed the impact on costs to be compared with the impact on benefits. For example, if we want to understand the level of employment that is decided on by a firm, we can compare each additional worker's impact on production and revenues with their impact on costs. The firm will only choose to hire the worker if the former exceeds the latter (see Chapter 4). Total employment then can be analyzed in terms of the firm's decision to hire workers one at a time. This same logic can be applied to any economic decision.

The marginalists argued that the demand for commodities was determined by the utility or pleasure that the purchase would bring to the buyer. Although utility could not be seen or measured (and therefore could not be compared between individuals), the marginalists assumed that it existed for each person in discrete units called "utils." Just as supply was governed by profit maximization, demand was governed by utility maximization. As more and more of a particular good was purchased, additional utils created for the consumer must fall. This is called the law of diminishing marginal utility. For example, if you decide to buy an ice-cream cone on a hot day, the first cone gives you a great deal of pleasure (e.g., 10 utils). However, the second cone gives you some but not as much pleasure (e.g., 6 utils), because your need for ice cream has already been slackened by the first cone. The third gives you almost no pleasure (e.g., 1 util), and the fourth cone makes you sick so you do not consume it (e.g., 0 utils). Because the additional pleasure created by additional purchases falls, the price that the consumer is willing to pay also must fall.

The marginalists made an analogous argument with respect to supply. They believed that costs would rise as production increased, because some factor of production is usually fixed (e.g., land or a factory). Higher costs of production would force suppliers to raise their prices to maintain their profits. Prices and the quantity of supply therefore must rise together. Based on this type of reasoning, it is possible to show that price changes cause corresponding changes in the quantity of supply and the quantity of demand in a manner that results in systematic prices and levels of output in various markets.

Pareto and Efficiency

The argument that the interplay of supply and demand drives economic outcomes achieved its clearest expression in the early 20th century work of Italian sociologist Vilfredo Pareto, who sought to establish that competitive markets were efficient in the sense that neoclassical economists now use the term. By efficiency, Pareto meant a condition where, without comparing the utility of any individuals, we can show that no individual can be made better off without making someone else worse off. Also, because competitive markets allow individuals to choose the jobs and consumer goods they as individuals value most highly (assuming that the jobs are available and the goods affordable), there can be no superior situation to competitive markets.

As an implication, if we believe a market is reasonably competitive and find inequality in the distribution of income or jobs, then any governmental action to alleviate that inequality will necessarily be inefficient and make some individuals worse off. Given the presumption that we cannot compare the utility levels achieved by different individuals, we cannot even say that the poor are worse off than the rich!

Thus, Pareto used the logic of those preceding him to provide a powerful and persuasive defense of Smith's predilection for competition in the market.

ENDNOTES

[1] For further discussion, see Charles Schultze, *The Private Use of Public Purpose*. Washington, D.C.: The Brookings Institution, 1977.

[2] See Robert Crandall, "Import Quotas and the Automobile Industry," *Brookings Review*, Summer 1984.

[3] Bad externalities such as smoke or noise mean the government should restrict the production or use of the product. By the same token, good externalities such as the smell of flowers mean the government should subsidize and promote production of the product. Education may be an example of a product with good externalities.

[4] Intuitively, public goods can be thought of as having "superexternalities" of the good kind.

[5] See Maria Gallucci, "California's Model Climate Policies Will Maintain Momentum in Obama Second Term," InsideClimate News, Nov. 8, 2012 (insideclimatenews.org).

WORK AND WAGES IN THE NEOCLASSICAL MODEL

INTRODUCTION: THE MARKET FOR WORK

Most neoclassical research on discrimination looks at labor markets and, particularly, wages. If the labor market were similar to the chewing gum market, we could skip this chapter and move directly to the question of labor market discrimination. Using the tools of supply and demand from Chapter 3, we would analyze differences between blacks and whites or men and women as if they simply were different flavors or brands of gum.

Work, however, is not the same as chewing gum. When a pack of gum is sold, the producer no longer cares whether it is chewed, resold, or thrown away—when a worker sells his labor, he would not be happy about being chewed, resold, or thrown away. When people buy gum, they usually do so because they like chewing—employers buy labor to turn a profit.

These facts imply that we need to look specifically at supply, demand, and equilibrium in the labor market. Then, having done so, we ask whether wages would be unequal even if discrimination was absent. The answer is "yes," which in turn means that some—or all—of gender and race wage differences may have nothing to do with discrimination. To get to the neoclassical understanding of wage discrimination requires that we first understand why differences would exist without it. This chapter serves that purpose, and also examines unemployment. After all, it does not matter whether you would earn a high or a low wage if you are out of a job. We conclude by looking at wage differences among groups that may have nothing to do with discrimination.

THE DEMAND FOR LABOR: WHY FIRMS EMPLOY PEOPLE

In contrast to demand in the chewing gum market, economists call the demand for labor a "derived demand." Firms do not hire employees because they like them, prefer them, or maximize some unknown utility through hiring. Firms hire to produce something that is sold to make a profit. Firms maximize profits by hiring people for the indirect gain. Stated differently, a firm's demand for labor is related to its supply on the output market.

Derived demand for labor: Firms hire people to produce goods and services that can then be sold

The road to maximum profits seems to be straight enough. Profit is the difference between the revenues from selling and the costs from producing. This implies that managers should strive to increase revenues and reduce costs. But what if you are deciding whether to hire another employee? This should result in more revenues, but could not possibly reduce costs. How should the decision be made?

The answer in neoclassical theory is that the firm hires up to the point where the marginal revenue product for the last worker equals the wage (either in per-hour or per-day terms). The marginal revenue product tells the firm how much money in sales (revenue) the last (marginal) worker will generate (produce) by working. The wage tells us how much the worker costs, so the trick to maximizing profits is to hire every worker who brings in more money than she or he costs, and not to hire any worker who costs more than the money brought in.

The law of demand holds in the labor market for several reasons. First, if the last person hired was producing just enough marginal revenue to cover his or her wage and the wage goes up, the firm will no longer find that employee profitable. If higher wages translate into fewer workers, then the law of demand holds. Second, if the wage rises, the firm will find its costs going up. Provided there is competition, the only way that the output price will rise is if the market supply falls. Remember, consumers are only willing to pay more if less is available in the market (by their law of demand), so the only ways to cover higher wages is to reduce production. Third, if the wage goes up, the firm has an incentive to find technology that replaces workers, again leading to fewer employees.

Law of demand for labor: As wages rise, the number of workers hired falls

Consider a hypothetical example to see how the law of demand works in the labor market. Workers at ABC, Inc. produce magazines. They neither write nor sell the magazines, just print them. ABC is doing well in the business, and this becomes known to a field representative of the typographers' union. She spots an opportunity and organizes the workers at ABC into a local of the typographers' union, promising that they will have grievance procedures to protect them against arbitrary managers and seniority rules so that, as workers age, their jobs will be more secure. And, yes, she promises higher wages. Later, a collective bargaining agreement is signed between the union local and ABC management, and sure enough, ABC employees receive higher wages. Is management likely to take this lying down? The law of demand says no. First, ABC managers may find some barely-profitable production runs—for example, for local city-based magazines—and shut those down. The marginal revenue product on these jobs is lower than the wage, so some workers lose their jobs. Second, ABC managers may be able to crank up the price that they charge to produce some magazines. This sounds great, but ABC will likely end up producing fewer magazines as consumers balk at paying more for the same old product (the law of demand again). Employment falls once more. Third, ABC managers may start looking for high-tech equipment to replace many of their typographers. A year earlier such equipment didn't make sense, but with higher wages, it does—and again, employment falls.

This story of the law of demand should sound familiar. It echoes the argument of Chapter 3 that competition reduces the ability of anyone, either on the supply or the demand side, to influence price. Here, we see employees trying to raise the "price" of their labor (i.e., the wage) through a union and running afoul of the law of demand. Even if workers can raise the wage, the cost will be steep: fewer jobs.

We have painted a picture of the demand for labor that makes it sound very impersonal. There is no room for loyalty or friendship in a firm whose sole purpose is to maximize profits. While this sounds harsh, it also implies there is no room for treachery or prejudice. The bottom line of profit is the only yardstick when it comes to hiring workers, and as Chapter 5 will show, there is little room for discrimination in competitive labor markets.

BOX 4.1
THE MALE AND FEMALE SUPPLY OF LABOR

Does the law of supply hold for labor? The short answer used to be "yes" for women and "sort of" for men. This finding from empirical studies meant that as the wage rose, a large number of women entered the labor force, but only a few more men did. Conversely, as the wage fell, only a few men quit their jobs, but many women did. The supply of women tended to be more sensitive than the supply of men to the wage.

Many studies have been performed to check the effect of wages on the labor supply. In a summary of earlier research undertaken by Mark Killingsworth, he concluded that the quantity of labor supplied by men is largely unaffected by the wage, while for women, a 1% increase in the wage draws in 0.6% more women into the labor market. Stated differently, a 1% drop in the wage would have no effect on how many men wanted to enter paid employment, but it would drive out 0.6% of women.

The difference in female and male labor supply can be looked at graphically. Figures 4.1 and 4.2 show labor supply for women and men. Start with a wage of $5 per hour. Coming across to the labor supply curves and down to the labor quantity axes, we discover that 2000 women and 2000 men wish to work at this wage.

What happens if the wage rises to $10 an hour? Here is where the greater sensitivity of women comes in. The female supply curve is relatively flat compared with that for men. Coming across from the $10 wage to the labor supply curves and down to the labor quantity axes, we find that the $5 wage increase draws 1200 more women into the labor force but no more men.

FIGURE 4.1
FEMALE LABOR SUPPLY

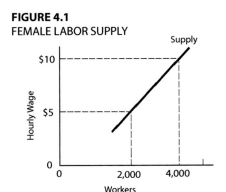

FIGURE 4.2
MALE LABOR SUPPLY

By the 1990s, however, women had begun behaving more like men, and their labor supply was only half as responsive to wage increases or decreases as in the past. Today, most adults need to work, regardless of wage levels.

Sources: Mark Killingsworth, *Labor Supply*, Cambridge, England: Cambridge University Press, 1983, 185; and Francine Blau and Lawrence Kahn, "Changes in the Labor Supply Behavior of Married Women: 1980-2000," *Journal of Labor Economics* Vol 25, 2007, 393-438.

THE SUPPLY OF LABOR: WHO WANTS TO WORK, AND HOW PRODUCTIVE ARE THE WORKERS?

The Work Decision

When a firm supplies a product to the market, the profit motive rules. When a worker supplies labor, however, we are back to utility, preferences, and opportunity costs.

If you are thinking about taking a paid job, you face a labor–leisure choice. As you mull over the decision, the major factors are that you will have more money if you work, but less time to relax and enjoy life. In a word, you face a problem of "scarcity." From Chapter 3, we know that the neoclassical answer to scarcity is to be rational, to weigh the utility of leisure against the utility from being able to buy more, and, perhaps, even save a little.

> ***Labor–leisure choice: For many people, the opportunity cost of work is more time off***

Individuals weigh the opportunity cost of paid employment against leisure in several ways. First is the question of whether to take any job. Second is the issue of whether to work full- or only part-time. Third is whether to show up for work each day. And, finally, in some cases the decision of whether to work overtime emerges. These decisions are not made on a simple basis like profit maximization; instead, they involve feelings or preferences. You wake up some mornings and think, "Maybe I won't go to work today." You ponder "how do I feel" and then decide whether the money is worth more than the pleasure of sleeping in, going out, or whatever else you might do (less the aggravation from the boss for missing work).

The question of labor supply often is simplified from the four issues just discussed to the simpler question of how many hours people want to work. Focusing on the question of labor hours supplied, it turns out that the law of supply may not apply in the labor market. People might even want to work less for a higher wage. This argument may strike you as nonsense; after all, if someone offered you a job earning truly astounding wages, such as $1,000 per hour, you would surely accept the job. Even if it meant quitting college, most people would have a hard time saying no. These people fit the law of supply, but in other circumstances, the law of supply makes less sense. For example, once you have the $1,000-per-hour job, this provides you with enough income to vacation abroad, take up deep-sea fishing, or follow your favorite performers on tour. Now, suppose you get a raise to $1,100 per hour. Are you likely to work more or fewer hours? If you said, "Fewer hours, I'll take a trip to Paris," you just violated the law of supply.

> ***Law of supply for labor? The law of supply—that more people seek jobs at higher wages—may not be true for labor***

As this example suggests, the law of supply may not hold in the real world. One of the most studied cases of labor supply is that of white men and women in the United States. In general, these studies show that women used to obey the law of supply. However, men have never been as obedient, and women have become less so (Box 4.1).

The working-hours decision turns on many aspects of life. Family and community commitments, wealth, social background, and one's like or dislike of work, all are relevant, but neoclassical economists consider an individual's rate of time preference to be one of the most important determinants of working hours. This is an interest rate that each of us carries in our head, and it will be different for different people. It depends on how much an individual values enjoying something today versus in the future. Individuals with a low rate of time preference save for their retirement. Individuals with a high rate spend their money when they are young.

Rate of time preference: Low for people who value the future and high for those who value the present

What do the terms high and low mean in this context? Basically, we can calculate rates of time preference by asking, for example, what interest rate on a savings account would coax you into saving one-fifth of your income. Some people will save one-fifth of their income no matter what—they have a zero rate of time preference. Others will require an interest rate of 5%—they have a 5% rate of time preference. Still others will require a 10% interest rate, while a few might require a 100% return before they would hand over one-fifth of their money to a bank.

What does the rate of time preference have to do with labor? It influences how much we work, how hard we work, and how much we save when we are young. Someone with a very low rate doesn't much care about the present, so he or she will take a very tough job with long hours and high wages to ensure a comfortable retirement in the future. Others with a very high rate of time preference take easy jobs with short hours and then spend the income from week to week because the present is more important to them.

One of the most crucial roles that time preference plays is in the education decision. We focus on this issue next.

Human Capital

The neoclassical view of education was developed in large part by Gary Becker. Becker won the Nobel Prize in economics in 1992 partly due to his work on education, but his research is also at the core of the neoclassical understanding of home production (examined in the next section) and discrimination (examined in Chapter 5).

Before Becker's work, formal education was viewed by economists as consumption. The rich went off to elite colleges, where they learned about the finer things in life. Becker transformed this view by arguing that education is an investment.

Becker posited that if capitalists spend or invest money to receive a return, why not view education as a process with an investment that also yields a return? College is not free and the opportunity cost is often quite high given that students could instead be earning money. The only reasonable neoclassical explanation for college is that it somehow enhances our ability to produce once we get a job. We invest in human capital through schooling and later receive a return in higher wages.

Human capital: Improved productive capabilities due to investments in education

The notion of education as human capital, which was largely alien to students 20 or 30 years ago, now seems common. Just ask yourself whether you would be in college today if you did not expect to raise your earning power as a result. Or, looked at differently, ask yourself whether you would be willing to take out a hefty loan to pay for tuition if you did not expect to earn more than people who did not attend college.

Estimates suggest that human capital is critically important to our economy. Comparing the costs and returns of formal education in terms of higher wages to investments in physical capital, such as workplaces, tools, and machinery, suggests that human capital may account for more than half of all "capital" existing in the U.S. economy.[1]

Here is where the rate of time preference comes into play. The decision to "invest" in human capital is similar to the decision to save. Those with a low rate of time preference invest in education and those with a high rate do not. Estimates of the returns from a college education (and there are many) suggest that the effective rate of return is between 5% and 15%. People with lower rates of time preference view college as a bargain, and people with a higher rate prefer to go directly into the workforce.

Human capital is critical to the neoclassical understanding of discrimination. Suppose that some group chooses college attendance less frequently than others, and earns less in the labor market. This outcome may simply be the product of a high rate of time preference rather than of discrimination. On the other hand, if the market for student loans is imperfect because banks worry about students defaulting, then college education will be constrained by parental income and wealth, which could allow past racial discrimination to affect present opportunities.

Human capital also feeds back into the question of labor supply. Individuals with high levels of education expect to earn a return, but they cannot if they do not work. Therefore, we can predict that individuals who acquire education plan to supply their labor to the market later.

Both the decision to supply labor and the education decision are complicated by the existence of another form of work—unpaid and at home.

Household Production

Following much debate in the late 1800s, the U.S. Bureau of the Census reached a decision that has remained in place to this day: women working at home are counted neither as employed nor as contributing to the economy.[2] While it is difficult to put a dollar figure on work done in the home, it is odd that two women working in their own homes would be counted neither as being employed nor as being productive. By hiring each other to do the same work in each other's homes, both would suddenly be counted as employed and productive. What's the difference? According to Gary Becker's theory of household production, there is no meaningful difference. Parallel to his argument that college students might be engaged in a valuable activity, Becker argued that if women stay at home, there must also be an economic rationale: household production is as important as work done for a firm.

Household production: Unpaid work, as opposed to leisure, in the home

Becker's model starts with the observation that both work and leisure occur in the home, and then adds Adam Smith's assertion that the division of labor can improve economic efficiency. If one spouse cooks and the other cleans, each will become expert at that particular task. Additionally, a clear division of labor reduces the costs of coordinating work in the home; we need not begin each day by deciding who cooks and who cleans. These claims imply that families confront not only a choice between market work and leisure time but also one between using money or our own time at home to produce goods for consumption. If both spouses are employed, more money may be spent on child care, but if only one works for wages, the other can "produce" child care directly.

Looked at differently, Becker suggests that time and money are substitutes in the home. We can wash dishes by hand or save time at home by working for pay to buy an automatic dishwasher. Similarly, if you are at home a lot, you might learn to cook from scratch, but if you are working full-time, you might buy a microwave oven and stick to frozen dinners and take-out.

Few, if any, economists would quibble with the notion that a division of labor in the home can improve family welfare. Such a division, however, need not imply that either spouse will specialize in housework. To conclude that individuals will specialize, we must further posit that there exist economic advantages to working "full-time" in either paid employment or the home. Some evidence suggests that employers favor such specialization, on average paying 40% lower hourly wages for part-time as opposed to full-time workers.[3] Part of the reason for the large wage advantage accruing to full-timers may lie in the fixed costs of employing workers. Firms providing health, pension or insurance benefits, or with expensive machinery and equipment, may find that these costs are the same regardless of how many hours a particular employee works. These costs can be spread over more hours as the employee's working time increases, thus giving a cost advantage to full-time employment.[4]

If someone is going to specialize in home production, who will it be? Most of us have a pretty good idea that the answer is "the wife," but why should this be so? While we consider discrimination later, there are other neoclassical explanations for women tending to specialize in home production.

First, it may be that women have a greater preference than men for tasks that are performed at home. Catherine Hakim suggests as much by arguing that women in our society care more about children than men do.

Second, it may be that women have a comparative advantage over men in home production. Recall that comparative advantage means one party is relatively more productive at some task compared with another. Regarding work in the home, comparative advantage could imply that because of biology or socialization, women are better at most household production tasks, such as child care. Instead, or additionally, men may have a comparative advantage in paid employment.

In the labor market, it makes little difference whether women simply prefer or exhibit a comparative advantage in home production, nor does it matter whether preferences or comparative advantage result from socialization or biology. What matters is that by the time people enter the labor market, it may be efficient for women to specialize in home production and for men to take paid employment. Historical evidence suggests that a division very much like this has existed across many societies (Box 4.2).

To see why this pattern of specialization is efficient, imagine if we reversed traditional gender roles so that most men stayed at home and most women took paid employment. Each partner may receive lower utility in his or her new role, or total productivity may fall. In either case, the family would be worse off as a result. Of course, some couples may have different preferences or comparative advantages, but competitive markets do not stop them from choosing what is best for them (assuming there is no discrimination).

The sexual division of labor and Becker's theory of home production help to explain two important phenomena. First, a wave of women entered the U.S. labor force starting in the 1960s. Becker predicted this phenomenon by noting that as the price fell for purchased goods such as dishwashers, electric stoves, vacuum cleaners, and so on, people would increasingly move away from work at home toward work in the market. Purchased goods would be substituted for work in the home as the opportunity cost of taking paid employment fell.

Second, as noted earlier (Box 4.1), the law of supply seems to hold more for women than for men. This makes sense given that the opportunity cost of taking paid employment may be home production for many women but not for most men.

BOX 4.2
THE SEXUAL DIVISION OF LABOR ACROSS CULTURES

Have men and women everywhere always exhibited the same division of labor we see to-day? The answer is that for many tasks, the division of labor is remarkably stable across a host of societies historically.

Roy D'Andrade summarized a series of early studies on the matter and found that with some exceptions, many of the same jobs are dominated by either women or men in most societies. For example, in a study of subsistence activities in 224 societies, men performed the following tasks, either always or usually, in at least 90% of the societies: pursuit of sea mammals, hunting, trapping small animals, herding, metalworking, weapon-making, boat-building, manufacture of musical instruments, work in wood and bark, work in stone, and work in bone, horn, or shell. Women dominated activities to a similar extent in the cases of: grinding grain, carrying water, cooking, preserving meat or fish, and gathering herbs, roots, or seeds.

Whether because of physical differences, preferences, comparative advantage, or discrimination, men and women have historically performed different tasks. However, this historical division does not necessarily imply that it will continue forever. For example, if subsistence societies differentiate in terms of physical attributes, we might expect this division to break down as we move toward less physically strenuous white-collar occupations in the workplace.

Source: Roy G. D'Andrade, "Sex Differences and Cultural Institutions," in *The Development of Sex Differences*. Eleanor E. Maccoby, ed. Stanford, CA: Stanford University Press, 1966.

In other words, some women may have a productive option outside of the labor market—home production—that may not be readily available to men, and therefore they may be more willing to enter or exit the labor force as wages rise and fall.

This last argument can help to explain why women entered the labor force in the post-World War II period. Women's wages rose (see Chapter 2), thereby driving up the opportunity cost of home production and motivating women to seek paid employment. Note also that this argument has nothing to do with discrimination. Indeed, the argument suggests that, like the consumer who is better off because of a wide range of substitutes in the market, women may be better off than men because women can substitute home production for work through the labor market.

How much is household production worth? In 2003, for the first time, the U.S. government collected data on how Americans spend their time. The data suggest that estimated output would be around 50% higher if household production were included. Given that Gross Domestic Product was $13.84 trillion in 2007, this means that almost $7 trillion worth of unpaid work was performed in the home.

EXPLAINING WAGE DIFFERENCES

Having looked at supply and demand, human capital, and home production, we now can think about wage differences that are generated by competitive markets.

Firm-Specific and General Human Capital

Earlier, we discussed education as a human capital investment. Gary Becker labeled this general human capital. By "general," Becker meant that it was transportable, so it could be taken from one job to another or one firm to another. A college education fits the notion of general human capital and is closely related to earnings differences in the United States.

General human capital: Investments that make a person more productive at many jobs or firms

Becker argued that human capital can take on another form, that of firm-specific human capital. These are skills that are usually acquired during the early stages of employment. Such skills are also specific to the firm—knowing who to contact in case of foul-ups or emergencies, how particular machines work, how to operate within a particular bureaucracy, and where the lunch room and restrooms are located. For example, if you take a job managing a factory, you would have to get to know everyone, learn something about the machines, the accounting system, how wages and personnel decisions are made, who can decide on new investments, what to do with customer complaints, and so on. Much of this knowledge could be used in another factory owned by another firm, but much could not. Other companies are likely to have different people, machines, accounting systems, and so on. So, as you acquire human capital as a manager, much of it is firm-specific.

Why should we care about general as opposed to firm-specific human capital? Because the implications for training and wages are quite different. General human capital is typically paid for by the employee. If you want a college degree, you apply to a college, do the work, and pay the tuition and living expenses. In turn, you receive higher wages as a reward for your investment, assuming you can find a job. This is not true with firm-specific human capital. The firm knows that it is worthless elsewhere and therefore need not reward your higher productivity with higher wages. It may represent a coup to get a major proposal through a firm's bureaucratic red tape, but you may not be able to take that skill elsewhere.

Firm-specific human capital: Investments that make a person more productive at one particular firm only

Becker resolved these issues by arguing that workers choose to invest in general human capital and are rewarded by the market, but that firms and workers split the costs of firm-specific human capital. The reason for the split is that the only way firm-specific capital pays off is when the worker remains with the firm for a long period of time. If both the worker and the firm pay for and benefit from the initial investment, both have a strong incentive to maintain the relationship.

An implication of this argument is that the firm can simply take the most qualified applicant if general human capital is important. With firm-specific human capital, however, managers need someone who is qualified and likely to stay with the firm for many years.

Who is likely to stay with the firm over the long haul? One conclusion from the theory of home production is that women may have more productive opportunities than men outside the labor market and be more ready to leave the firm if wages fall. Therefore, employers may not provide as much firm-specific human capital to women as to men. As a result, women will earn less because they are less productive. This is an example of "statistical discrimination," which we explain in the following chapter. Note also that as women's commitment to paid employment has increased in recent decades, we would expect employers to respond by providing greater amounts of firm-specific training to women.

As with general human capital, we may find differences across groups in terms of firm-specific human capital. The example here suggests that women may receive lesser investments because of a lesser commitment to paid employment. This same argument could be extended to different cultures or races if they also diverge in their commitment to the firm, which is a point we take up later in this chapter.

Compensating Differences and Hedonic Wages

Neoclassical economists believe that hard work and sacrifice will generally be rewarded through the mechanism of compensating differences. If the firm sets wages equal to the marginal revenue product, then people who work harder should receive higher wages. The difference that is attributable to hard work is called a compensating difference.

Compensating differences: Higher wages for jobs that are difficult, dirty, disgusting, or dangerous

Compensating differences may apply to many characteristics beyond how hard an employee works. If there are jobs that most people find repulsive, such as being a coroner or working in a meat-packing factory, the supply of labor will be low for those jobs and a compensating difference paid to attract people into the workplace. Similarly, jobs that are boring or that require trust or attention to detail should pay a compensating difference. This same argument applies to dangerous jobs as well. Indeed, estimates suggest that at a dangerous workplace with 1,000 employees, the total wages could be reduced by between $35,000 and $500,000 per year by a safety program that saved (on average) one life every ten years.[5] A firm tolerating such dangerous conditions may pay a compensating difference to do so.

There is a problem with compensating differences. Many occupations where we would expect to find compensating differences are associated with low pay. Few of us can imagine employment more stressful than working the counter of a fast-food restaurant at rush hour, yet these jobs pay close to the legal minimum. Nor are there many jobs dirtier than picking up garbage, yet these jobs are also not known for high wages. Do these cases imply that the theory is wrong? Neoclassical economists have responded to this problem by modifying the theory of compensating differences with the concept of hedonic wages.[6]

Hedonic wages: Wages that reflect the preferences of a particular worker in a job and not those of the general public

The idea of compensating differences starts from the notion that some jobs are simply bad or good. Hedonic wage theory suggests that we should look at the preferences of workers in the actual occupation. If some people do not mind picking up garbage (perhaps their sense of smell is poor), then a compensating difference will not be required to coax enough workers into this job. Similarly, some people might find that the stress of rush hour at a fast-food restaurant alleviates boredom. Therefore, as long as enough people can be located who have a relatively low distaste for such characteristics, compensating differences also will be relatively low.

A Norwegian study of wages and safety fits this story. The study found mild evidence of compensating differences—higher wages for more dangerous work. It found much stronger evidence of a trade-off between wages and safety *within* particular labor markets.

At heart, hedonic wage theory is about the advantages of the division of labor. Part of the magic of the market is dividing tasks to improve productivity, but another part is that markets improve efficiency by matching individuals to the particular jobs they find most inviting or least onerous. Not surprisingly, when it is suggested that some jobs are underpaid because of discrimination, some neoclassical economists respond that because of hedonic wages, jobs cannot be compared; wages reflect the preferences of people who hold those jobs and not the likes and dislikes of the general populace.

Inheritance

Some people are born with a silver spoon in their mouth. If you were a daughter of Bill Gates, your labor market opportunities would likely be improved by your father's holdings of $66 billion.[7] You could afford the best schools, the most extensive job search, and if all else failed, simply start your own business. Few neoclassical economists believe that such differences are fair, but many believe they are efficient. If LeBron James is a very successful basketball player because of biology or social inheritance, we might say this is unfair, but most of us would not respond by watching less talented players or by calling for James to take a pay cut. As Thomas Sowell argues,

> [T]here is no more individual merit in having received a windfall gain in the form of brain cells rather than in the form of encyclopedias or private schooling. Each individual is born into a world he never made, with a brain he never made ... [H]is value to society is the same, whether that value originated inside his head, or inside his home or school, or among his companions [Sowell, 145].

While inherited wealth, culture, and ability make a great deal of difference regarding earnings potential, it is the market that motivates people to use those advantages in a productive fashion. The magic of the market prevents us from having a society that produces shoddy goods. That magic may result in wage differences that relate to either biology or social inheritance, but are still efficient.

Finally, a few studies have been performed concerning the effects of inheritance. One shows that around half of the positive or negative economic effects of inheritance disappear in the next generation.[8] This is consistent with the notion that inheritance is far from the most important determinant of wage differences, leaving a broad scope for individual choice and initiative regarding how much we will earn.

UNEMPLOYMENT

There are other reasons for wage differences than those outlined earlier. These have to do with disequilibrium and the related phenomenon of unemployment. Human capital, home production, and hedonic wages are all facets of how wage differences emerge in equilibrium. Now, we turn to wage differences that are largely byproducts of the economy moving toward equilibrium (but not quite getting there). There are three major forms of unemployment in neoclassical economics: structural, frictional, and seasonal. We take these up in order, link them to wage differences, then look at the Keynesian challenge.

Structural Unemployment

Structural unemployment is caused by changes in the economy that make some jobs obsolete. These changes can stem from various sources: new technologies may reduce the need for certain types of jobs, consumers may decide they no longer wish to purchase certain types of goods, firms may relocate production to low-tax or low-wage areas, or a new product with different production techniques may push aside old products. For example, a skilled typist could earn good money almost anywhere during the 1960s; in the 2000s, almost anyone can use a word processor (with a spell-checker) to accomplish the same results. When consumers decided they wanted more small, fuel-efficient cars and fewer SUVs in 2007 and 2008, tens of thousands of U.S. auto workers who produced the gas-guzzlers found themselves out of work while the

Japanese firm Toyota became the world's largest automaker in part by producing small cars and the hybrid Prius.

Structural unemployment: Job loss resulting from changes in technology, consumer desires, or product innovation

Structural unemployment is painful but efficient. The pain felt by the thousands of auto and steel workers who lost their jobs in 2008 is undeniable, so much so that the government provided extended unemployment benefits. On the other hand, any attempt to stem structural employment would mean holding on to inefficient technologies, producing goods that consumers have no interest in purchasing, and denying consumers access to new and better products. As it turned out, the $80 billion government bailout of the industry saved as many as 1.5 million American jobs, and returned GM and Chrysler to profitability by 2012.[9]

Frictional Unemployment

Frictional unemployment stems from the fact that it takes time and money for firms to identify high-quality workers, and for workers to find where they are most productive. Workers have an incentive to search for the job where their marginal revenue product is highest, because then their wages also will be highest. Firms have an incentive to identify potential employees with the highest marginal revenue product. Such searching by firms and workers is costly for society because job searchers are not producing goods and they are using scarce economic resources in their search for new jobs. If a worker wants to quit a job and wait a few months before looking for another, this creates frictional unemployment (the firm searching for a replacement and the worker eventually for a new job), but this is efficient as both the worker and the firm are given the freedom to make these choices.

Frictional unemployment: Lack of employment caused by firms seeking high-quality workers and workers searching for high wages

Frictional unemployment sounds relatively painless in theory—in practice, it is often every bit as horrible as structural unemployment. Looking for work can be frustrating, especially when firms do not hire the first applicant because they are also searching. Furthermore, once a job is taken, the firm may discover that it hired the wrong person, or the employee might realize that the job was a mistake; in either case, the new job is quickly gone. Even a successful job search may conclude with a family moving from one state or nation to another, so the issue of home production is also linked to frictional unemployment. Indeed, one study showed that among husband-wife pairs who switched states, the man's earnings rose by an average of $4,254 and the woman's fell by $1,716.[10] Because overall family income rises in this process, the move may be efficient, but it is not painless for the women involved.

Like structural unemployment, frictional unemployment is efficient—unless the government intervenes. Studies show that by providing unemployment insurance and training programs for the unemployed, the U.S. government has inefficiently lengthened the amount of time that individuals spend looking for work. There is less reason to take the first available job if the government will pay you to keep on looking.[11] This does not mean that unemployment insurance should be abolished, because it alleviates much real pain and suffering. However, there are costs for maintaining the system.

Seasonal Unemployment

Seasonal unemployment is exactly what it sounds like. Retail clerks can find virtually round-the-clock employment during the Christmas shopping season, as can peach pickers during the early summer in the southern United States. The rest of the year, some of the retail clerks and the agricultural workforce will be unemployed. Knowing they will be unemployed so much of the year, why would anyone take a seasonal job? The neoclassical answer is that individuals selecting this type of employment may value their leisure very highly. For example, a campground worker in the Catskills who winters in Florida might not complain too loudly about a low wage at the campground, or a worker with children in primary school might want a job as cafeteria worker, school teacher, or crossing guard, with work being scheduled around school attendance. Alternatively, the job might pay a compensating difference to make up for the lack of work during part of the year. This brings us back to the issue of wages.

> ***Seasonal unemployment: Lack of certain types of jobs at predictable times of year***

Linking Unemployment and Wages

Neoclassical economists view the three types of unemployment discussed above as efficient but painful. Unemployment of these types also can be viewed as fair—in the sense that it may be random. No one knows who is going to lose his or her job, so we all take our chances. If we all buy lottery tickets, we view it as fair that one person wins, and this same argument can be applied to unemployment.

Unemployment also may be fair in a deeper sense—if the market pays us extra for being unemployed. Obviously, you do not receive a wage increase while you are out of a job, but what about after or before unemployment? In the case of frictional unemployment, the entire reason that workers search for jobs is to improve their wages, and firms who find the most productive workers available can afford to pay higher wages. In the case of seasonal unemployment, as suggested earlier, workers may receive a compensating difference because the job is temporary. Similarly, to the extent that structural unemployment is predictable, workers also should receive a compensating difference. For example, anyone taking a job at a U.S. automobile factory producing SUVs during the 2000s should have seen the writing on the wall: the jobs were largely temporary. If more secure employment was desired, it had to be sought outside the auto industry, or producing more fuel-efficient vehicles.

THE KEYNESIAN CHALLENGE

While the three main types of unemployment as analyzed by neoclassical economists are efficient, and even fair to a limited extent, other economists, called Keynesians (for economist John Maynard Keynes), believe that some unemployment is both inefficient and unfair. With Keynesian unemployment, the government may need to intervene.

Keynesians, such as Nobel Prize-winner Paul Krugman, believe that people often experience involuntary unemployment, which means that people are willing but unable to find jobs at the market wage.[12] Neoclassical economists see involuntary unemployment as an oxymoron. After all, how can workers claim they cannot find a job when all they have to do is to accept a lower wage, after which they will find plenty of work?

Involuntary or Keynesian unemployment: A lack of jobs because sales are down across the economy

Keynes and his followers believed that even if workers were willing to take wage cuts, jobs still might be unavailable. For example, suppose that consumers slow down their purchases, perhaps because they are worried about losing their jobs or they want to buy a car or a house but cannot, or don't want to, get a loan. Producers see declining sales and lay off workers, and now we begin a process of positive feedback. With fewer people working, sales fall yet again. People may become fearful and, even if they have jobs, cut spending just in case they become unemployed. This is what Keynes referred to as insufficient aggregate demand—the inability of consumers to purchase enough goods and services to keep the economy humming. This is precisely what Keynes believed happened in the 1930s and what Krugman and others argue happened in 2008.

Positive feedback: Where an adverse economic event causes more adverse events, or beneficial events cause more beneficial events

What about wage cuts? According to Keynes, even if workers try to generate more demand for their labor by taking wage cuts, this may not work. Following a wage cut, workers have less money to spend, so sales may fall yet again. Keynesian unemployment with positive feedback effects can help to explain why unemployment kept going up in 2008 and 2009.

Because Keynesians see the economy as generating involuntary unemployment through positive feedback, they also see a role for an activist government in curbing unemployment. The problem of involuntary unemployment emerges from a lack of sales, and the government can increase sales by either buying more or taxing less, as the Obama administration did with the economic stimulus legislation of 2009.

Neoclassical economists believe that market economies generate negative feedback. If unemployment occurs, the laws of supply and demand will work to return us to equilibrium, and in equilibrium, everyone who wants a job can find one. In other words, an adverse event such as increased unemployment sets in motion a process (i.e., wage cuts) that solves the problem by increasing employment opportunities.

Negative feedback: Where an adverse or beneficial economic event is corrected by the economy to return us to equilibrium

THE FAIRNESS OF INEQUALITY: WAGE DIFFERENCES AMONG GROUPS

This chapter began by asking why firms hire people and why people work for firms. Firms hire to make a profit, and they employ and pay people precisely according to their marginal revenue product. When people decide to seek a job, they make a labor–leisure trade-off, with people who value leisure less and working more than those who place a higher value on leisure.

Then, we confronted a series of explanations for why some people make more money than others. First is the issue of time preference and general human capital. People who value the future have a low rate of time preference and are willing to sacrifice when they are young—by staying in high school or shelling out for college—so they are more productive and earn more later in life. Specialization in household production also may affect wages, because those who specialize are less skilled at paid employment. Nonetheless, such specialization is rational and efficient, perhaps more for women than for men, even if women's earnings suffer as a result.

Other explanations for wage differences include firm-specific human capital, where the firm invests in a worker's skills and both the firm and worker benefit later. Firms also may pay higher wages in the form of compensating differences for jobs that are difficult, dangerous, or otherwise undesirable. Such differences may be small, however, because of hedonic wages: if enough people can be found who do not object to the seemingly undesirable conditions, then wages need not be higher than those for other jobs. Inheritance, whether in the form of money, biology, or socialization, may give some people an advantage when it comes to wages as well.

Finally, we examined unemployment. Some unemployment—frictional—leads to higher wages as people search for better jobs and firms search for better workers. Other types—structural and seasonal—also may be related to higher wages (when people work), which compensates for the higher risk of losing jobs and income. Keynesian economists challenge these arguments by suggesting that unemployment often is involuntary.

With this knowledge in hand, we consider the question of why some groups experience systematic differences in wages and employment even if there is no discrimination. Much of the earlier discussion regarding household production can help to explain such differences between men and women. If women have a comparative advantage or simply prefer household production relative to men, then we should not be surprised if women earn less than men. Part of this difference may result from women specializing in "training" that is less valuable in the labor market than in the home, another part may result from women's greater willingness to leave the workforce when wages fall, and yet another may result from women shunning higher education because it is not as valuable in the home as in the labor market.

Standard models of human capital suggest that over half the difference between the wages that men and women receive can be accounted for by educational achievement and experience on the job. Thus, if women wished to earn the same as men, around half the current difference could be wiped out if women switched their educational patterns to mimic those of men and did not interrupt their careers for childbirth. Recent evidence suggests this change is already occurring. While women were less than two-thirds as likely as men to attain a bachelor's degree in 1960, women were more likely than men to achieve the degree by the end of the 1980s (Goldin, 1990). That trend continued. In 1980, 5.5 million women and 5 million men were enrolled in colleges and universities, with the figures rising to 11.2 million for women but only 9.1 million for men by 2011.[13]

The education gap between men and women closed, so neoclassical economists would expect wage and employment differences to have disappeared as well. Evidence for this claim can be found by the drop in the male/female wage gap: white men's median annual earnings for full-time, year-round employment were almost twice as high as the equivalent figure for white women in 1967, but were only one-third higher by 2008 (see Chapter 2). By historical standards, this is a rapid decline in inequality. Not only could women who worked expect to earn more, but the proportion of women in the labor force rose as well, with the proportion of white women rising from under 50% in 1973 to around 60% in 2008. Over that same period, the proportion of white men in the labor force fell slightly, from around 80% to under 75%. In his model of household production, Gary Becker (1965) forecast precisely this sort of change: It became relatively cheaper to substitute store-bought goods for those produced in the home, so women went to work and rationally started acquiring the types of education that were rewarded by higher wages.

The discussion thus far has not addressed racial or ethnic divergence in wages, but it can. If a group of immigrants arrives in the United States, will they become rich or poor? Does group membership tell us how they will perform economically as individuals? The neoclassical answer is that if group membership matters, it is at least partly attributable to culture and the economy from which the group derives. Indeed, to the extent that the group's culture emphasizes education, hard work, and savings, we would predict that the group would become wealthy precisely because the market is operating in a fair and efficient fashion.

The analogous story for black and Hispanic as opposed to white Americans is less heartening. In terms of education, the proportion of whites between the ages of 25 and 29 holding a college degree rose from 25% in 1980 to 35.5% in 2007, but comparable figures for blacks were 11.6% in 1980 and 19.5% in 2007. For Hispanics, the figures were 7.7% in 1980 but only 11.6% in 2007. As of 2007, both blacks and Hispanics were less likely to have a college degree than even whites back in 1980.[14]

Neoclassical economists focus on two major reasons for the very distinct trends affecting gender and race (both unrelated to discrimination). First, during the 1980s and 1990s, the returns to education increased dramatically in the United States. No one really knows whether increasing returns to education have resulted from changes in the supply of college-educated workers, the disappearance of high-wage factory jobs, changes in technology, or other causes, but the facts are clear. For year-round full-time workers, the earnings of college graduates were around 50% higher than those for high-school graduates in the late 1970s, but rose to almost a 100% advantage by the year 2000. Because the educational attainment of women surpassed that for men while that of blacks and Hispanics remained far below that of whites, it is not surprising that the earnings gap by gender tended to close over the period while that by race increased.[15] Second, as women became more likely to work, their commitment to staying at work increased as well. Women's labor-force participation rose fairly steadily from 43.3% in 1970 to 58.1% in 2011 (with some recent decline due to the Great Recession).[16] If gender and racial differences in earnings and employment are caused in large part by differences in human capital, which in turn are related to formal education and experience on the job, then discrimination in the labor market cannot necessarily be blamed for these differences.

A third factor that also suggests the distinct labor market experiences for gender and race groups are not the result of discrimination concerns learning by these groups over time. For example, differences in education levels, occupations, and experience by group may appear to reflect differences in rates of time preference (as people with a high rate of time preference ultimately earn less because they invest less when they are young), which might in fact represent a response to historical and external conditions. If women specialize in housework, their absence from business courses might have nothing to do with time preference, instead signaling a rational response to the fact that knowledge of high finance does not pay off in the world of child-rearing. Similarly, individuals living in societies with a low average life expectancy usually would not live long enough to experience high earnings from obtaining a Ph.D. To the extent that immigrants carry the values from such societies into a developed economy, or that women who will be entering the labor market are socialized by mothers who did not, these groups may appear to be more present-oriented than males of the historically dominant ethnic group in the economy. Therefore, these groups will earn less. Nonetheless, over time, they will discover the value and returns for human capital. For immigrants to the United States, and women who have entered the U.S. workforce during the last several decades, Thomas Sowell and Claudia Goldin provide some evidence that over time, these groups do develop such expectations, and that their education and earnings improve accordingly.

Many neoclassical economists believe the labor market functions as an efficient and impartial mechanism for motivating individuals to contribute productively to the economy and to receive commensurate rewards. To the extent that this is true, the government should engage in laissez-faire policies with respect to both race and gender, permitting the market to work its magic. Other neoclassical economists, and probably a majority, believe that markets sometimes fail because of imperfect competition, externalities, and public goods. By extension, many of these economists believe that discrimination can exert real effects and, in some cases, persist in providing some groups with reduced economic opportunities. We analyze this possibility in the next chapter.

DISCUSSION QUESTIONS

1. Why is the demand for labor called a "derived demand"? Can you imagine a case where labor demand is not derived?

2. What are the opportunity costs for you to hold a full-time job (whether you already do or do not hold such a job)? What sorts of labor–leisure choices do you make on a day-to-day, week-to-week, or year-to-year basis?

3. What does it mean to say that men often "break the law of supply" in the labor market? Why would they not follow the law of supply?

4. Does the idea of a "rate of time preference" imply that individuals who choose to attend college usually will save more of their earnings? Does it imply they will save less?

5. What sorts of policies would a firm need to implement if it wished to reduce the extent to which women specialize in home production?

6. When families move from one city or state to another, does the theory of home production help us to predict how men's and women's wages are likely to change in the process?

7. Can you identify jobs where general human capital is important? Where firm-specific human capital is important?

8. Janitors perform many dirty and boring tasks. Should they be paid a compensating difference for these adverse conditions? Why might a neoclassical economist argue that no compensating difference should be paid?

9. If you have known someone who was unemployed for a time, do you think he or she was unemployed for structural, frictional, seasonal, or Keynesian reasons?

SUGGESTED READINGS

Becker, Gary. 1965. "A Theory of the Allocation of Time." *Economic Journal* 75, September.

Becker, Gary. 1975. *Human Capital*, 2nd ed. New York: Columbia University Press.

Dale-Olsen, Harald. 2006. "Estimating Workers' Marginal Willingness to Pay for Safety using Linked Employer-Employee Data." *Economica* 73, 99-127.

Frazis, Harley and Jay Stewart. 2006. "How Does Household Production Affect Earnings Inequality? Evidence from the American Time Use Survey." Working paper 393, Washington, DC: U.S. Bureau of Labor Statistics.

Goldin, Claudia. 1990. *Understanding the Gender Gap*. New York: Oxford University Press.

Hakim, Catherine. 2001. *Work-Lifestyle Choices in the 21ˢᵗ Century: Preference Theory*. New York: Oxford University Press.

Kantrowitz, Mark. 2007. "The Financial Value of a Higher Education." *NASFAA Journal of Student Financial Aid* 37, 1.

Krugman, Paul. 2013. *End This Depression Now!* New York: W.W. Norton.

Rosen, Sherwin. 1974. "Hedonic Prices and Implicit Markets." *Journal of Political Economy* 82, January-February.

Sowell, Thomas. 1983. *The Economics and Politics of Race*. New York: Quill.

ENDNOTES

[1] Figures in this paragraph and the next are from Ronald G. Ehrenberg and Robert S. Smith, *Modern Labor Economics*, 4th ed. New York: HarperCollins, 1991, Chapter 9.

[2] See Nancy Folbre, "The Unproductive Housewife," *Signs*, Spring 1991.

[3] See Chris Tilly, "Short Hours, Short Shrift," in *New Policies for the Part-time and Contingent Workforce*. Virginia L. duRivage, ed. Armonk, NY: M.E. Sharpe, 1992.

[4] This argument implies that in gay or lesbian households, we would find a similar degree of specialization, with one person staying at home and the other going to work.

[5] Figures from Ronald G. Ehrenberg and Robert S. Smith [1991, op. cit.], p. 276.

[6] Hedonic is defined as "pertaining to pleasure," or "of or related to hedonism or hedonists" [*Webster's New Twentieth Century Dictionary*, Unabridged 2nd ed. New York: Simon & Schuster, 1979].

[7] See the Bill Gates Wealth Clock at http://philip.greenspun.com/WealthClock.

[8] See W. Stanley Siebert, "Inequality of Opportunity," in *Microeconomic Problems in Labour Economics: New Approaches*. Robert Drago and Richard Perlman, eds. London: Wheatsheaf, 1989.

[9] See "A Million Jobs" (editorial), *New York Times*, Feb. 25, 2012 (nytimes.com).

[10] See Solomon W. Polachek and Francis W. Horvath, "A Life-Cycle Approach to Migration," in *Research in Labor Economics*. Ronald Ehrenberg, ed. Greenwich, CT: JAI Press, 1977.

[11] See Ronald G. Ehrenberg and Ronald L. Oaxaca, "Unemployment Insurance, Duration of Unemployment and Subsequent Wage Gains," *American Economic Review*, Vol. 66, December 1976.

[12] Structural, frictional, and seasonal unemployment usually are not viewed as being involuntary in this sense.

[13] See U.S. Bureau of the Census, "School Enrollment," CPS October 2011 – Detailed Tables, Table 01-01.

[14] See U.S. National Center for Education Statistics, *Digest of Education Statistics 2007*, Washington DC, Table 200.

[15] Discrimination could play a role here if black Americans believe education is only rewarded if you are white. In other words, positive feedback effects could occur such that discrimination causes low wages and leads people to acquire less education, thus reducing wages even further.

[16] See U.S. Bureau of Labor Statistics, *Women in the Labor Force: A Databook*, 2012 edition, Washington DC, Table 2.

5

DISCRIMINATION IN THE NEOCLASSICAL VIEW

INTRODUCTION: DIFFERENCE AND DISCRIMINATION

A white man works at a fast-food restaurant that is part of a large national chain with standardized pricing, cooking machinery and methods, and standardized portions. This employee gives extra portions to white customers and the expected portion to black customers. Is this discrimination? Clearly, the answer is "yes."

This small story can be used to illustrate the neoclassical understanding of discrimination. The employee gave extra portions to whites because he was averse to the skin color of the black customers. It didn't matter whether black customers were nicer, smarter, more honest, or more hard-working than the average white person—all that mattered was their skin color.

Discrimination: Adverse treatment of an individual based on group membership instead of productivity

Looking below the surface, a key that helps unlock the neoclassical model of discrimination is the possibility that both parties suffer from the discriminatory act. Black customers get short-changed relative to whites, and the white employee may "pay" for his discrimination—if the boss finds out about the extra portions for whites, the employee will likely be fired.

Like all illustrative stories, this one is incomplete, because discrimination can have major impacts on the jobs, promotion opportunities, available housing, incomes, education, and the health of those who are subject to it. Discrimination is inequitable. That is the bad news. The good news is that the story also suggests a way in which the ill effects of discrimination may be wiped out: even if the boss doesn't care about discrimination, the boss can make more money by firing the discriminating employee and replacing him with someone who does not discriminate and hand out extra food for free.[1]

Discrimination occurs when the economic opportunities of some well-defined group are limited by virtue of their group membership rather than their potential or actual economic contributions. If "ascriptive" or unimportant characteristics of a group affect their position in the economy, discrimination may be the culprit.

As with household production and human capital, economist Gary Becker was at the forefront of explaining discrimination from the neoclassical perspective. Considering a story like the one described here, his logic suggests that we seek an explanation for such behavior through rational individuals maximizing their utility or, stated more simply, exercising their preferences. Those with preferences that generate discrimination must have a "taste for discrimination," and if you have a taste for any good (or here, "bad"), this should show up in a willingness to pay for it.

Once discriminatory tastes are admitted, they enter the market in much the same way as any other taste. The market allows each of us to have unique tastes and to act on those tastes. In the neoclassical market economy—one that is populated by individual self-satisfiers—any individual consumer, worker, or business owner can make economic decisions based on discrimination. Anyone can choose products or services based on race, gender, ethnicity, religion, or sexual orientation, because the market permits them to do so. If people would benefit from ending discriminatory behavior, they would rationally do so.

Now we confront a puzzle. If markets allow each of us the freedom to discriminate at will, how can it be that competitive markets will stamp out the adverse effects of discrimination? While much of this chapter is devoted to putting this puzzle together, a hint at the solution lies in the fact that discrimination can occur in labor markets. As argued in Chapter 4, labor markets are unlike other markets, so tastes for discrimination within labor market settings may have unexpected effects.

We begin our analysis of the neoclassical model by explaining the results of labor market discrimination. Basically, discrimination in labor markets is inefficient and inequitable, and these problems show up in three ways: unequal wages, unequal employment opportunities, and occupational crowding. Then, we introduce neoclassical models of discrimination. Three of the models are based on tastes for discrimination held by consumers, employers, or employees; the other model concerns statistical discrimination. With these models in hand, we can solve the puzzle of how markets permit discrimination yet ameliorate its adverse effects. Further, if the "magic of the market" works to eliminate the effects of discrimination, the economy gains in terms of both efficiency and equity. We then examine measured discrimination, particularly regarding wages. Because studies almost universally find discrimination affecting wages and employment for women and minorities, we are left with another question: if competitive markets can solve the problems of discrimination, why hasn't it happened yet? We outline a variety of answers then consider government policies to deal with discrimination.

The Inefficiency of Discrimination

In trying to understand the neoclassical approach to discrimination, it is important to separate market discrimination from differences in taste, abilities, and effort. Neoclassical economics celebrates individual differences and diversity. It is precisely because we all have such different tastes and preferences that there is so much variety in consumer goods and occupations. Indeed, markets thrive in response to different tastes and preferences. Producers strive to identify products that are desired by consumers and low-cost methods to produce those goods, and simultaneously search for employment and personnel policies that will attract talented people.[2]

Discrimination is a different circumstance altogether. Like most people, neoclassical economists condemn discriminatory practices that affect people on the basis of their gender, race, ethnicity, or religious background. Moreover, if discrimination exists in markets, this is an economic as well as a moral problem. Discrimination results in both inequity, leading to unfair opportunities and outcomes, and inefficiency, meaning that at least one person can be made better off without making anyone else worse off. With discrimination there may be no trade-off between equity and efficiency, because both will improve if the effects of discrimination are eliminated.

The inequality of discrimination is obvious in unequal pay and unequal employment opportunities, but inefficiency is not so obvious. Inefficiency is seen most clearly when capable people are not allowed to hold certain jobs because of discrimination. Consider the following scenario. Imagine you are a talented fashion designer—one who can create the most beautiful and intricate gowns in the world. Because of discrimination, however, clothing manufacturers refuse to hire you or to purchase your designs. To support yourself and your family, you resort to working as a waiter. Unfortunately, you are a bad waiter, often forgetting orders and spilling drinks on customers; as a result, you receive virtually no tips. The reason this outcome is inefficient is that you suffer direct wage losses and, at the same time, society is robbed of your talents as a fashion designer, thus enjoying less total output than if you had been a fashion designer. Both you and those who purchase high-fashion clothing (not to mention the restaurant diners) would be better off if discrimination were eliminated.[3]

Inefficiency of discrimination: Income for those experiencing discrimination is lower and commodities are more costly

Although discrimination is inefficient, ridding our economy of it is difficult. The problem is that labor markets generate substantial inequality in wages and efficient employment (see Chapter 4). In the neoclassical view, inequality generated by competitive markets is desirable because it serves as a powerful motivator—providing you with incentives to save, invest, work, and locate the job where you are most productive. These sources of inequality, which are efficient because they motivate people, will be fused in the real world with inequality which is inefficient because of discrimination. Because it is so difficult to pull apart the efficient and inefficient sources of inequality, attempts to alleviate labor market discrimination might even reduce efficiency. Efforts to reduce or eliminate labor market discrimination may simply return us to the "trade-off" between equity and efficiency (see Chapter 3). We can make the economy more equal or more efficient, but not both.

For example, suppose that the government required "blind" hiring of all new employees and did not allow employers to know the name, age, work experience, education, or anything else about prospective employees. This would stop inefficient hiring discrimination and make the economy more equitable, but it would create new inefficiencies—the most qualified and productive employees would often be missed. In actual economies, it may be difficult to end inefficient discrimination without creating new inefficiencies.

Three Outcomes from Discrimination

Inefficiency because of discrimination in labor markets can take three forms: lower wages for some types of workers as opposed to others performing identical tasks, higher unemployment or underemployment rates for groups with similar characteristics, and job segregation or crowding of a group into a few jobs that pay less than other, comparable jobs.

Three results of discrimination: Lower wages, un- or underemployment, and occupational crowding

For an example of wage discrimination, return to our fashion designer scenario. Suppose that a clothing manufacturer recognizes the value of your work and decides to hire you as a designer. Because your only other option is waiting tables, the employer could offer you lower wages than those of other designers performing the same work. You have little choice other than to take the job at low pay. Furthermore, the employer would not be maximizing profits if he or she paid you the higher going wage. You receive a lower wage because of discrimination.

The fashion designer might instead (or additionally) suffer from unemployment or underemployment. If no employer will hire you, you could end up without any job—unemployed. A more likely scenario, however, and the one depicted earlier, finds you taking a job for which you are less qualified, waiting tables, in which case you are underemployed. A different form of underemployment would occur if you could not find full-time employment as a fashion designer and so either accepted a part-time designer job or acted as a part-time designer in your home. Whether you are unemployed or underemployed, you suffer, as do consumers who are deprived of your work.

Underemployment: When a person is employed in a job where her or his abilities, skills, or preferred working hours are not fully used

A third set of outcomes from discrimination is job segregation and occupational crowding, an idea developed by Barbara Bergmann.[4] There is nothing inherently wrong with job segregation per se. If men wish to work with other men and women with other women, this is not necessarily a problem. Men and women may voluntarily "crowd" into different types of jobs and workplaces. What Bergmann noted, however, was that crowding may be involuntary and inefficient—discrimination may be at work. What if women or minorities are restricted to a few occupations because of a lack of promotion opportunities in some jobs and employment discrimination in others? The supply of women or minorities to these few occupations then rises, and wages must necessarily fall as we move down along the demand curve in response (recall from Chapter 3 that any time supply increases, the equilibrium price will fall). This implies that for equally qualified workers, those in crowded occupations will receive lower pay than those in other types of jobs. For example, if becoming a fashion designer and a skilled machinist require the same amount of training and effort, but members of your group are limited to a few occupations (e.g., being a designer, waiter, or secretary), you will experience lower wages as a fashion designer than as a skilled machinist.

Occupational crowding: When a group is limited to a few occupations and so receives low wages

The key insight of Bergmann's crowding model is that voluntary segregation by gender or race does not explain wage differences between groups. After all, if you could change occupations and, given the same amount of human capital, make more money, wouldn't you try? Only discrimination can explain why women and minorities are limited to a few occupations and receive lower wages than others as a result. Stated differently, is it accidental that groups who are crowded into a few occupations today were legally prohibited from voting in the 1789 presidential election? Bergmann suggests that such crowding is not voluntary, but instead results from past and present discrimination.

Now that we have the outcomes from discrimination, let's go back to the causes.

MODELS OF DISCRIMINATION BASED ON PREJUDICE: CONSUMERS, EMPLOYERS, AND EMPLOYEES

Discrimination as an economic topic was introduced most forcefully into the neoclassical realm by Gary Becker in his 1957 work, *The Economics of Discrimination*. Using the central building blocks of neoclassical theory—self-interested, individual behavior—Becker showed that different labor market outcomes based on prejudice against a group could fit into the neoclassical model of utility maximization. He argued that if individual consumers, employers, or employees exhibit a "taste for discrimination," then these prejudices could result in economic inequality. Having a taste for discrimination means that a person experiences disutility from association with people he or she doesn't like. As a result, people with the taste are willing to pay (in the form of shoddy goods and services, lower profits, or lost wages) to avoid contact with people in that group.

> ### Taste for discrimination: A "willingness to pay" to avoid connections with members of a particular group

Becker argued that three distinct groups—consumers, employers, and employees—might engage in discrimination, and we analyze these three cases here. Another form of discrimination—"statistical discrimination"—is considered in the following section. A final type of discrimination exists outside of labor markets and is labeled "premarket discrimination." Because labor markets neither cause nor solve premarket discrimination, we discuss it at the end of this chapter.

Consumer Discrimination

Start with consumers who have a taste for discrimination. Assume, for instance, that you have a "distaste" for bald newscasters and refuse to watch them when they appear. If many others share your distaste for bald newscasters, TV stations who hire bald newscasters will lose a large portion of their audience. To satisfy advertisers who demand a large audience share, TV stations will hire only full-haired broadcasters. As a result of this widespread taste for discrimination, competent newscasters—who also happen to be bald—will not be hired. With the effective supply of broadcasters now restricted to the full-haired, wages will be higher than they otherwise would be. To pay these higher wages, the TV station has to show more insipid commercials or hire incompetent but full-haired newscasters who are willing to work for lower wages. For consumers, the price of discriminating takes the form of less, or worse, news. For bald broadcasters, the cost is much higher—no jobs as broadcasters. Therefore, if discrimination is part of people's tastes and preferences, the economy will be both inefficient and inequitable.

> ### Consumer discrimination: When those making purchases refuse to buy goods or services made or sold by members of certain groups

Two pre-existing conditions must be met if consumer discrimination is to have economic effects. First, consumers must know who is on the other end of a purchase. While this is almost always the case with retail sales (except for those made over the phone, by mail, on online), it will rarely, if ever, be true for manufactured goods or utilities such as water, sewage, or electricity. Second, a large group of consumers, with sufficient buying power, must have the same taste for discrimination. Residents of Montana might share a taste for discriminating against people and products from California, but there are too few Montanans to affect the market. These conditions help to explain when consumer discrimination may be relevant, and who is in a position to discriminate effectively.

Employer Discrimination

Consumers are not the only ones who might have a taste for discrimination. When employers have the "taste," it can result in one group of workers receiving different wages than another group. For the sake of illustration, assume that the owner of a private hospital has a distaste for women doctors. This distaste is so strong that he is willing to pay male doctors a premium for working at his hospital. Further, assume that many hospital administrators feel this way as well. The result is that the demand for women doctors will be low, as will their wages. A taste for discrimination by employers can result in wage differentials, unemployment for female doctors, or women being crowded out of doctoring and into other professions.

> *Employer discrimination: When employers refuse to hire, or will only pay lower wages to, members of certain groups*

In his 1957 work, Becker suggested that employer discrimination was more prevalent than consumer discrimination. The reason is not hard to find: consumers often do not know who produced the goods and services they purchase, but employers know for certain who is working for them. Moreover, it is easy for most of us to see ourselves in a position where we would willingly engage in employer discrimination. How? Suppose you start a small business. Are you likely to employ your partner, children, aunts and uncles, nieces and nephews? If you're like most people, the answer is "yes." However, when you do this, are you also likely to exclude individuals who are not of your own race or ethnicity? Unfortunately, the answer here also is "yes." Finally, returning to Becker's definition of discrimination, would you be willing to pay your mother or brother a little more than you might a stranger to perform the same quality of work? If the answer is "yes," then you would be discriminating. As a result, total output for society and wages for excluded groups will suffer, leading to an economy that is both inefficient and inequitable.

There is an important qualifier here, one that is shared with the consumer discrimination story: for employer discrimination to be effective, most employers will need to share the same prejudices.

Employee Discrimination

Employees may also have a taste for discrimination. Again, take the case of doctors. Assume that male doctors have a distaste for working with women doctors. Male doctors may be willing to take a lower wage to avoid working with female doctors, or they may be willing to incur the cost of a long commute to an employer who only hires males.

> *Employee discrimination: When skilled employees of one type prevent people of another type from obtaining skills and jobs in those fields*

In this situation, neither employers nor consumers have any incentive to oppose employee discrimination. If employee discrimination prevents you, as an employer, from hiring the most qualified employees, then your discriminating employees must be willing to accept lower wages to make up for their lack of productivity (i.e., they must be willing to pay). From a profit standpoint, employee discrimination is not a problem. By the same logic, products that are generated by discriminating employees will come into the market with the same price and quality as they otherwise would. Indeed, the effects of employee discrimination should be wiped out by competitive markets through the creation of segregated workplaces. In our medical example, unless the male doctors can collude to keep women out of the profession, some hospitals will hire only male doctors and others only female doctors, so the wages for both female and male doctors should be equal.

If the market can solve employee discrimination, then where are the inefficiencies? The answer lies in skill monopolies. If male doctors refuse to train female doctors and there are few, if any, female doctors to begin with, or if male carpenters refuse to train female apprentices, or male professors to train female graduate students, then inefficiency rears its ugly head. In this case, the only people who are available for hiring are male, and they do not need to suffer low wages when exercising their prejudices.

The example of doctors is no accident. Male doctors successfully kept women out of the prestigious American Medical Association until 1915, and out of Harvard Medical School until 1945.[5] As a result, women's position in the medical profession was minimal for many years. In theory, the result of this discrimination is poor medical care—consumers suffer from shoddy products and services as some of the most potentially productive individuals are kept out of an occupation.

Some evidence regarding discrimination by consumers, employers, and employees is provided in Box 5.1.

A final note on the taste for discrimination: regardless of whether it is consumers, employers, or employees who have the taste, actual discrimination will almost always look like the employer's fault. After all, it is employers who hire people and set wages, even if they are responding to consumer or employee discrimination. For example, Daniel H. Hamermesh found evidence that "beautiful" people are favored and "homely" people experience discrimination in wages, though it is difficult to know whether such "looks" discrimination results from employers, employees, consumers, or all three!

STATISTICAL DISCRIMINATION

In the 1970s, some neoclassical economists developed alternative explanations for discrimination. These explanations require that we relax one of the basic assumptions of competitive markets—that there is complete and perfect information—to see if it alters the predicted outcomes. Under conditions of imperfect and incomplete information, there is uncertainty in economic transactions, which can induce economic instability and discriminatory outcomes.

The Transaction Costs Problem

"Transaction costs" is the term that economists give to the expense of entering into and conducting market exchanges. These costs include those for discovering relevant information. Consider the following example: you have decided to buy a high-definition TV. Of course, you want the best one in your established price range. Because a TV is a relatively big purchase in your budget, you decide to do a little research—reading reviews of different models on the web, and actually going and looking at TVs in the store to compare their performance. All of this takes time—perhaps even time away from studying (a costly way to spend your time!)—and,

---

BOX 5.1
DISCRIMINATION IN MAJOR LEAGUE SPORTS

Partly because performance is measurable, and maybe because most neoclassical economists have historically been male, many studies of discrimination analyze professional
sports. Lawrence Kahn summarized these studies and he uncovered evidence consistent
with each of the three types of discriminatory outcomes described earlier. Until the 1940s
and 1950s, blacks were banned from all major professional sports in the United States (i.e.,
unemployment). Nonetheless, after the color barrier was formally broken, studies found
blacks receiving lower wages for identical productivity, particularly in basketball (i.e., wage
discrimination) and being relegated to less prestigious positions, particularly in hockey,
football, and baseball (i.e., occupational crowding).

   More recent studies suggest that discrimination has lessened, but still exists. For example, a study of the National Basketball Association found that white players attracted
larger audiences in the 1990s (holding performance constant), generated higher television
advertising revenues, and therefore received higher salaries for identical performance. Another study, however, found no racial salary differences over that same time period. Still
other studies of professional baseball find evidence of past discrimination that has dissi-
pated, with all-star voting and election into baseball's Hall of Fame no longer demonstrating
any race effects. Nonetheless, discrimination may not have disappeared. As of 2013, 67% of
NFL players were black, but less than 10% of head coaches (3) were black.

Sources: Mark Kanazawa and Jonas Funk. 2001. "Racial Discrimination in Professional Basketball: Evidence from Neilsen Ratings." *Economic Inquiry* 39, 599-608. Barton Hamilton. 1997. "Racial Discrimination and Professional Basketball Salaries in the 1990s." *Applied Economics* 29, 287-296. Andrew Hanssen
and Torben Andersen. 1999. "Has Discrimination Lessened Over Time? A Test Using Baseball's All-Star
Vote." *Economic Inquiry* 37, 326-352. R. Todd Jewell. 2003. "Voting for the Baseball Hall of Fame: The Effect of Race on Election Date." *Industrial Relations*, January, 87-100. Natelege Whaley. "NFL Did Not Hire
African-American Head Coaches in 2013." Black Entertainment Television (BET.com). Jan. 18, 2013.

---

in effect, increases the cost of a TV. If you decide to purchase a used TV through Craigslist or
at a flea market, you are likely to incur additional costs in terms of the time it takes to negotiate
the selling price and determine the quality of the second-hand product.

> *Transaction costs: Time or money that is spent trying to identify and
> negotiate the price, quality, or location of commodities, employers, or
> employees*

   When the notions of incomplete information and transaction costs are applied to labor
markets, there may be fairly large information gaps between employers seeking qualified
employees and potential employees searching for the best jobs, then negotiating wages, benefits,
and working conditions. Efforts to overcome this information gap impose large transaction
costs on both employees and employers. When looking for a job, you require information on
where the jobs are, who to talk to, and what skills are needed for each one. You need to line
up recommendations and make sure you know what the appropriate clothes are to wear for
a particular interview. This quest for information makes your job search longer and costlier.
Further, you need to think about what sort of package you might negotiate or demand in terms
of wages, health and dental care, training opportunities, pensions, and so forth.

   Most immediately, this information problem creates frictional unemployment, because it
requires time for employers to identify good employees, for employees to identify good jobs,

and for both to negotiate an employment contract. With people out of work in the meantime, frictional unemployment occurs. Such information problems also can generate statistical discrimination, which is the problem we turn to next.

The Problem of Statistical Discrimination

Given the information problem, rational employers will use whatever information on potential productivity they can find, and efforts to use all relevant information can produce *statistical discrimination,* an idea developed by Nobel Prize-winning economist Michael Spence. This type of discrimination is not based on tastes or prejudice. Instead, it occurs when employers judge an applicant's abilities based on known characteristics of the group that individual belongs to, rather than on the applicant's individual abilities. An employer is especially likely to do this when there is imperfect information about prospective employees, or the cost of obtaining more information is high. So, instead of conducting extensive and expensive tests, the employer ascribes what he or she knows about similar applicants to the person in front of them in making hiring decisions.

Statistical discrimination: Applying group information to an individual member of that group

Education provides a case of statistical discrimination. Researchers at the U.S. Census Bureau found that graduation from high school adds an average of $1.3 million in lifetime earnings (compared to dropping out), getting an associate's degree adds another $420,000, and getting a bachelor's degree adds an additional $550,000.[6] The statistical discrimination part is that the estimates for an extra year of school are not even calculated, because it is degrees, rather than years of schooling, that translate into big earnings advantages.

The good news with the case of high school or college graduation is that as an individual, you exert some control over whether you are in or out of the high-wage group. When it comes to race or gender, there is less choice. In the 1960s it was common for a married woman in her twenties to be denied a job because employers assumed she was going to get pregnant and leave.[7] Employees who quit cost firms money—especially if the job requires skills that the firm must provide to the worker (i.e., the firm-specific skills discussed in Chapter 4). So, employers who invest in workers' firm-specific skills have a profit motive for hiring workers who will likely stay with the firm for many years. In the 1950s and early 1960s—the height of the Baby Boom—most young, married women had children and left the labor force. While any particular woman may not bear children, or may have no intention of leaving work once a child is born, this makes little difference if statistical discrimination is at work. As long as the statistical average points to women quitting more often than men, employers will assume that any individual woman also is likely to quit. Young or married women will have a hard time finding a job, and their wages will be lower or their unemployment rates higher—just as predicted by Becker's very different theory of discrimination.

An additional source of statistical discrimination, which is similar to that associated with education, can also affect women. Suppose that you have a child right after college and work as a homemaker for the next ten years. Then you decide to enter the workforce, but find you have little information to give to employers regarding your skills. Whether you are extremely competent or extremely slow, it will be costly for the employer to find out, and you will face difficulties obtaining a good job.

These two sources of statistical discrimination represent two general types. In the first case, an employer may know that, on average, one group is less productive than another, and therefore avoids hiring members of the less productive group. In the second case, the employer knows that, on average, both groups are equally productive, but he or she has less information about one of the groups, and therefore avoids hiring from that group.[8]

Two sources of statistical discrimination: 1) One group is less productive on average, or 2) less is known about one group

For a simple example, suppose you are taking applications for a job managing a group of clerical workers when two rather unusual candidates show up. The first is a 10-year-old girl; you immediately think, "She's too young to do this job." On average, this assumption would be correct, so you reject this applicant based on her membership in a low-productivity group (by age). Next, you find a Martian has applied for the job. You are polite to the visitor from outer space, but cannot quite bring yourself to hire "it," because you know so little about Martians. In each of these cases, you statistically discriminate, but for very different reasons.

There has been much speculation about why and how statistical discrimination occurs. Even if a young woman promises an employer that she will not quit to raise children, the employer might believe that if she does give birth, she is more likely than a man to be absent because of a sick child or might put more effort into working at home and thus be less productive on the job. In the case of minorities, employers may believe that nonwhites in general, and blacks who grow up in the inner cities of the United States in particular, receive an inferior education or are more likely to experience problems at home or in their communities, reducing their expected job performance in either case. For either minorities or women, if managers who make hiring decisions are white males, it is possible that they find it easier to pick up relevant information from white males during the interview process. A white male manager might be less comfortable with, and less able to pick up information from, interviews with women or people of color.

Statistical discrimination is often efficient. Employers are simply using all available information in a case where the costs of eliminating statistical discrimination by gathering more information outweigh the benefits in terms of hiring more productive employees. To end statistical discrimination in these cases would mean reducing total output to pay for additional tests and interviews. In this circumstance, society loses in terms of efficiency if we try to eliminate statistical discrimination.

There are two cases where statistical discrimination is inefficient, however, and should be eradicated on grounds of both equity and efficiency. First, there may be externalities or public goods aspects of testing. If all prospective employees have taken a particular type of test, employers will know what a certain score implies. However, if a single employer gives the test, she or he may not know how other prospective employees might score. Further, once a test has been taken, if the scores are held by only one employer, inefficiency occurs, since the economic cost of giving the score to other firms is close to zero. Here there is a clear efficiency gain if the government steps in, pays the costs of testing, and distributes results to all interested employers.

A second case where statistical discrimination is inefficient occurs when group behavior changes but employers do not know. For example, when an immigrant group enters a country, they may bring their cultural values and previous patterns of behavior with them. If these values and behaviors are not very productive, then statistical discrimination will follow. Now, what if the next generation of the group changes their behavior? They may still experience statistical discrimination even though it is unwarranted. If these values and behaviors do not match those that employers want, then statistical discrimination will follow.

Because of the two possibilities outlined here, statistical discrimination may be either efficient or inefficient. To complicate matters further, it will often be difficult to tell whether such discrimination is efficient and the government should stay out, or whether it is inefficient and the government could improve matters, for example by gathering and disseminating better information on prospective employees.[9]

Comparing Prejudice and Statistical Discrimination

A central difference between statistical discrimination as outlined earlier and Becker-type models of discriminatory tastes lies in their implications for efficiency. Statistical discrimination by employers is sometimes efficient, but discriminatory tastes always lead to inefficient discrimination.

Discrimination and efficiency: Consumer, employer, and employee discrimination are inefficient; statistical discrimination may be efficient or inefficient

Recall that in the cases of consumer, employer, or employee discrimination, the discriminator pays. Discriminating consumers end up with low-quality or overpriced products, discriminating employers end up paying higher wages than they could or should, and discriminating employees receive lower wages than others. With statistical discrimination, employers profit from discriminating—this is where transaction costs come in. If a ten-year-old child applies for a managerial position and you, as the employer, try to avoid statistical discrimination, you will spend time and money on testing, interviews, reviewing job applications, and so on, that you could have avoided. It is inefficient for you to do so because you know beforehand that few, if any, ten-year-old children are capable managers.

Statistical discrimination may be inefficient from society's view if testing has externalities, such that the total benefits of all interested employers receiving the results outweigh the costs of administering the test, but the costs to the individual firm of giving the test are greater than the benefits. Similarly, statistical discrimination is inefficient if group characteristics have changed but employers do not know.[10] In either case, there may be an efficiency-improving role for government. Discrimination because of prejudice, however, is always inefficient.

THE MAGIC OF THE MARKET TO THE RESCUE: ENDING DISCRIMINATION

Now we are ready to solve the puzzle posed earlier: if everyone is free to discriminate in a competitive market economy, how does competition erode the adverse effects of discrimination? The answer takes us back to the magic of the market first discussed in Chapter 3. Basically, because the market is impersonal, it penalizes those who discriminate and rewards those who do not.

Initially, we look at how models of prejudice break down in the presence of competition. Then, we consider how the market erodes statistical discrimination.

Ending Discrimination Because of Prejudice

At first glance, it appeared that Gary Becker successfully explained why discrimination persists: as long as consumers, employers, or employees are willing to pay to exercise their prejudices, discriminatory outcomes will be sustained. Consumers with the taste for discrimination end up paying more for goods or services (or getting less of the good than they might have without discrimination), discriminating employers must pay a higher wage to employees, and employees with a taste for discrimination could conceivably end up with a lower wage.

As Nobel Prize-winner Kenneth Arrow and others have argued (and as Becker himself later recognized), there is an inconsistency in Becker's model: if there is just one employer who does not have a taste for discrimination, then Becker's original model of employer discrimination cannot hold in the long run. Wage discrimination will be bid away. Arrow argued that if there is one employer who is indifferent to whether black, white, or even green people are hired, and there are no skill differences according to skin color (or gender or religion), then the non-discriminating employer will be able to hire cheaper workers and make higher-than-average profits (because costs are lower than the industry average). The existence of super-high profits for employers without a taste for discrimination will mean that more and more non-discriminating employers will enter the market and that those with a taste for discrimination will be forced out of business because they are less profitable. Eventually, employers will have to raise the wages of workers facing discrimination (as the demand for these workers rises) until, in the long run, wages will be the same for equally productive workers. Indeed, as a practical matter, an employer who does not wish to associate with certain groups can achieve this end while still making average profits by investing in the stock market, where the employer will not have to associate with anyone beyond a broker. In the long run, there's just no money to be had by employers who discriminate.

Erosion of effects of prejudice: Competitive markets reward consumers, employers, or employees who have no taste for discrimination

Somewhat differently, if employees are discriminatory, this doesn't necessarily need to result in adverse outcomes for anyone. Instead, firms could operate segregated workplaces, with some for black women, others for white men, and so forth. The separate groups could exercise their prejudices but no one group would receive lower wages for identical levels of productivity, because in that case, employers would build more factories to employ these low-wage workers, and increase their demand for workers in this group until wage equality exists. Furthermore, if training is such a problem that members of certain groups cannot enter a field, then open admissions policies both at schools and for apprenticeship programs should end this practice (as eventually happened with the American Medical Association and Harvard Medical School).

Concerning discrimination by consumers, consumers typically have no idea who produced the goods they buy, because of our highly integrated and global economy. Even with services such as health care, education, and security, the consumer often does not know exactly who the providers are, so discrimination will be difficult or impossible.

Even in instances where consumers can identify employees, consumer discrimination should still break down over time. Assume there are two labor markets, one for women and one for men, in which equilibrium wages are higher in the men's market and lower in the women's because of consumer discrimination. Now, introduce a small group of non-discriminating consumers. They will be able to purchase women-produced goods at a lower price and so should drive up the demand in the women's labor market. At the same time, if some traditional consumers drop out of the market, demand in the men's labor market should fall. In the long run, the wages should be equal. At the extreme, one might find segregated workplaces, but not wage differences.

The point here is that coupled with competition, differences in tastes and preferences ensure that the unequal and inefficient economic effects of discrimination on wages among equally skilled workers will be bid away. Because of self-interest in better and cheaper consumer goods, higher profits, and higher wages, discrimination that results in wage differentials or unemployment will dissipate over the long run if markets are competitive. Indeed, if all else fails, those who experience discrimination should be able to start their own firms, produce at substantially lower costs, and receive higher profits than firms that permit discrimination.

This argument has become so pervasive in neoclassical economics that many often argue for competitive markets as the cure for discrimination—precisely because discrimination is not profitable. Milton and Rose Friedman bring home this point through a discussion of the production of pencils in their 1979 treatise *Free To Choose*. They describe a pencil assembly process that brings together lumberjacks and woodcutters from California, miners extracting graphite in Ceylon, and rubber tappers from Indonesia: "These people live in many lands, speak different languages, practice different religions, may even hate one another—yet none of these differences prevented them from cooperating to produce a pencil."

Ending Statistical Discrimination

Although statistical discrimination may be efficient and exist even if no one is prejudiced, it does not need to last forever. Firms have an incentive to come up with better and cheaper predictors of individual productivity, or better tests to gauge the qualifications of job applicants. Firms that do so will make more money for two reasons: 1) they can cheaply identify and hire highly productive women or minorities who are passed over by firms that perform less extensive tests, and 2) as long as statistical discrimination still exists, the employer can pay women or minorities less than equally qualified whites or males receive. Therefore, we should see fewer and fewer instances of statistical discrimination over time.

Erosion of statistical discrimination: Competitive markets reward employers for finding productive individuals in groups subject to statistical discrimination

There is some evidence on both the employer and employee side that statistical discrimination is being eroded. First, for employees, evidence suggests that women or minorities who are willing to spend the money to signal their value to the firm experience much larger returns than whites or males do. Women and minorities experience larger increases in earnings from college graduation than white males, suggesting there is less wage discrimination against women and minorities who graduate from college (Goldin, 1990). By improving the information that is available to employers, these individuals themselves help to stamp out the adverse effects of statistical discrimination.

Second, even if education is used to signal high employee capabilities and motivation, employers have an incentive to learn quickly about an employee's productivity, eventually eliminating the effects of statistical discrimination. Joseph Altonji and Charles Pierret (2001) tested for such effects, and found that the effects of statistical discrimination by race disappear in a matter of a few years after college graduation.

Does this evidence suggest that competitive markets have effectively combated discrimination? Maybe not. Recent polls suggest that whites and males, but not others, believe this to be true. Polls taken after the election of President Obama in November 2008 showed that 38% of whites, but only 20% of black Americans, believed that racial equality had been achieved. At the same time, 32% of men, but a full 48% of women, believed there are continuing advantages in our society for males.[11]

Who should we believe? To get an answer, let's look at some numbers.

MEASURING WAGE DISCRIMINATION

How much discrimination actually occurs in labor markets? Thousands of studies have attempted to answer this question. Here, we examine how typical studies are performed, look at some representative findings, and finish by examining some problems associated with this line of research.

How to Measure Wage Discrimination

For neoclassical economists looking at the issue, wage discrimination is measured by taking actual wage differences between groups and breaking them down into those caused by discrimination and those independent of discrimination. Economists do this with regression analysis, using a technique called the residual method. The idea of a regression is that we can use some characteristic of people to predict an outcome for those same people. For example, a regression analysis might show that people who live in the suburbs of large cities earn 25 cents an hour more than those who do not, and that people with prior military service earn ten cents an hour more than others. This does not mean that everyone who has served in the military earns exactly ten cents more than the average. While many will earn more or less, we focus on the average.

> ### Discriminatory wage differences: What is left over (the residual) after accounting for human capital and other market-generated wage differences

Now, we come to the residual part. Suppose that, on average, young workers receive 50 cents an hour less than older workers, but that there are more older workers who live in the suburbs and have served in the military. Calling the 50-cent differential "discrimination" would miss the possible influence of these other factors. After accounting for the fact that some older workers have never served in the military or lived in the suburbs, we could use the regression to show that fifteen cents of the differential results from suburban residence, and that five cents results from different military service experiences. The final result is that 30 cents (i.e., the residual) of the difference between what young and old workers receive can be attributed to discrimination.

This example is a bit silly. On the one hand, young workers likely have less work experience (hence, less firm-specific capital), so much of what looks like discrimination (30 cents) may result from productivity characteristics we did not account for. Discriminatory differences, then, are overstated. On the other hand, it is possible that real estate agents in the suburbs discriminate against young home buyers, so part of what looks like an objective factor (i.e., suburban home ownership) is really caused by discrimination. Further, just having a regression does not ensure that causality is correct. If workers with higher wages move to the suburbs (rather than suburban residence influencing wages), then the entire model is wrong. Regardless of these problems, neoclassical economists typically view the residual from a wage regression as capturing the effects of discrimination.

Looked at slightly differently, a regression partitions wage differences between people into those that result from discrimination and those that result from differences in productivity. Drawing on Becker's work on human capital, neoclassical economists first partition off productivity differences associated with education. Wage studies usually control as precisely as possible for levels and types of education, and this explains much (although far from all) of the wage differences that usually are identified. If education indeed makes people more productive (as the theory of human capital holds), then such differences should not be attributed to discrimination.

A related source of wage differences concerns experience on the job, or job tenure. As discussed in the previous chapter, there are two reasons why individuals with lengthy job tenure receive higher wages. First, investments in firm-specific training may occur over time, thus increasing the worker's productivity and, hence, wages. Second, once a firm has invested in a worker's human capital, it has an incentive to pay workers who stay with the firm more than others so that the workers do not quit.

An additional cause for workers to receive higher or lower wages stems from compensating differences. If some workers desire flexible hours and no heavy lifting, they will pick occupations that pay less money but offer these advantages. Again, we might not want to attribute related wage differences to discrimination.

A final cause of wage differences that neoclassical economists focus on has to do with the specific labor market that a worker is in. Workers in the southern United States typically earn less than workers in the northeast (and pay less for consumer goods as well), but this may have nothing to do with discrimination. Similarly, wages may be higher in urban areas or for employees of Fortune 500 firms, and again, discrimination may not play a role. If such factors are unrelated to discrimination, they should be included in regressions so that their effects are excluded from the discriminatory residual.

How Severe Is Wage Discrimination?

Francine Blau and Lawrence Kahn (2006) presented a representative study of gender wage differences that used the methodology outlined earlier. Here, they sought evidence on the "gender gap" in wage differences, or why men earn more than women. Table 5.1 presents their results.

The bottom of the table shows that the gender wage gap is a little over 20%—meaning that women earn around 80 cents per work hour for each dollar that men earn. The rest of the table breaks down this difference into components adding up to 100%. Since women have higher levels of education than men, the education effect is negative (reducing the difference almost 7%). If education were all that mattered, women would earn more than men. Women, however, tend to work shorter hours and take more time out of the labor force for children, so end up with less experience (and presumably less human capital) as a result, a difference that explains 10.5% of the gender gap. Race explains a small fraction of the gender gap, but occupation explains over one-quarter of the gap. Of course, if women are crowded into a few occupations due to discrimination, then this part of the gap is actually due to discrimination. One fifth of the gap is explained by the industries where women are employed—like retail services and nursing homes. A small fraction is explained by women's lower rates of union membership (and unions

TABLE 5.1
THE GENDER GAP IN WAGES

Percentage of the Wage Gap Between Men and Women Explained by Differences in Characteristics

Characteristics	Percentage
Educational Attainment	-6.7
Labor Force Experience	10.5
Race	2.4
Occupational Category	27.4
Industry Category	21.9
Union Status	3.5
Unexplained	41.1
Total	100
Wage Differential (%)	20.3

Source: Francine Blau and Lawrence Kahn, "The Gender Pay Gap: Going, Going... But Not Gone," in Francine Blau, Mary Brinton and David Grusky, eds., The Declining Significance of Gender? New York: Russell Sage Foundation, 2006.

raise wages), but over two-fifths of the gap is unexplained—and can be thought of as the effects of discrimination. If that figure is accurate, and if occupational crowding is not occurring, then discrimination causes women to earn 92 cents on the dollar relative to men (i.e., this figure represents 40% of the 20% difference).

As mentioned, it could be that discrimination—in the form of occupational crowding—may cause us to understate the size of the discriminatory wage differential. Instead, the discriminatory gap may be overstated if sources of productivity differences are ignored. For example, the types of data that are used in these studies rarely distinguish between workers who attended Harvard University or a community college, or even between A and C-average students, but employers often use this sort of information to gauge the likely productivity of a prospective employee.

For both gender and race discrimination, there is a problem which a few recent studies have uncovered—wage differences get larger with age (see Box 5.2). These studies are consistent with political economy models of discrimination analyzed in Chapter 8, but are difficult to explain in a neoclassical framework.

BOX 5.2
TO AVOID WAGE DISCRIMINATION: STAY FOREVER YOUNG

Claudia Goldin created a minor sensation among labor economists when she discovered that discriminatory wage differences by gender were smallest for young men and women, which she took as evidence that discrimination was diminishing over time. But there turned out to be a catch: more recent data continue to show that discriminatory wage differences are smallest when workers are young. For example, a study using data from 1991 to 2001 found young white women earning 10% less than equivalent white men, but the difference almost doubled for white women in their 30s, as shown in Table 5.2. That same doubling pattern appears for black men and for black women.

TABLE 5.2
DISCRIMINATORY WAGE DIFFERENCES AMONG COLLEGE GRADUATES, 1991-2000

	Ages 20-29	Ages 30-39
White men	100%	100%
Black men	89.9%	79.5%
White women	90%	82.9%
Black women	84.8%	72.8%

Source: Weinberger and Joy (2007). Note that the estimates control for work experience, work hours, education and region.

The table also shows (again) that race and gender are not additive effects. If they were, then young black women would report earnings at 79.9%, and black women in their 30s would report earnings at 62.4%. Black women still receive the lowest wages out of the four groups, but we could not predict their earnings from the experience of black men and white women.

Looking over a longer time period reveals that discriminatory differences have been declining for white women. Using 1980-1990 data for people in the 30s, Weinberger and Joy found that white women's earnings were only 76.4% of white men's (the newer figure is 82.9%). But the race story is different. For that same time period and age group, black women's earning were 71.4%, meaning they rose by a meager one percent in the more recent decade. The figure for black men was 82.9% during the 1980s, a decline of over 3% during the 1990s. It appears that discrimination against black men might have worsened during the 1990s.

Problems with Measures of Wage Discrimination

There would not be a mini-industry devoted to studies of wage discrimination if everyone believed the numbers in Table 5.1. Indeed, there is much disagreement as to the accuracy of such studies, and most centers on two issues. First is a reverse causality problem, which causes us to understate discrimination. For example, suppose we believe that as people become more experienced on a job, their productivity rises, and so should their wages. Following this logic, we would control for experience and might find that part of the male-female or black-white wage difference results from males or whites having more experience on the job. However, what if you, as a woman or a black, find it hard to obtain a job in your preferred field due to discrimination, or find that you are subject to discrimination in promotions or layoffs? Because of any or all of these forms of discrimination, you are less likely to gain as much experience as whites or males, so it would appear that you choose to be less experienced when in fact discrimination is at work.

The second problem with the residual method is that we might ignore real differences in productivity that are not measured. In this case, we would overstate discriminatory wage differences. For example, suppose that men work harder than women because of women's greater commitment to home production, as Becker (1985) suggests. If Becker is right but we have poor measures of how hard people are working, it will look like discrimination is present when, in fact, productivity differences are responsible for the wage difference.

Most neoclassical economists resolve this issue—the understating of discrimination because of reverse causality, and the overstating of discrimination because of unmeasured productivity differences—by arguing that some discrimination exists and that we need better indicators of individual performance to be more precise about its effects. The studies of wages in sports (see Box 5.1) go a long way toward resolving this problem because measures of productivity are readily available for that industry.

In sum, even with all the problems that afflict studies of discriminatory wages, most neoclassical economists believe the problem is real. However, if competitive markets can eliminate the ill effects of discrimination, why hasn't it happened yet?

WHY DISCRIMINATION PERSISTS

If the market should eliminate the effects of discrimination, why do we still encounter evidence of the phenomenon in today's economy? Basically, four general arguments have been used by neoclassical economists to answer this question:

1. Discriminatory effects are apparent only, and are not real. As Becker's theories of human capital and home production suggest, it may be that observed differences in the economic circumstances of different groups result entirely from objective differences in productivity among these groups (Sowell, 1983; O'Neill, 1990). For example, blacks may inhabit a culture with little emphasis on training and careers and, hence, earn less as they are less productive than whites. Women may be efficiently emphasizing home production at the expense of market wages. There may indeed be discrimination in a society, but the market has already stamped out any economic effects.

2. Discrimination is disappearing, but this takes time. While markets may be acting to stamp out the effects of discrimination, the market may be sluggish or slow (Goldin, 1990). For example, if women began entering business schools in record numbers in the 1980s, we might not expect to see them evenly represented in high-level management positions for another two or three decades.

3. Consumer discrimination can persist. In markets where employees are highly visible to the public, consumers can easily identify and discriminate against those they dislike. If most people in an economy dislike bald newscasters, a TV station will never hire anyone with less than perfect hair. (Check this on your local station, and see if we are right.) The key to this persistence is that the discriminating group must have substantial purchasing power (money or majority status in the population) and the ability to monitor whether their will is being enforced. Evidence from professional sports is partially consistent with this possibility (see Box 5.1).

4. Monopoly power can sustain discrimination. If a group controls some product or input that others cannot provide, that group will be able to translate monopoly power into discriminatory outcomes. For example, if workers in a labor union prevent others from gaining skills that are needed to perform the job, the workers can keep their wages high by limiting the supply of skilled workers to one firm, industry, or area and crowding all other workers into other jobs. The American Medical Association, for example, does this by limiting the number of students who are permitted to enroll in medical school. Typically, the remaining jobs require fewer skills and, hence, pay less (Bergmann, 1989).

This last case is important because it suggests that unions may use their monopoly power to discriminate unfairly. Evidence from the U.S. trucking industry suggests that such behavior has indeed occurred. Until the late 1970s, interstate trucking was limited by the U.S. government to a few large companies, virtually all of which had collective bargaining agreements with the powerful Teamsters union. Then the government deregulated the industry, allowing anyone to enter the market. As a result, the Teamsters lost power, its membership waned, and wages for truck drivers fell. Most importantly, the wage difference between black and white drivers narrowed dramatically, suggesting that the union had been discriminating against black drivers (Peoples and Saunders, 1993).[12]

In general, most neoclassical economists agree with one or more of the four arguments presented here: either discriminatory effects are already gone, gradually disappearing, prevalent only in a few occupations where consumer discrimination persists, or exist in only a few select occupations where employees, unions, or governments permit discrimination to continue.

This general view does not, however, mean neoclassical economists believe that discrimination no longer exists, nor does it imply that nothing should be done about it (i.e., that laissez-faire policies are needed). After all, "gradually disappearing" could take a long time. Neoclassical economists who do believe that government intervention is warranted make their case on the empirical grounds that the costs of intervention are low and the benefits high.

Next we turn to the arena where most, if not all, neoclassical economists agree that discrimination is a problem—outside the labor market.

Discrimination outside the labor market cannot be solved by competitive labor markets, because the market is not involved. Logically, such discrimination occurs before an individual's entry into the labor market, so it is called pre-market discrimination. From a strict neoclassical viewpoint, "discrimination outside of the labor market is beyond the scope of labor economics" (Hamermesh and Rees, 1993; 471). We discuss these issues now because many social scientists who work basically within the neoclassical framework do, but it is worth warning you that we are moving into murky waters.

One way to view group differences resulting from factors outside the labor market is to view them as supply-side factors. Discriminatory tastes mean that identically qualified women or minorities are treated differently in the labor market; the demand for equally qualified women and minorities is less than that for white males. Supply-side factors mean that women and minorities are actually different from males and whites when they enter the labor market.

Hamermesh and Rees place these supply-side differences outside of labor economics in part because even a perfectly fair, perfectly competitive labor market could not possibly alter these things; if women are less productive than men, the market will consistently and efficiently generate lower pay for women. On the other hand, if equally qualified women are paid less than men (i.e., demand-side discrimination), then market competition should alleviate the problem, as occurred in the interstate trucking industry.

Supply- vs. demand-side differences: Discrimination in labor markets affects the demand for labor; external differences (including premarket discrimination) affect the supply of labor

The supply-side factors that we examine fall into two categories. The first is labeled pre-market discrimination. This is real discrimination, but it occurs outside the labor market. The second is cultural or biological differences among groups. This second set of factors has nothing to do with discrimination, but it could generate outcomes that look an awful lot like those produced by discrimination. An amalgam of these arguments appears in literature on the underclass, the final topic in this section.

Pre-market Discrimination

Pre-market discrimination occurs when a group of people are denied opportunities because of discrimination in the form of laws or attitudes.[13]

An example of pre-market discrimination is the Jim Crow laws that existed in the United States from the late 1800s until the 1960s. These laws sanctioned "separate but equal" facilities for black and white Americans. As a result, many colleges and universities refused to accept black students, and because of this pre-market discrimination, blacks were denied opportunities to improve their human capital.[14]

A more recent example is the connection between the legacy of legally-sanctioned racial housing segregation and unequal educational opportunities. In most places in the United States, public education is funded through local property taxes. Residential racial housing segregation and high housing prices leave many black families in poorer neighborhoods than many white families. One consequence is that inner cities tend to have a lower tax base than white suburbs. A lower tax base means higher tax rates to raise the same amount of funds for schools than in the suburbs and/or reduced spending. Poorly funded public education leaves many children with lower skills entering the labor market and makes it harder for them to go to college. Court cases have challenged this mechanism for funding, and in many cases states have redistributed income to schools in poorer communities; however, inner-city schools still tend to lack the range of facilities and offerings that exist in suburban schools. There is an additional and important economic impact of the legacy of racial housing segregation in the United States. For most people, the largest piece of wealth they own is their home. Segregated neighborhoods have left black families with fewer and lower-value assets than white families. The high costs of early education and care (for pre-school children), after-school programs for school-aged children, and college—even at public universities and colleges—means that many families must dip into their savings (i.e., cash out some of their assets) in order to pay for these important investments in their children's human capital. Families with less wealth cannot afford the same kind of investments. Unequal access to human capital would explain how blacks might have lower earnings based on lesser educational attainment.

Another example is that girls receive less attention in the classroom than boys. For whatever reason (e.g., individual teachers may prefer boys to girls, boys act up more than girls and require more attention), if less attention translates into less learning, then girls will be at a disadvantage relative to boys once they enter the labor market.[15]

Somewhat differently, Linda Grant found evidence from elementary schoolrooms that black girls are typically expected to be helpers, ignoring academic pursuits to help keep the classroom clean, help students locate materials or lost items, or help teachers maintain order in the classroom.[16]

Pre-market discrimination: Unequal treatment or opportunities in non-market settings that cause unequal labor market opportunities

Regarding the gender gap specifically, pre-market discrimination can take the form of discriminatory tastes, or instead be a rational response to discrimination. Causality could go either way. The discriminatory tastes argument fits the stereotyping found in schools and discussed earlier. There also is evidence that women respond to discrimination when they are young through their choice of, for example, college major.[17]

If you believe that men will make life as a female engineer difficult, why even try to enter that field? Therefore, part of the phenomenon of pre-market discrimination could be discrimination proper—women being discouraged from becoming engineers—and part could be a response to labor market discrimination—giving up before the career even begins since the labor market is stacked against you.

This reverse causality problem makes our understanding of home production, as outlined in Chapter 4, look somewhat naive. For example, part of the gender earnings gap could result from women specializing in home production and receiving appropriately lower wages through the mechanism of statistical discrimination—discrimination that is more apparent than real. Extending this argument, Becker suggested that employers might efficiently pay women less (i.e., statistically discriminate) for reasons beyond the likelihood that women will quit to have children. Even women with ongoing careers may be more likely to miss work because of an ill child, parent-teacher conferences, or the like, and might be less focused on the job or work less hard because of a relatively greater concern with children. For example, public health researcher Jody Heymann found that women are more likely than men to be interrupted at work to care for their own children, grandchildren, parents or other adults (men were more likely to interrupt work to care for an ill spouse or partner). Employers who are aware of relevant commitments may statistically discriminate. On the other hand, if discrimination in the labor market implies that women will earn less than men for the same skills and education, it is rational (but inefficient) for women to specialize in home production.

Many neoclassical economists argue that pre-market discrimination should be eliminated. For example, laws that promote discriminatory behavior could be overturned. Once pre-market discrimination is gone—for example, if schools are desegregated and all students admitted and treated based on merit, not gender or skin color—then economic outcomes should converge. In fact, many neoclassical economists point to the fact that the wage gap between blacks and whites has narrowed since the 1950s (see Chapter 2), and take this as evidence that the removal of legal restrictions on education for blacks in the United States has indeed alleviated much pre-market discrimination.[18]

Of course, that argument is less plausible in light of the increasing wage differences experienced as black and white men age (see Box 5.2).

Cultural and Biological Differences

Some neoclassical economists question whether pre-market discrimination exists at all, or if instead, lower wages for women and minorities are really caused by different preferences or abilities. These are the cultural or biological differences among people, which may in turn create inequality in the labor market (although not because of discrimination). Take the case of boys receiving more attention than girls in school. It is possible that, on average, boys are biologically more active and aggressive than girls. Boys then command more attention from their teachers. In our society—where education and attention from teachers pay off—boys' biological traits lead to higher-paying jobs.

> ### *Cultural or biological differences: Differences that are not discriminatory, but can cause different group outcomes in labor markets*

Biological or cultural differences can carry into the neoclassical understanding of wage differences because of factors considered in Chapter 4: time preference, human capital, and compensating wage differentials. If women or minorities have higher rates of time preference relative to white males, this could result in white males ultimately earning more as they are more future-oriented. Concerning human capital, cultural or biological differences can explain why women or people of color choose not to invest in themselves. Time preferences for cash today versus in the future, an ethnic group's historical emphasis (or de-emphasis) on education, and the knowledge that one will need to leave the labor force to raise children have all been promoted as explanations for differences in self-investment. Once in the market, individuals are solely responsible for their economic position, but outside the market, gender or race could determine what an individual desires from or is capable of in the market. The culture and community that one grows up in also could alter desires and abilities. Thomas Sowell (1983) argues that immigrants from China typically exhibit a high level of interest in obtaining education and frequently become entrepreneurs. As a result, this group often holds some of the most prestigious jobs and earns more than natives, even in countries like Malaysia, where the government has passed laws that explicitly discriminate against the overseas Chinese.

One study of the UK helps to tease out some of these productivity differences, by focusing on the value of fluency in English for recent immigrants (Shields and Price, 2002). That study found lower wages for immigrants from some specific countries, such as Bangladesh (18.5% penalty), but those differences may have to do with either productivity or discrimination. More importantly, English proficiency generated a 16 to 18% increase in wages (controlling for education, occupation, etc.), suggesting that productivity is heavily affected by language skills.

Whether differences in group behavior (i.e., supply-side differences) result from biology or culture determines whether we, as individuals or through government policy, can improve matters. If we are poor because of bad genes, there is little that can be done. If we are poor because of our culture, however, this can be changed. (Whether it should be changed is another question.)

Regarding male-female differences in earnings, recall from the last chapter (see Box 4.2) that anthropological research found the division of labor between men and women to be fairly stable across a large number of societies. This suggests that biology may play a role—inherent mental or physical differences between men and women may help to explain the gender gap. If this is the case, the gender gap will always be with us in a competitive market economy, as sociologist Catherine Hakim has argued (see Chapter 4).

Most relevant research, summarized by Blau and Ferber (1992), suggests that biology plays at most a minor role in determining the division of labor between men and women.

For example, studies of primates find that among chimpanzees, which are the most socially advanced primate aside from humans, females do not occupy subordinate positions. Moreover, more recent studies of people suggest that the sexual division of labor varies widely across societies. Blau and Ferber conclude that the division of labor found today, as in the crowding of "female" occupations, is "not shaped by biology alone." Instead, they suggest we look at "the interaction of technology, the role of women in production, and a variety of social and political factors" (1992; 31). Not surprisingly, one of the factors which Blau and Ferber consider to be relevant is discrimination.[19]

Undoubtedly, some neoclassical economists will never be deterred by the evidence, and will continue to search for biological explanations for wage differences. For example, Inas Rashad (2008) argues that height can help to explain wage differences across lines of race and gender, since, on average, white men are taller than black men, women are shorter than men, and black women are shorter than white women. Of course, the study admits that height discrimination might be involved, but also suggests that taller people tend to be healthier, and thus more productive.

POLICIES AND PRESCRIPTIONS

As argued in previous chapters, the general neoclassical prescription for social problems is for the government to take a laissez-faire stance, allowing impersonal market forces to sort out matters. This same argument is usually applied to the labor market. If discrimination is temporary and the market can bid it away, it is best to not intervene and let the market do its work. However, in instances where discrimination persists or pre-market discrimination exists, there might be a case for government to intervene.

Since virtually all legal barriers to economic opportunities for women and minorities have been removed, there are few reasons for neoclassical economists to argue that racial and gender discrimination precludes market success. Further, the levels of individual discrimination are much lower now than even two or three decades ago. After all, the United States elected its first black President (whose closest contender for the Democratic Party's presidential nomination was a woman). In this "post-racial" world, discrimination is not the reason for wage inequality. The problem is a lack of human capital investment. Therefore, neoclassical economists would argue that if the goal is to reduce wage inequality, we should pursue policies that promote human capital development, regardless of race or gender, and that do not interfere with market mechanism.

Underperforming schools should be shut down and replaced with more efficient ones. Neoclassical economists would support market-based solutions such as charter schools and other school choice efforts. The argument is to use public funding of education to promote more competition among local schools, thereby working to improve outcomes. Lower wages mean less wealth, and with the high cost of pre-market human capital investments, efforts to boost savings are in order. Instead of providing assistance for specific goods and services (like food or housing), governments and private charities should use funds to promote asset development among low-income families. One popular reform is the creation of Individual Development Accounts (IDAs). When a low-income family in an IDA program saves money, the amount is matched and can be withdrawn, usually for educational purposes or for a down-payment on a house.

With the increase of women in the labor market and recent scientific research on brain development, neoclassical economists are rethinking the role of early education and care as an important public good. Brain research convincingly shows that high quality care and stimulation shape how very young children learn now and later in life. Small public investments in their care and education can reap large individual and societal results. Nobel-Prize-winning economist Joseph Stiglitz (2012) is just one of many neoclassical economists who support the idea of more comprehensive investment in early childhood programs. And while these programs would benefit all children, government funding in this public good would disproportionately help the children of low-income women and minorities.

SUMMARY

This chapter opened with a puzzle: if free markets allow you or anyone else to discriminate against anyone or anything else, how can it also be that free markets eliminate the ill effects of discrimination? Part of the answer is that outcomes from discrimination inside of the labor market are inefficient. Whether groups experiencing discrimination are paid less, unemployed, underemployed, or crowded into a few occupations, we would all (potentially) benefit from ending such discrimination. Four types of discrimination exist inside the labor market: as Becker argues, consumers, employers, or employees may have a "taste for discrimination," and statistical discrimination may occur. Statistical discrimination itself takes on two forms: one group is on average less productive than another, or less is known about one group than another. The solution to our puzzle lies in the magic of competitive markets rooting out inefficient discrimination. Consumers without a taste for discrimination will be able to purchase better products at lower prices, non-discriminating employers will earn higher profits, non-discriminating employees will earn higher wages, and employers who are able to overcome statistical discrimination through better testing and interview procedures will earn higher profits.

The vast majority of studies to date reveal continuing wage discrimination, although debate about its extent continues. Some of this difference may result from pre-market discrimination, such as laws or attitudes that restrict opportunities for women or minorities outside the labor market. Competitive labor markets cannot solve pre-market discrimination—only government or community action can. Some of this difference may also result from biological or cultural differences among groups. The vast majority of neoclassical economists discount biology arguments, but some believe that culture indeed plays a role. If culture is relevant, at least some of what looks like discrimination inside the labor market is not caused by labor markets and cannot be solved by labor market policies.

At the end of the day, many neoclassical economists believe that some discrimination does exist inside of labor markets and seriously harms women and minorities.

The simple view of supply and demand in competitive markets suggests that the effects of discrimination either have been, will be shortly, or will eventually be wiped out, because markets reward people who do not discriminate, whether they are consumers, employers, or employees. In this case, laissez-faire government policies are the appropriate response to discrimination.

We finished by asking what policies neoclassical economists might promote to reduce wage inequality based on discrimination. Because discrimination is primarily the result of individual prejudice and legal restrictions, the precipitous decline in both requires a smaller role for the government to counteract these forces. Instead, wage inequality is seen as a problem of insufficient investment in human capital. Race-blind and gender-blind policies that are consistent with market-based solutions can promote increased human capital, like school choice, asset development incentives and childhood educational programs.

DISCUSSION QUESTIONS

1. Suppose you started your own business and hired only family members. Why would this strategy be inefficient?

2. Have you ever been involved in a situation where you believe that you experienced discrimination because of someone's taste or prejudices? Was it because of statistical discrimination?

3. Suppose a car salesperson charges a higher price to black than to white customers. Is this likely to result from discriminatory tastes or statistical discrimination? How would it change your answer if the salesperson were black?

4. If people voted in national and local elections for only candidates of their own race, would this be inefficient? If so, how might the "market" for votes solve the problem?

5. Many whites and males believe there is "reverse discrimination" and, as a result, they receive fewer opportunities than minorities and women. How can they believe this when the vast majority of studies show continuing discrimination against minorities and women?

6. A problem with measuring wage discrimination using the "residual method" is that part of the residual may result from unmeasured productivity differences. Can you imagine a test that would solve this problem?

7. If a parent purchases a Barbie doll for a young daughter and a WWE wrestling doll for a young son, is this an act of pre-market discrimination?

SUGGESTED READINGS

Aigner, Dennis J. and Glen G. Cain. 1977. "Statistical Theories of Discrimination in Labor Markets." *Industrial and Labor Relations Review,* January.

Altjoni, Joseph and Charles Pierret. 2001. "Employer Learning and Statistical Discrimination." *Quarterly Journal of Economics* 116(1).

Arrow, Kenneth. 1973. "The Theory of Discrimination." In *Discrimination in Labor Markets,* Orley Ashenfelter and Albert Rees, eds. Princeton: Princeton University Press.

Becker, Gary S. 1957. *The Economics of Discrimination.* Chicago: University of Chicago Press.

Becker, Gary S. 1965. "A Theory of the Allocation of Time." *American Economic Review* 75.

Becker, Gary S. 1985. "Human Capital, Effort, and the Sexual Division of Labor." *Journal of Labor Economics* 3(1, supplement).

Bergmann, Barbara. 1974. "Occupational Segregation, Wages and Profits When Employers Discriminate by Race or Sex." *Eastern Economic Journal,* April- July.

Bergmann, Barbara. 1989. "Does the Market for Women's Labor Need Fixing?" *Journal of Economic Perspectives,* Winter.

Blau, Francine and Marianne Ferber. 1992. *The Economics of Women, Men and Work.* 2nd ed. New York: Prentice-Hall.

Blau, Francine and Lawrence Kahn. 2006. "The Gender Pay Gap: Going, Going... But Not Gone," in Francine Blau, Mary Brinton and David Grusky, eds., *The Declining Significance of Gender?* New York: Russell Sage Foundation: pp. 45-66.

Ehrenberg, Ronald G. and Robert S. Smith. 1991. Modern Labor Economics, Theory and Public Policy. 4th ed. New York: HarperCollins.

Friedman, Milton and Rose Friedman. 1979. *Free to Choose.* New York: Harcourt, Brace, & Jovanovich.

Goldin, Claudia. 1990. *Understanding the Gender Gap.* New York: Oxford University Press.

Hamermesh, Daniel S. 2006. "Changing Looks and Changing "Discrimination": The Beauty of Economists." *Economics Letters,* 93, 405-412.

Hamermesh, Daniel S. and Albert Rees. 1993. *The Economics of Work and Pay.* 5th ed. New York: HarperCollins.

Heymann, Jody. 2000. *The Widening Gap: Why America's Working Families Are in Jeopardy and What Can Be Done About It.* New York: Basic Books.

Kahn, Lawrence M. 1991. "Discrimination in Professional Sports: A Survey of the Literature." *Industrial and Labor Relations Review,* April.

O'Neill, June. 1990. "The Role of Human Capital in Earnings Differences Between Black and White Men." *Journal of Economic Perspectives* 4(4).

Peoples, James and Lisa Saunders. 1993. "Trucking Deregulation and the Black/White Wage Gap." *Industrial and Labor Relations Review* 47(1).

Rashad, Inas. 2008. "Height, Health, and Income in the U.S., 1984-2005." *Economics and Human Biology* Vol. 6, 108-126.

Shields, Mark and Stephen Wheatley Price. 2002. "The English Language Fluency and Occupational Success of Ethnic Minority Immigrant Men Living in English Metropolitan Areas." *Journal of Population Economics* 15(1), 137-160.

Sowell, Thomas. 1983. *The Economics and Politics of Race.* New York: Quill.

Stiglitz, Joseph. 2012. *The Price of Inequality.* New York: W.W. Norton.

Weinberger, Catherine and Lois Joy, (2007). "The Relative Earnings of Black College Graduates, 1980-2001," in Marlene Kim, ed., *Race, Work and Economic Opportunity in the 21st Century*, New York: Routledge.

Wilson, William J. 1987. *The Truly Disadvantaged: The Inner City, the Underclass, and Public Policy.* Chicago: University of Chicago Press.

ENDNOTES

[1] Notice the story still works if the employee gives white customers the standard portion and gives short portions to black customers. The latter are still short-changed, and the employee could be fired for driving away paying (black) customers.

[2] Of course, some markets thrive on mass production, which provides similar goods to a large number of people (e.g., McDonald's hamburgers). In these cases, technology may dictate similar products to achieve low costs. Even here, however, the market still permits diversity (e.g., gourmet or vegetarian burgers), but at a price.

[3] We ignored the person who got "your" job as a fashion designer because of discrimination. Would that person be better off if discrimination were eliminated? Not directly, but in principle, the higher output resulting from eliminating discrimination could be redistributed so that, in fact, everyone would be better off afterward.

[4] Earlier, Gary Becker suggested the possibility that discrimination might affect some occupations more than others, but Bergmann is usually credited with developing this idea.

[5] See Blau and Ferber, 1992; 157–158.

[6] Carnevale, Anthony P., Stephen J. Rose, and Ban Cheah (2011). *The College Payoff: Education, Occupations, Lifetime Earnings.* Washington, D.C.: Georgetown University, Center on Education and the Workforce. Available at: www9.georgetown.edu/grad/gppi/hpi/cew/pdfs/collegepayoff-complete.pdf.

[7] Even earlier, women in many occupations were required to quit if they so much as got married, because their role as a "wife" demanded it (Goldin, 1990).

[8] For those with a statistical bent, the average productivity-difference case concerns different mean productivity, while the less-knowledge case concerns different productivity variance.

[9] In theory, prospective employees could engage in statistical discrimination against firms.

For example, if prospective employees know that promotion opportunities are more limited in small firms, they may target their job search at big, Fortune 500 firms—even if a particular small firm might provide greater promotion opportunities.

[10]This argument follows standard treatments of statistical discrimination, such as those found in Ehrenberg and Smith (1991) or Hamermesh and Rees (1993). A different form of "statistical discrimination," where initial employer prejudices become inefficient, self-fufilling prphecies, is discussed by Stephen Coate and Glenn C. Loury in "Will Affirmative-Action Policies Eliminate Negative Stereotypes?" *American Economic Review* 83(5), December 1993.

[11]Sources: ABC News/*Washington Post* Poll, Jan 13-16, 2009, CBS News/*New York Times* Poll, Jan 11-15, 2009.

[12]There also is direct evidence in that the U.S. government sued the Teamsters during the 1970s for discrimination against minorities.

[13]We use the term pre-market discrimination because it is accepted. It is not quite accurate, however, because it covers more than just young people "before" they enter the labor market (e.g., Jim Crow laws affected adults as well).

[14]The Jim Crow laws were one of many legal challenges by southern whites to the abolition of slavery in the 1860s. By 1883, the U.S. Supreme Court overturned legislation guaranteeing blacks equal access to public accommodation. Then, in 1896, the principle of "separate but equal" was accepted by that same body. See Teresa Amott and Julie Matthaei, *Race, Gender, and Work*. Boston: South End Press, 1991.

[15]See Bernice R. Sandler, "The Classroom Climate for Women," or Rita Kramer, "Are Girls Shortchanged in School?" both in *Race and Gender in the American Economy*. Susan F. Feiner, ed. Englewood Cliffs, NJ: Prentice-Hall, 1994.

[16]Linda Grant, "Helpers, Enforcers, and Go-Betweens: Black Females in Elementary School Classrooms," in *Women of Color in U.S. Society*. Maxine Baca Zinn and Bonnie Thornton Dill, eds. Philadelphia: Temple University Press, 1994.

[17]Thomas N. Daymont and Paul J. Andrisani, "Job Preferences, College Major, and the Gender Gap in Earnings." *Journal of Human Resources*, Summer 1984.

[18]See Robert Higgs, "Black Progress and the Persistence of Racial Economic Inequalities, 1865–1940," in *The Question of Discrimination: Racial Inequality in the US Labor Market*. Steven Shulman and William Darity, Jr., eds. Middletown, CT: Wesleyan University Press, 1989.

[19]Blau and Ferber's textbook cited here is explicitly neoclassical. However, much of their other work arguably falls between the neoclassical and political economy views presented here.

PART THREE

THE POLITICAL ECONOMY APPROACH

6

THE BASICS OF POLITICAL ECONOMY

INTRODUCTION: A DIFFERENT WORLD-VIEW

In the political economy world-view, people are not simply rational, calculating individuals. They are members of groups, and membership in particular groups predicts whether any particular individual will get a fair shot in the labor market or elsewhere in the economy. From the moment you are born, you enter an economy with an unlevel playing field. Each of us may have the opportunity to try hard and be the star player on our respective teams, but overall, the teams do not have equal resources and the rules of the game favor some over others.

This chapter begins our exploration of political economy. Parallel to our overview of neoclassical economics in Chapter 3, we overlook some important differences among political economists for the sake of simplicity of exposition. Nonetheless, we believe this material will give you an accurate understanding of the basic principles that unify this school of thought (see the Appendix to this chapter for more on differences among political economists).

This chapter first introduces the lens through which political economists view society: the "Four C's" of political economy—context, collective behavior, conflicting interests, and change. The Four C's are key concepts that provide a way to examine society and help to distinguish political economy from neoclassical economics. We then focus this lens on three critical divisions in society: class, race, and gender. These divisions are used by political economists to inform their analysis of almost any economic issue: global warming, economic development, raising children, or, in our case, discrimination and wage inequality. In political economy, these divisions are directly connected to different forms of oppression and particular places (i.e., sites) where that oppression primarily occurs. We explore the issue of why such divisions continue even if they are unfair, immoral, and inefficient by first asking whether market competition can break down these barriers and, second, by asking how, in general, social change occurs. Chapter 7 discusses work and wages in the political economy view; then we apply the tools of political economy directly to the question of discrimination in Chapter 8.

THE FOUR C'S: CONTEXT, COLLECTIVE BEHAVIOR, CONFLICTING INTERESTS, AND CHANGE

What is "political" about political economy? Why is it not just called "economics"? Neoclassical economists use markets and competition to analyze not only economic phenomena, but also institutions such as the family and government, as well as behaviors such as crime and divorce. For neoclassical economists, society as a whole can be explained directly by market behavior and competition, or indirectly as an analogy to markets and competition.

Political economists argue that behavior is not only individual but social as well. We are both individuals *and* members of social groups (such as blacks, women, or workers), and our behavior represents a response both to what we as individuals value and to what the groups we are affiliated with value. "Political" enters here because political economists perceive important social groups within our society as being related to each other by unequal power and uneven access to resources. Whites hold power over blacks, men over women, and capitalists over workers. When one group holds power over another, it means it controls the other. The dominant group can say "yes" or "no" and have their decision stick. Political economists call those relations oppressive. It is this group control or power that explains the "political" in political economy. To understand how such inequalities are played out and contested in an economy where actors are both individuals and members of social groups, we introduce the Four C's that link the thinking of political economists: context, collective behavior, conflicting interests, and change.

> ***Political economy: An approach to studying societies that emphasizes unequal economic power***

Context: It Isn't Just the Economy

As our discussion of the word "political" suggests, political economists believe that a narrow focus on markets and competition cannot explain how the economy works. Instead, we need a broader view of economics, one that includes the social and political context for economic decisions. In the simplest view, context means that the past influences the present—in other words, history matters.

Now hold on, you say. If I decide to buy a package of chewing gum, how is this influenced by the past? First, whether you can afford to buy the gum can loosely be predicted by how much money you have, which in turn depends on how much money your parents had, which can be predicted by their race, gender, and class. Second, before you purchase the gum, you will probably think about where you can chew it. If you have a big meeting or are on your way to a mosque, maybe chewing gum wouldn't be appropriate. Where do the rules for what is appropriate originate? They emerge from history.

> ***Context: The history and institutions that shape and constrain behavior***

For political economists, context is broader than simply saying "history matters." Context includes customary beliefs about social roles, such as whether women should work outside the home. It includes institutional configurations, such as the size and role of government; popular ideologies, such as the celebration of wealth or consumption; and property rights, such as the private ownership of capital. Context also includes the distribution of wealth and power in society, which determines far more than who can afford chewing gum. So, for political

BOX 6.1

CONTEXT MATTERS: NEOCLASSICAL ECONOMICS VS.
POLITICAL ECONOMY ON UTILITY, TASTES, AND PREFERENCE

To see an important difference between political economy and neoclassical economics, consider the most basic of assumptions in the neoclassical model: that people are by nature out to satisfy their individual desires; people are self-satisfying and individualistic (i.e., utility- and profit-maximizers). Political economists argue that people are not inherently selfish and greedy. Instead, they believe that our economic system rewards self-satisfying behavior and those who promote it, thereby encouraging people to act selfishly.

The differences parallel the two views' starting points: individuals vs. groups. Political economists stake their view on humans' desires to be members of, and identify with, groups (e.g., classes, races, genders) and to want to transform nature into useful things. Once in a group, collective effort brings its rewards, but the rewards are not always, or even necessarily, monetary.

For example, people who put a lot of time into volunteer organizations such as Habitat for Humanity (where people build or reconstruct housing for the poor) may find it a very emotionally rewarding experience, and it certainly is necessary. However, there are few economic rewards and increasingly less and less time to perform such activities. Even so, the fact that people do often join volunteer organizations and donate money, time, or materials to these groups implies that people are not consistently selfish. Indeed, it is hard to imagine how a society could function if everyone—in the home, community, or work-place—strived to do whatever it took to get ahead. Political economists go further and argue that a different economic system—one that rewarded cooperative behavior—might create an entirely different set of behaviors we call "human nature." There is a small neoclassical literature on altruistic giving, but the vast majority of neoclassical models assume that people behave selfishly. How bad is the problem? So bad that students who study neoclassical economics tend to become more selfish in the process!

Perhaps a bigger difference in the two models, however, is the assumptions of why people want what they want (i.e., where tastes and preferences come from). In the neoclassical model, an individual's desires are just that—individual. They are not influenced by what other people want or made in tandem with other people's desires. In fact, in the neoclassical model, where desires come from is not of much interest; they are assumed to be determined exogenously, or outside the purview of the economist's world. Political economists, on the other hand, argue that outside influences are perhaps the most important determinant of what people want to purchase. In sum, context is everything.

As an example of this last point, think about the attire you purchase. While this is an individual choice—no one made you buy jeans instead of running clothes—your desires are intimately connected with society. Today, young men and women often have tattoos and piercings, but for young men during the 1950s, wearing so much as an earring was to invite derision at best or even a fight (hardly "individual" decisions). Many of the young men who desire and purchase earings and other piercings would not have done so during the 1950s and, arguably, wouldn't have wanted the earrings even if they were handed over on a silver platter!

Corporations are well aware that what you want is in large part socially determined. As recently as 1981, U.S. corporations spent over $60 billion on advertising, a figure that rose to over $279 billion in 2007.

Sources: Douglas Galbi, "Annual U.S. Advertising Expenditures Since 1991," available at http://www.galbithink.org/ad-spending.htm, and Robert H. Frank, Thomas Gilovich, and Dennis T. Regan, "Does Studying Economics Inhibit Cooperation?" Journal of Economic Perspectives 7(2), Spring 1993.

economists, markets do not operate in a vacuum. Rather, they vary with, and can only be understood within, the historical and cultural contexts in which they occur.

Let's look at a more substantial example. Consider how a family with two adults and young children decides to acquire the goods and services it needs. Certainly, the family will try to "economize" by selectively looking for items on sale. When looking for employment to pay for the items, they will avoid lower-paying jobs, if possible. These aspects of decision-making are shared by the neoclassical and political economy views.

The political economist, however, argues that many other components enter into this decision. The cultural and customary standard of living will determine how much a family thinks it needs to consume (for example, one car or two?). The role of shopping and acquiring goods and services in society as a whole will matter. Political economist Jeremy Rifkin found that productivity in Europe is close to that for the United States, but incomes are less than three-quarters as large—and most of that difference is attributable to Europeans demanding and getting more leisure, while Americans have more money for shopping. As part of U.S. society, this family also is likely to want to shop until they drop, so they will need a lot of money (and a credit card or two). The need for money to do all this buying may dictate that the children be placed in child care so the two adults can work for pay. However, this strategy may run up against cultural stigmas attached to women working outside the home while their children are young. As sociologist Pamela Stone argues, the media often signal to women that they should feel guilty for having a career at such times, while a man is supposed to feel better to the extent that he can earn more money to support his family. A woman's desire for economic independence also may be a factor, which in turn is influenced by whether her friends or female relatives are economically independent. None of these issues can be taken as "given" unless we are willing to abstract from the most concrete questions concerning the decision to work.

If political economists are correct that the context of social life largely determines human behavior and not the other way around, then the sources of tastes and preferences, as well as the constraints on behavior, take the center stage in economic analysis (Box 6.1).

While context may sound abstract, many of its results are easily understood. If your parents were nice to you as a child, you will likely be nice to your children as well. If your grandparents lived in a society where forks, spoons, and knives were common eating utensils, then you probably will as well. And, to get a bit ahead of our story, if blacks and other minorities (as well as women) experienced discrimination historically, they likely will today as well.

It follows from the notion of context that political economy is very broad. The danger here is that we might end up arguing that "everything causes everything." Nonetheless, if you follow the story, a pattern emerges. It is not as precise as neoclassical economics, but political economists believe these patterns provide believable and, ultimately, powerful explanations for how economies function. By recognizing that history and institutions are important in explaining and understanding economic phenomena, political economists believe they provide a more complete basis for interpreting the consequences and causes of economic actions.

Collective Behavior: Who We Are Is What We Are

All social theories must begin by making some assumption about the categories through which causality occurs. This assumption largely determines how a theory explains the world around us. Theories that begin with the individual will produce explanations that are rooted in individual motivations. Theories that begin with groups will produce explanations that are rooted in group relationships. The problem of choosing an analytical unit cannot be avoided, but it is a chicken-and-egg situation. Are groups merely the sum of individual actions, or do groups determine what individuals want and do?

Neoclassical economists have many disagreements among themselves, but they all agree that economic behavior can be understood best in terms of the decisions of rational, self-interested individuals. They dismiss the notion that groups are more fundamental, for the simple reason that groups do not make decisions, individuals do. Only the individuals who comprise groups can be called decision makers. Group behavior therefore is perceived to be a function of the decisions made by many individuals, and it is those decisions that neoclassical economists perceive to be the most fundamental.

Collective behavior: Actions resulting from group influence or membership

The neoclassical perspective has an intuitive appeal, so it is worth pausing to explain why political economists reject it. In political economy, individuals cannot be taken as the basic unit of analysis, because their tastes, interests, knowledge, judgment, and, ultimately, their actions are largely the product of their social experiences and circumstances. Their choices are frequently self-interested, but self-interest is context-dependent. After all, individual decisions are influenced by factors such as advertising, community standards, job expectations, judgments of friends and relatives, and ideologies such as consumerism or religion. In other words, individual decisions are no more basic than the context in which they occur. To use our earlier analogy, you as an individual can strive to be the best member of a team, but the team that you are assigned to by your race, class, or gender is equally important for predicting your future success or failure. Political economy focuses on the structure and dynamics of that context, and it emphasizes the ways in which people jointly influence economic outcomes.

For example, Judith Lorber argues that individual behavior is not prior to group behavior, because groups predate individuals. Would a rational male choose to wear a suit and tie? Like spike heels for women, ties are uncomfortable, yet some men continue to buy them and put them on in the morning. Only the long-standing, group practice of wearing a tie can explain such apparently irrational behavior.

Most of us, most of the time, will share much of our identity and desires with members of our family, neighborhood, apartment complex, village, town, or country, and we will often confront collective concerns or decisions as members of these groups. We consist of those relationships in the sense that our thoughts, feelings, and actions take place in terms of them. Nothing we do is—or could be—separate from them. Just try going out to the woods sometime and not thinking about other people, or buying clothing without thinking about how other people might respond. Each of us exists in a web of relationships. Instead of focusing on the individual, political economy focuses on the relationships that comprise and sustain the individual, and the role that collective behavior plays in motivating economic behaviors and outcomes.

The final reason why political economists choose groups as the basic unit of analysis stems from an understanding of unequal power in our society. Political economists believe that disparate power relations are based on differences in access to the political and cultural resources and institutions of our society, and gaining control of economic and other resources requires more than individual action—it requires the concerted action of many people with shared interests. Only groups can effectively gain and maintain power.

Conflicting Interests: Winners and Losers

Political economists argue that society combines different groups with conflicting interests. These are not conflicting interests in the simple sense that if you can talk your mechanic into charging you $20 less on repairs, then the mechanic loses the $20 you gain. Following our discussion so far, you should guess that these conflicting interests in political economy instead exist between groups.

> *Conflicting interests: Group goals that, if met, mean one group gains at the expense of another*

The significance of conflicting interests stems from political economy's analysis of groups and emphasis on group dynamics. Serious conflicts often result from one group having power over another group.

Conflict in political economy may take many forms, and political economists sometimes disagree over what constitutes real (as opposed to perceived) conflicts. One conflict that all political economists see as important, however, is one based on people's relationship to production. Those who own the means of production, such as land, rights to natural resources, plant, and equipment (called capitalists), have distinct goals and interests in terms of how these forces are used, compared with those who only own their own labor power (called workers) and must obtain a job from those who own the resources. Workers want the highest wages they can get, while capitalists want to pay the lowest wages possible. Capitalists want workers to be as productive as possible, while workers may perceive few, if any, rewards for doing so.

You might believe that competitive markets will wash away the effects of conflicting interests, but this will only be true in some cases. As economist John Roemer argues, if one group has more money at the beginning of an economic game, then that group is likely to end up much richer at the end, even if the "game" is perfectly fair or competitive.

Going further, conflicting interests often destabilize markets. An obvious example is when workers go out on strike. Another case is when a firm moves a plant from a high-wage to a low-wage country, but then finds that the unemployed workers in the rich country can no longer afford the company's products. Economic activities become games in which we cannot know the outcome beforehand because we cannot know which strategies will be employed. Indeed, making sure that others do not know your strategy before a game starts often is a key to winning. Political economy views such conflicts as being inherent in most economic systems.

There are many other important conflicts: among different types of capitalists, such as financial vs. industrial, goods-producing vs. service-producing industries, and small vs. large; and between different types of workers, such as high-skill vs. low-skill and male vs. female. Furthermore, there are important conflicts that exist between capitalists and those outside the production process, such as conflicts over the environment. Finally, there are conflicts that exist both inside and outside production, such as between men and women, whites and blacks, gays and lesbians and straight people, and between Jews, Moslems, and Christians.

In this book, we have chosen to highlight the conflict between workers and capitalists (what is often described as class conflict), between whites and blacks, and between men and women. We believe that these three conflicts help to explain both wage levels and inequality in a way that other conflicts do not. And while we see these conflicts as being somewhat separate, they are very much shaped by the same context—the historical development of an economic system in which a relatively few, propertied white men have wielded the lion's share of control over productive resources and people.

Change: It Wasn't Always This Way

The final unifying component of political economy is the importance of change. Political economists emphasize that collective behavior in a conflict-ridden context can only result in struggles and, with it, change. In other words, the nature of unequal power generates conflict, which, in turn, leads to change. All varieties of political economists view society as a dynamic entity. Change is the one thing on which there is always certainty, although the direction and the outcome of that change is never certain.

Change: Instability created by conflicting interests

For political economists, inequality is built into the economic system. It is an inevitable byproduct when a relatively small number of capitalists own most of the productive resources of society. In addition, as we argue later in this chapter, such inequality is systematically linked to race and gender as well as to class. This inequality is based on group membership rather than individual efforts and, as a result, creates group conflicts over the rules that govern distribution of resources and power. In turn, these conflicts create the impetus for economic and political change.

Consider something as simple as income taxes. The old saying is that "the only certain things in life are death and taxes." In the political economy view, however, it also is certain that income tax rates will change in your lifetime. The rich will seek limits on income tax rates, and middle-income workers may wish to see overall income taxes reduced. On the other hand, those who use public schools, or see value in antipoverty programs, national defense, parks, roads, and so on, will want the government to collect enough taxes to pay for these things. These groups will constantly strive to improve their position and, as they discover new tactics, put together different coalitions. As related events unfold, they will be in stronger or weaker positions to change income taxes. The result is guaranteed change, because these conflicts will not go away.

The Four C's of political economy provide general guidelines for understanding an economy or society and for distinguishing political economy from neoclassical economics. However, for political economists, further context is required before examining concrete issues such as wages and discrimination. That context is provided by looking at three key social relations—class, race, and gender—that political economists view as central to understanding our economy.

CLASS, RACE, AND GENDER

Historically, working people with little or no wealth, people of color, and women have been oppressed groups in the United States. Their position at the bottom of the totem pole is nothing new. Men have dominated women, whites have dominated blacks, and the rich have dominated everyone else ever since Europeans first landed on these shores.

Class, race, and gender are social categories. This does not mean there cannot be other interpretations, nor does it mean all people are biologically identical. It does mean, however, that differences by class, race, and gender take their meaning primarily from society rather than biology. Therefore, what matters are the ways in which societies treat biological differences, and the various ways that race or gender are made into social categories.

Some people believe that race combines both social and biological components, however; it is worth considering that other societies do not define "black" and "white" as we do. In Brazil, for example, a person with any amount of white ancestry is considered to be white (or at least not black), while in the United States, a person with any amount of black ancestry is considered to be black. Human beings are rarely purely black or purely white; most of us are something in between, as the U.S. Census Bureau discovered when they allowed people to identify themselves as having multiple racial or ethnic identities. Thus, people cannot be neatly divided along racial lines on a strictly biological basis. There must be a social determination on the issue, and how this determination is made and affects the groups in question is what interests us here.

Class, race, and gender are groups into which an individual fits at birth. They are what economist Nancy Folbre labels as "given." You are born into a given group but can join a "voluntary" group (e.g., Habitat for Humanity or a bowling league). The significance of these groups may shift over time as a result of political, ideological, technical, or economic developments. Further, unlike race or gender, class is not completely "given" at birth and can be changed by occupational mobility or marriage. Nonetheless, each of these categories will have a great deal to do with the resources (social as well as financial) that are available to us as individuals, the reactions that we will face from other individuals, and our self-image. This is true for all of us, white as well as black, male as well as female.

Groups exist in relation to other groups. This is intrinsic to the very idea of the "group." White implies black, male implies female, and wealthy implies poor. To analyze group behavior means to analyze a group's relation to its counterpart group. The phrase "social relation" expresses this inherent connection between counterpart groups. By implication, we can also explore the group's relationship to non-counterpart groups. For example, we might be interested in the economic circumstances of women. To construct an explanation, we would begin by pointing out what is unique about women's circumstances by comparing them with the circumstances of men (i.e., the counterpart group). Then, we could complicate the picture by bringing in the other relationships that intersect gender, such as class and race (i.e., non-counterpart groups), by showing how women's circumstances are influenced by their distribution between class and race groups. We will explore these connections further after examining class, race, and gender in relative isolation.

Counterpart groups: Where the definition of one category implies, and is implied by, another

Class, race, and gender relations in the modern United States are marked by different types or forms of oppression. To see why, we might start by arguing that capitalists exert their power over workers to receive money or profits, but this cannot explain a holy war between nations, where one group wishes to eliminate another (not much profit there). In addition, neither profits nor hatred can explain why a man might wish to keep "his" wife at home and provide for her financially. Nonetheless, the wife in this case may be oppressed, controlled by her husband, and limited in her opportunities.

To conceptualize these diverse relations, we use the term "forms of oppression." The basic idea is that oppression can be for purposes of one group making money from another (exploitation), achieving submissive behavior from another (domination), or limiting the location or opportunities of another group (exclusion). We define these terms more carefully later.

The relationship between counterpart groups also occurs in a particular context. In other words, relations of class, race, and gender are associated with practices and behaviors that occur at a particular site or location.[1] A site gives us a very general notion of which aspects of context are most important for interpreting social relations. The idea of sites allows us to analyze counterpart groups by first examining their individual sites, and then looking at the impact of one site on others. For example, the community is the primary site of race relations in the United States largely because of geographic segregation. We can also look at the connections between sites and, particularly, how practices are carted between sites. The transportation of practices is one way in which oppression can be maintained, but it can also provide a method for creating social change.

Sites: The primary physical locations where social relations are played out

Class: The Rich Get Richer . . .

Karl Marx and Frederick Engels wrote about classes in capitalist societies.[2] For them, class was the most important social and economic category of analysis. A class is a group of people who have the same relationship to the "means of production" and the generation of surplus. The means of production are what people need to produce goods and services—machinery, communications equipment, buildings, and the know-how to successfully market a product as well as finance and manage the firm. Surplus is the amount of product left over after enough is set aside to assure reproduction of the people and equipment that produced the product.

Surplus: Output above that needed to replace the capital and labor used in the production process

In capitalism, there are two primary classes: the capitalist class, and the working class. The capitalist class is defined as the group that owns the means of production and, by virtue of that ownership, holds property rights to the surplus, which in capitalism means profits. The working class is the group with nothing to bring to market except its capacity to work—it produces the entire product but receives only a portion of it as wages. This is not to say that capitalists do not play an important function in the production process, or that they do not necessarily work. Capitalists typically make investment decisions. Some work in managing the day-to-day operations of work; others do the work of hiring managers. The point is that capitalists have control over productive resources while the workers do not (except their own ability to do work).

In this view, creation and struggle over the surplus is at the heart of the economy. In turn, conflict over surplus sets into motion a process of constant struggle and change. While some political economists argue that classes are not so neatly defined, they nonetheless still assign an important role to the decision-making power that capitalists, as a group, have over workers and other groups in society.[3]

Surplus isn't all bad. If a society produces more than is needed to replace worn out machinery and keep workers fed, clothed, and housed, that sounds like a pretty good society. We could take the remaining surplus and use it to put a woman on Mars, build pyramids, or commission great works of art. However, if one economic class controls the surplus, then inequality and oppression are bound to follow. That class may be a group of slaveowners, government officials in a dictatorship, or a group that decides whether workers can have a job (capitalists). In any of these cases, those who produce the surplus do not get to keep it, so they have no long-term incentive to keep producing it.

Class: Relationships defined by control vs. production of surplus

Another slant on this relation is found by arguing that capitalists exploit workers. While we look more closely at this issue in the following chapter, the basic logic is simple. Capitalists have all the options that workers have—to purchase any consumer goods on the market, to seek employment anywhere and, in democratic societies, to vote. However, capitalists also have more options than workers—the ability to hire and fire people, the ability to survive without employment by others, and the money to contribute to political campaigns. These extended options provide capitalists with the power to strike an unequal bargain with workers. Capitalists benefit quite a bit by receiving and controlling the surplus that workers produce.

An important site where exploitation occurs is inside the firm. Class relations influence communities and families, but the act of creating surplus as well as struggle over that surplus mainly occur in the arena that connects employers to employees (i.e., the firm). Class aspects of community development (e.g., capital flight) are unlikely to make sense unless we first understand what is going on inside of firms.

Exploitation: Control by one group of another's work for monetary or material gain

To pin these ideas down, let's ask where you fit. Do you (or your parents) receive enough income from owning stocks or bonds so that you will never have to work for someone else? Do you work for someone else who has the money to hire you? If you're like most people, you are in the working class and not a capitalist.[4] Assuming that you're a member of the working class, will you be exploited? That is, when you get a job, is the owner of the firm likely to make money off your work? And, finally, where will this exploitation take place? Like a growing number of people, you may find yourself working with a computer and a wireless connection from home, but for most people, you are likely to go to work inside a firm.

Race: Exclusion and Solidarity

While race and ethnicity often are thought of as relating to biological differences in skin color or the shape of facial features, it is the transformation of these features into race or social relations that is important here. The United States was colonized by Europeans in the 16th and 17th centuries. Since that time, racial differences have been used to justify the appropriation of land, labor, and wealth from a wide range of racial and ethnic groups. In extreme cases, it has even justified genocide.

Race: Social relations that are associated with cultural or ethnic divergence

When people of color go to work in a firm, they are as likely to be exploited as any white worker, and possibly even more so.[5] As workers, they are members of the group of all workers, so they share common interests with other workers, such as in higher wages and obtaining control over the surplus. These interests are not identical, however, because white Americans have systematically sought to exclude people of color.

Gary Becker's notion of a "taste for discrimination" captures an element of exclusion: whites may seek to avoid contact with blacks. In the political economy view, however, acts of exclusion generally have a broader basis in collective behavior and context. Regarding context, political economists believe that the shadow of slavery can indeed stretch into the present (Darity and Meyers, 1994). Regarding collective behavior, whites may perceive it as normal to exclude blacks since "everyone does it."

Exclusion: Physical or social isolation of a group to diminish their roles and opportunities

The process of exclusion has led most directly to residential and geographical segregation. As a result, community or regional location is key to understanding the establishment of race relations in the present-day United States. Stated differently, communities are an important site where race relations are played out because of segregation: whites and blacks overwhelmingly live in separate communities, primarily resulting from the refusal of whites to accept integration, but also because Supreme Court decisions in the last two decades have weakened school desegregation efforts. For example, political economist Gary Orfield (2009) found that the average black student was in a public school that was 35.2% white in 1988-1989, but that figure fell to 29.4% by the 2006-2007 school year. By dividing communities along color lines, whites have been able to restrict use of their tax dollars to their own communities, particularly with respect to schooling and other public services. Segregation establishes residential and voting patterns that divide the tax base and electoral districts, which in turn allows whites to concentrate resources in their own communities.

Given segregation and unequal resources, conflict is certain to follow. These conflicts, both between and within communities, often concern the distribution of public resources: white communities have the good schools, white communities are near the areas of greatest job growth, white communities provide social networks that inform the residents about job openings, white communities have the votes to influence local and state politicians, white communities have basic public services. Black and Latino communities in general have few or none of these amenities, nor are they likely to get them in an era of budget cuts and urban fiscal crises.

We do not minimize the importance of race within the site of the firm or family (discussed later). Nonetheless, in the political economy view, we cannot hope to understand racial differences in jobs or incomes without considering the impact of geographical segregation.

The flip side of exclusion and segregation is group identity and solidarity. This too distinguishes race relations from class relations (discussed earlier) or gender relations (discussed later). Managers at work and men at home may make it difficult for workers to gather as workers or women to gather as women, respectively. This is not as big a problem for minorities in the United States, who are constantly bombarded with the message that they should stay with "their own kind." For all its ill effects, exclusion also facilitates group culture, whether it is the passing of Native American languages and religious practices from generation to generation or the development of gospel music, blues, rhythm and blues, jazz, and rap or hip-hop music in the black community. Similarly, it is doubtful that the election of so many black officials in major U.S. cities would have occurred without geographical segregation.

Exclusion is not required for the development or maintenance of distinct ethnic cultures, nor should it be a prerequisite for minorities to exercise a political voice. A society that valued and celebrated the richness of experiences, ideas, and cultures that ethnic and racial diversity make possible would, however, look very different from what we see in the United States today.

In sum, race is a social relation that in the present-day United States, as in the past, is largely based on the processes of excluding minorities socially, politically, and physically. As a result, the site of the community is largely segregated in the United States.

Gender: "A Woman's Place"

Everyone knows that there are differences between men and women, but for political economists, the important aspect of gender is that men and women often do different things that are, at most, only loosely connected to biology. This view stems from the argument that what men as opposed to women do varies from generation to generation (i.e., change) and across societies (i.e., context). Most societies exhibit a sexual division of labor—women perform very different tasks than men—but the tasks vary according to the social context. What does this division look like in the United States?

Gender divisions appear in wages and occupations (see Chapter 2), but they are crucially linked to roles that are established inside the family. They have an important impact on firms and communities, but their roots lie in the sexual formation of identity and division of labor within the family (Bergmann, 1986). In other words, parallel to class and the firm and to race and the community, our understanding of gender relations will be enriched greatly when we examine the site of the family.

Gender: Socially created distinctions between men and women

Gender relations inside the nuclear family—with a wife, husband, and child or children—often do not look like exploitation or exclusion. Typically, neither women nor men marry just for the money, nor do women and men often live in segregated communities. Instead, we apply the term domination to relations of oppression between men and women. Domination in this case refers to the ability of men to assert their authority or to rule over the women in their lives.

Domination: Social roles or forms of coercion which assure that one group is submissive to another

Domination can take many forms. Practices such as foot-binding in East Asia, pornography, or wife-beating are obvious examples of domination. Domination also might appear as sexual harassment in the firm, where specifics might include men hitting on women, or expecting women to make coffee, take notes, be quiet at meetings, or just not giving much credence to women's suggestions. Domination also could be embodied in the wealthy husband discussed in Thorstein Veblen's 1899 classic *Theory of the Leisure Class*. The husband wishes his wife not take paid employment, perform household tasks, nor wear comfortable clothing—any or all of which would reflect poorly on the man's ability to make money and "properly" show off his wife to the rest of society. The shared aspect of all these cases is the control of women by men and submission by women to male authority—in short, domination.

Domination of women is different than both race and class, because women and men often are combined within families. When a woman lives with a man, she will have the same legal access to public and private resources. However, her access is dependent on her family connection. If she leaves her husband or he leaves her, she is likely to experience a drastic fall in her standard of living. Indeed, recent studies suggest that on average, the standard of living for a mother drops by 34% following a divorce, and is still below the pre-divorce level six years later (Page and Stevens, 2002). Within the family, it is typical for the woman to spend far more time than the man cleaning, cooking, and raising children. Thus, men have physical and financial leverage over women as well as access to free female labor in the household.

Until the last five decades, women's economic status in capitalist societies had been severely restricted. White married women were not expected to work and, in many cases, were barred from jobs. The types of jobs that any particular woman could hold were very limited and also delineated by race. Further, women's wages have always been lower than men's and usually not enough to support a single person, let alone a family. Since the 1960s, the position of women in the economy has changed dramatically, and women now have significantly more economic independence from men. However, some things still remain true: women are primarily responsible for providing caregiving in households, and women still make considerably less than men when they do work for wages.

Connecting Relations and Oppression

So far, we have seen how political economy expands our vision of the economy beyond the workplace and simple economic explanations for behavior. Capitalists exploit workers in the firm, whites exclude blacks from communities, and women are dominated by men in the home. However, the picture is seriously incomplete.

The idea of connecting class, race, and gender to the respective sites of the firm, community, and home fits white, male, middle-class stereotypes and experiences. Ask such a person about work, and he probably thinks about getting up in the morning, kissing his spouse and children goodbye, and going to the office. Ask him about women, and he is likely to think about his wife or mother in the home. Ask him about race relations, and he is likely to conjure up images of blacks in the inner city or the community (although not "his" community).

These stereotypes obscure the fact that the majority of each relevant counterpart group participates in activities at all three sites. Most adult men and women—and adult blacks and whites—work for wages, have some type of family life, and live in communities. These stereotypes also hide the possibility that men can exclude women, bosses dominate workers, and whites exploit blacks.

To think about the variety of processes that people engage in, consider the "Matrix of Oppression" in Figure 6.1. In it, we see how the three relationships of interest—class, race, and gender—intersect with the three forms of oppression discussed earlier—exploitation, exclusion, and domination.

First, consider exploitation. In the subsection on class, we discussed ways in which capitalists exploit workers. Now, we extend that to include the possibilities that men exploit women and that whites exploit blacks. The potential for men to exploit women in the home is obvious; if men work fewer hours and control decisions about what the household will consume or how leisure time will be used, then men exploit women at home. Men also may exploit women at

FIGURE 6.1
FORMS OF OPPRESSION: CLASS, RACE, AND GENDER

	Exploitation	Exclusion	Domination
Class	Low wages, job loss threats	Legacy preferences at elite colleges	Rewards for worker obedience, status perks for managers
Race	Low minority wages, lack of employment	Housing segregation	Minorities limited to service jobs
Gender	Unpaid housework, women's low wages	Marriage bars, occupational segregation	Male control over household decisions

work if women receive lower wages for the same work as men and thus subsidize men's wages or contribute to profits (we call these "job competition" effects in Chapter 8). Similarly, whites may exploit people of color at work. In the community, whites might use their control over resources to ensure that amenities located in the city but often used by whites from the suburbs (e.g., museums, ball parks, convention centers) are maintained while public expenditures are diminished for the public schools and roads used by predominantly minority city residents.

Second, consider exclusion. While blacks are often excluded from white neighborhoods and white jobs, it also is true that many workers are likewise often excluded from the opportunities and activities of the wealthy. With few exceptions, most readers of this book can be confident that neither they nor their children will ever be admitted to elite prep schools such as Deerfield Academy or Exeter, to Ivy League schools such as Yale, Princeton, or Harvard, or to exclusive country clubs (although women were finally admitted to the prestigious Augusta National Golf Club in 2012). Women also are excluded from many activities, such as male occupations, many lucrative sports activities, and the presidency (although Hillary Clinton came close!).

Third, consider domination. Women may be dominated in the home or at work, but workers and people of color may, by virtue of group membership, also experience domination. If a worker does not voice her ideas for improving quality or reducing unnecessary paperwork, exploitation cannot provide an explanation (the firm makes less money than it could), but domination can. If she feels that her male colleagues don't take her seriously because she is a woman, she might not feel comfortable speaking up. Similarly, whites may often try to exclude blacks from society, and the occupations where black employment is relatively easy to find are those where the worker is subservient to the (typically white) customer—from shining shoes to serving meals to cleaning houses or buildings. While there may be elements of exploitation in such jobs, it also is clear that domination in the sense of submission enters the mix as well.

We have not introduced the sites of the firm, community, and home into the matrix of oppression. If we did, it would form a third axis (we do not show this in Figure 6.1, because it yields 27 cells in the matrix!). Domination, exclusion, and exploitation can occur at any of the three sites (i.e., the firm, home, or community), while relations of class, race, and gender also exist at all three sites. If you look back on the examples just used, you will see some of these interconnections.

While we omitted the notion of sites from the matrix of oppression, it is used extensively in the remaining discussion of political economy in this book. To see why, go back to the Four C's. Now, we can flesh these out a bit. Collective behavior concerns the actions of various counterpart groups—capitalists/workers, whites/blacks, and men/women. Forms of oppression, such as exploitation, exclusion, and domination, are the source of conflicting interests between these groups, and these forms of oppression and counterpart groups form part of the context for analyzing a society. Nonetheless, the simple matrix of oppression does not capture change. In fact, it looks static, as if men have always—and will always—dominate women. When we add the notions of practices occurring at sites, we admit that practices can change, whether because of conflicting interests or because practices can, and often are, transported from one site to another.

COMPETITION TO THE RESCUE—*NOT*

A neoclassical economist might respond to the material just presented by asking, "But what about the market?" If markets are competitive, why can't workers stop exploitation by threatening to switch employers or, better yet, by starting their own firms? Why can't women and people of color invest in their own education, get jobs and incomes equal to those of white males, and refuse to deal with men or whites unless domination and exclusion are halted?

The political economy answer is rooted in a different understanding of what competition means. Drawing from the work of Joseph Schumpeter, political economists view competition as a battle or a contest with winners and losers.[6] Suppose that you are selling a used car. You look in the newspaper to get some idea of the advertised price of similar cars. In the neoclassical view, the story ends with you selling the car at the market price. With many such cars and buyers on the market, you are anonymous. In the political economy view, however, you are engaged in a contest to sell your car. Whoever does buy from you (i.e., the winner) doesn't buy from someone else (i.e., the loser). Furthermore, you are unlikely to charge exactly the "market price." You might set your price a few dollars lower than others, hoping for a quick sale, or set your price higher, hoping to locate a hapless fool who will pay your price.

Competition in political economy: A dog-eat-dog process with winners and losers

What does this have to do with exploitation, exclusion, and domination? Regarding exploitation by capitalists, capitalists have resources (i.e., money), which give them an advantage in the labor market. Another advantage for capitalists in the labor market game is that there are relatively few capitalists but many workers. In most games, having more members on your team would be better, but in the labor market, the opposite holds true. Regarding exclusion and domination, it means bringing less power to market relationships, especially when there is competition. For example, one study found that new-car salespeople offer lower final prices to white men than to women or blacks (Ayres and Siegelman, 1995).

Does competition mean that you could become a successful capitalist and escape exploitation? Let's see. In 1980, the most profitable 20 corporations in the Fortune 500 earned $35.5 billion in profits out of $201.4 billion for all corporations. By 2012, the group of 20 with the highest profits received $238.8 billion, with all corporations generating $1,827.0 billion (in 2011). So getting into that group might be a good thing for you. In 2010, there were around 154 million Americans in the labor force, and nearly 6 million corporations in the United States. So there is approximately one corporation for every 20 workers. We'll make it easy and assume you can incorporate. What are your odds of ending up in the top 20? How about 1 in 300,000? And, yes, that is close to the odds of being struck by lightning (1 in 400,000).[7]

If dog-eat-dog competition favors those with money, it follows that not only capitalists, but whites and males (who typically have more money than their counterparts), are favored as well. This gives us some idea of why exclusion and domination are not eroded by markets, but a more complete explanation requires an additional distinction.

In addition to market competition, there also is firm-generated competition (Box 6.2). Market competition occurs when players, such as corporations, are forced into attempts to weaken or eliminate their market opponents. Someone is going to lose, and so each side strives to win. Firms that do not attempt to play the game of market competition, or who are not terribly successful, go bankrupt. Firm-generated competition occurs when a corporation (instead of the market) creates a game played by those who can help the firm financially (for example, employees, subcontractors, local governments, consumers, etc.). Here, one group of, say, employees wins while everyone else loses, one local government "wins" a plant while others lose, or one subcontractor receives work while others do not. Firm-generated competition is central to the idea of "divide-and-conquer," wherein capitalists divide workers along racial, ethnic, or gender lines and play each side off against the other. (We explore the concept of divide-and-conquer tactics further in the next chapter.)

BOX 6.2
MARKET COMPETITION AND FIRM-GENERATED COMPETITION

You see examples of competition every day. The Coca-Cola Corporation, PepsiCo and Cadbury Schweppes continue to advertise at a breakneck pace, even though they control around 89% of the U.S. market for nonalcoholic beverages, selling over $68 billion worth of drinks in 2005, with over $13 billion of that coming from sales of bottled water. Their continued advertising suggests they are very concerned that someone is going to take away their market share (i.e., market competition). At the same time, soft-drink and beer manufacturers often generate competition by allowing consumers to enter contests with winners going to Disney World or the Super Bowl. Of course, the latter type of competition seems pretty innocuous to most of us, but the firms would not generate this competition unless they thought that money could be made in the process.

Market competition can be brutal. When Folgers wanted to enter the market for coffee in Syracuse, New York, during 1974, it came in with guns blazing for Maxwell House, which controlled 33% of the market. The two battled with coupons, which ultimately reduced the price of coffee in Syracuse by almost 50%. After the smoke cleared and prices returned to normal, Folgers had gained 25% of the market, but Maxwell House still controlled 33% of the market. The losers? Small coffee producers like deLima, who saw their market share drop from 15% to 7% in the process.

The logic of firm-generated competition (i.e., divide-and-conquer) is close to a concept called the "prisoner's dilemma." In this scenario, the police capture two thieves, separate them (i.e., divide), and encourage them to confess. There are three outcomes: neither confesses, only one confesses, or both confess. If they both keep silent, they will get a light sentence (the best overall outcome for the thieves). If they both confess, they each get a harsher sentence (the worst outcome overall). If only one confesses, he will walk away, while his partner will receive a very long prison term. The usual outcome is that, fearing that the other will betray them, they both confess. Acting in what they perceive to be their self-interest, they end up with the worst outcome. They would both have served a lot less time in jail if they had cooperated.

In the real world, a manager can do much the same thing to get more work out of workers than they otherwise would provide—and for less money. The classic case is one where management enforces a strict policy that employees cannot discuss salary with each other. When it comes time for raises, each employee is told that she or he is receiving an above-average raise because of her or his exemplary performance. Only one problem here: everyone can't be above average (but everyone can work hard).

Sources: Beverage industry figures from Standard and Poor's *Industry Surveys: Foods & Nonalcoholic Beverages*, New York: Standard and Poors, 2006. Other material from Samuel Bowles and Richard Edwards, *Understanding Capitalism*, 2nd ed. New York: Harper-Collins, 1993.

In the political economy view, competition might tend to level the playing field in certain arenas, but this is not a general tendency. Where there are winners and losers, competition can turn slight differences in power and resources into larger ones. If men dominate women at home, they may be able to translate this into wage advantages in the firm, and competition may help them to do so. If whites can exclude blacks from their communities, this may give whites an "edge" in the labor market, which competition may reward heavily. If capitalists can draw more and more workers into labor markets, competition between workers helps the firm to become larger, more powerful, and better able to exploit workers. In other words, competition is unlikely to rescue groups from the oppression of exploitation, exclusion, or domination.

CHALLENGING OPPRESSION: IT AIN'T OVER TILL IT'S OVER

If people with power are a product of the context surrounding them and act collectively to maintain and extend that power, then where is the room for change? Are whites, males, and capitalists doomed from birth to oppress blacks, women, and workers? By the same token, are women, minorities, and workers bound to be oppressed? Will the "matrix of oppression" exist forever? Political economists respond with a resounding "no," because change is inevitable in an economy with inherent conflicts of interest.

The primary reason why change that reduces oppression occurs is that oppressed groups have no interest in maintaining their subordinate status. Over the centuries, workers have struggled to contain and control capitalists by joining labor unions, forming labor and socialist parties, and pressing for minimum wage, maximum hours, and occupational health and safety laws. Women have fought for equal access to voting, property, education, and jobs. Black Americans fought for freedom from slavery and equal access to public accommodations, jobs, and housing. For each of these groups, oppression has not been eliminated. The war has not been won, but this does not mean that battles are always lost—or that the battles are not worth fighting.

Related to the fact that oppressed groups have an interest in change is that market economies generate constant turbulence. People are moved in and out of jobs, new products are always under development, new technologies are being tried, and so forth. With such dramatic disturbances in the economy, opportunities are regularly opening and closing. For example, black and white women now work in much more similar jobs than was the case several decades ago, so there now are greater opportunities for these groups to organize under the same union or feminist organizational umbrella.

Marx provided another reason why people would ultimately abandon oppressive social relations: they are alienating.[8] Marx used the concept of alienation to express capitalism's separation of people from the results of their work (which are owned by the capitalist) and from control over their work. Marx also wrote about how capitalism reduced social relationships to money and things, and how this reduction inhibited people from fully developing their human potentialities. More generally, political economists view alienation as a sense of irrelevance and fragmentation caused by compartmentalizing one's life into "work" and "everything else." In this view, we are all victims of oppression, regardless of whether we are rich or poor, black or white, male or female, because relations of trust, love, loyalty, and friendship are undermined by the overwhelming importance that is placed on money by capitalism. Why else would people have to sign "prenuptial agreements" that guarantee a certain split of the money following a divorce from a marriage that is yet to occur? Why else would students fight—and even kill—fellow students over expensive basketball shoes or jackets?

Alienation: A sense of meaninglessness and the fragmentation of life

In Marx's view, such alienation can be eliminated only by abandoning oppressive relations. In other words, when men meet women and blacks meet whites as equals, we will each have greater opportunities for meaningful relationships. This view also provides a strong defense of democracy. Democracy is not simply our right as citizens; it also is necessary for our development as human beings. Democracy matters not just as a set of formal procedures, such as the right to vote, but also with respect to our ability to control the circumstances of our lives. Worker-controlled firms, for example, are seen as a positive alternative (with respect to both equity and efficiency) to the authoritarian organization of traditional, capitalist-controlled firms. Community-based organizations that strive to accommodate the needs of those who live in the community through representative and just mechanisms are an important part of the fabric of an enriched life. Similarly, valuing the work of families (rather than admiring family values) by recognizing and socializing the costs of child-rearing enhances our lives and enables all of us to be more effective participants in our families, communities, and workplaces.

The idea of alienation means that groups have more than just dollars driving them to act collectively to end oppressive relations. It expands our understanding of why people fight oppression—whether through the union movement, the feminist movement, or the civil rights movement. As highlighted in this chapter, oppression is not only about exploitation for profit, and groups that strive to end oppression often are concerned with more than monetary aspects of oppression.

Liberatory knowledge: Information that helps both the oppressed and oppressors understand the benefits of eliminating inequality

Also connected to the idea of alienation is the concept of liberatory knowledge, which is further linked to the notion of "institutional discrimination" that is discussed in Chapter 8.[9] Liberatory knowledge focuses on facts and social connections that explain the benefits of eliminating oppression. The notion of alienation may help to form the basis for liberatory knowledge, but there are other types of liberatory knowledge and other reasons to end oppression as well. For example, if a young girl is taught that she can perform mathematics as well as boys, or someday become the president or the pope, this would be a form of liberatory knowledge. Relatedly, many whites do not consider themselves to be discriminatory and will, if some discriminatory action is pointed out, be perfectly happy to change their behavior, as was perhaps shown most forcefully in the reelection of Barack Obama.

Finally, for a dose of reality, political economists recognize that oppression has existed for a long time and will not disappear overnight. In the political economy view, as opposed to that of neoclassical economics, capitalists, men, and whites have a powerful economic interest in maintaining inequality. It will take more than gentle philosophy and the presentation of a few facts to change that.

SUMMING UP

We began this chapter with the Four C's of political economy. Context reminds us that the past and the society in which we live are important for understanding both the present and the future. Collective behavior reminds us that although we may "feel" like isolated individuals, we are not only individuals; we are parts of larger groups that act and influence people's thoughts and actions. Conflicting interests stem from unequal power relations between groups and, in turn, drive change.

With the Four C's in hand, we turned to three sets of counterpart groups: capitalists and workers, whites and blacks, and men and women. We began by examining these in isolation, arguing that capitalists exploit workers in the firm, whites exclude blacks in communities, and men dominate women in the home. A richer approach permits all three forms of oppression to occur at all three sites and affect all three sets of counterpart groups. Then, men can exploit women at home or in the factory, whites can dominate blacks inside the firm or in the community, and capitalists can exclude workers in the community or the firm.

Counterpart groups—according to class, race, and gender—are those who act collectively, and the forms of oppression—exploitation, exclusion, and domination—are the primary reason for conflicting interests between groups. The particular groups that we examine, and the particular forms of oppression today, act as a backdrop or context for what follows.

Finally, we examined change. Looking at competitive markets, we asked whether these might break down forms of oppression. The answer generally is "no," but competition in markets of the political economy type—with winners and losers—does tend to cause dramatic changes in the economy. We finished by asking whether oppression will last forever and again answered "no," partly because of conflicting interests, partly because market economies are constantly changing, and partly because oppression is in many ways bad for everyone (but worse for some).

DISCUSSION QUESTIONS

1. Recall the last item that you purchased. Did context play any role in your decision? Do you think that other people in your class, race, or gender groups are more likely than those in other groups to buy the item?

2. Suppose that the audience for the "Rush Limbaugh Show" was mainly white and male. Would this imply that these white males are acting collectively?

3. Do you see conflicting interests in terms of class, race, or gender on your college campus? If so, what particular "battles" have occurred? Have these led to changes on campus?

4. Do you plan to or already have children? In making a decision, did you consider solely economic factors, or were you also influenced by others, such as family or friends?

5. Have you ever been exploited in the sense of producing more than you were paid? If so, was this in the firm, community, or home? Why was the other party able to get away with exploitation?

6. Could one person both dominate and exclude another at the same time? Try to find an example where this would be true.

7. Given their understanding of market competition and oppression, how do you think a political economist would respond to a government program such as WIC (Women, Infants, and Children) that improves average nutrition by providing free milk, bread, and other necessities to poor children?

8. If you were a white male, would you have any interest in seeing women and minorities receive job opportunities equal to your own? What if this meant that you would not get a good job or a promotion?

9. Are managers part of the working class? Why, or why not?

SUGGESTED READINGS

Amott, Teresa L. and Julie A. Matthaei. 1996. *Race, Gender and Work*. Boston: South End Press.

Ayres, Ian and Peter Siegelman. 1995. "Race and Gender Discrimination in Bargaining for a New Car." *American Economic Review*, 85(3).

Bergmann, Barbara. 1986. *The Economic Emergence of Women*. New York: Basic Books.

Bowles, Samuel and Herbert Gintis. 1986. *Democracy and Capitalism*. New York: Basic Books.

Bowring, Joseph. 1986. *Competition in a Dual Economy*. Princeton, NJ: Princeton University Press.

Darity, William A., Jr. and Samuel L. Myers, Jr. 1994. *The Black Underclass*. New York: Garland.

Folbre, Nancy. 1982. "Exploitation Comes Home: A Critique of the Marxian Theory of Family Labour." *Cambridge Journal of Economics* 6, December.

Folbre, Nancy. 1994. *Who Pays for the Kids?* New York: Routledge.

Hartmann, Heidi I. 1979. "The Unhappy Marriage of Marxism and Feminism: Towards a More Progressive Union." *Capital and Class* 8, Summer.

Humphries, Jane. 1991. "The Sexual Division of Labor and Social Control: An Interpretation." *Review of Radical Political Economics* 23, Fall & Winter.

Keynes, John Maynard. 1936. *The General Theory of Employment, Interest and Money.* New York: Harcourt, Brace.

Lorber, Judith. 1994. *Paradoxes of Gender.* New Haven, CT: Yale University.

Marx, Karl. 1967. *Capital, Vol. 1.* New York: International Publishers Co.

McLellan, David. 1973. *Karl Marx, His Life and Thought.* New York: Harper Colophon Books.

Myrdal, Gunnar. 1944. *An American Dilemma: The Negro Problem and Modern Democracy.* New York: Harper & Brothers.

Orfield, Gary. 2009. "Reviving the Goal of an Integrated Society: A 21st Century Challenge." Los Angeles CA: Civil Rights Project/Proyecto Derechos Civiles at UCLA. www. civilrightsproject.ucla.edu

Page, Marianne and Ann Huff Stevens. 2002. "Will You Miss Me When I Am Gone? The Economic Consequences of Absent Parents." Working paper #8786, Cambridge MA: National Bureau of Economic Research.

Rifkin, Jeremy. 2004. *The European Dream: How Europe's Vision of the Future is Quietly Eclipsing the American Dream.* New York: Penguin.

Robinson, Joan. 1962. *Economic Philosophy: An Essay on the Progress of Economic Thought.* New York: Doubleday.

Roemer, John. 2001. *Political Competition: Theory and Applications.* Cambridge, MA: Harvard University Press.

Smith, Adam. 1976 (originally 1776). *An Inquiry into the Nature and Causes of the Wealth of Nations.* Oxford: Clarendon Press.

Stone, Pamela. 2007. *Opting Out? Why Women Really Quit Careers and Head Home.* Berkeley: University of California Press.

Tong, Rosemarie. 1989. *Feminist Thought: A Comprehensive Introduction.* Boulder, CO: Westview Press.

Tucker, Robert C., ed. 1978. *The Marx- Engels Reader.* 2nd ed. New York: W.W. Norton & Co.

Veblen, Thorstein. 1973 (originally 1899). *The Theory of the Leisure Class.* Boston: Houghton Mifflin Co.

Wright, Erik Olin. 1994. *Interrogating Inequality: Essays on Class Analysis, Socialism, and Marxism.* New York: Verso.

APPENDIX: The Roots of Political Economy

Political economy combines several different traditions within economics and politics. Although many traditions in political economy differ in important respects, they are united in their belief that supply and demand are inadequate tools with which to understand economic dynamics and outcomes. Instead, they focus on forces such as conflict, power, and culture.

Political economy has its roots in four very different schools of thought. These four "legs" of political economy include the works of Marx, institutionalism, Keynesianism, and the protest movements of the 1950s to 1970s, which included the civil rights, anti-Vietnam War, and feminist movements. We focus on these four, because they embodied theories of economic activity and advocated change as well.

The Point of Departure

Neoclassical economists justifiably claim Adam Smith as their founder, because he was the first to articulate the principles of a self-regulating market economy. However, Smith also is considered to be the founder of political economy, because he did not limit his discussion of economics to supply and demand. In *The Wealth of Nations*, Smith raises three themes that lie at the core of political economy today: class conflict, wealth production, and human needs.

Smith's great intellectual breakthrough was his belief that labor, as opposed to agriculture or trade, was the source of national wealth. This belief allowed Smith to envision the process of economic growth in general without reducing it to any particular sector.

From Smith's notion of the wealth of nations, it follows that profits represent a deduction from the value that is produced by labor. The profit that capitalists receive is a surplus, an amount of products and services generated above and beyond the wages that are received by workers. This surplus theory of profits was later discarded by neoclassical economics in favor of the argument that profits are a return to the productivity of the capitalist. The dispute about the origin of profits continues today. Unfortunately, it cannot be resolved empirically, because there is no agreement on how to define or measure the productivity of capitalists.

Smith argued that the division of income between wages and profits was governed by a struggle in which the interests of owners and workers were diametrically opposed. "The workmen desire to get as much, the masters to give as little as possible. The former are disposed to combine in order to raise, the latter in order to lower the wages of labour."[10] Of course, other factors, such as the growth rate of the economy and the population, also influenced wages, but it was Smith's doctrine of class struggle between workers and owners that proved to be especially influential for political economists. His attention to the impact of worker and owner organizations introduced political and ideological elements into his economic analysis. It presented a picture of the economic system that was grounded in conflict rather than harmony, and it contributed to the more radical theories of Karl Marx.

Marx: Class Systems

Marx wrote during the mid-19th century, when England was experiencing the Industrial Revolution. He saw that small manufacturers were being swallowed up and displaced by large corporations. Technological change had become very rapid and, in conjunction with the expulsion of peasants from their land (called the "enclosure" movement), was contributing to widespread unemployment. Child labor, poverty, and industrial exploitation existed side-by-side with great wealth. Financial capital had become intertwined with industrial capital, making the economy more prone to speculative booms and busts. Therefore, Marx was much more critical of capitalism than Smith was; Marx believed it should be overthrown and replaced with socialism. He explained all of these developments in terms of domination by the capitalist class and subordination of all other aspects of society to its needs. Today, political economy follows in his footsteps with its focus on class relations and the domination of society by the wealthy, the transformation of competitive capitalism into monopoly capitalism, the destabilizing impact of technology, and the tendency of the economy to generate recurring unemployment.

Marx's other major contribution to political economy came from his philosophical training. As a young student, Marx studied philosophy in Germany. The first major contribution to political economy is Marx's method, referred to as historical or dialectical materialism, which developed out of both his attraction to and repulsion from Hegel's theories about the role of ideas in transforming the world. The materialism part of dialectical materialism came from Marx's rejection of the emphasis of German philosophy on ideas as the agent of social change. Marx argued that social life springs from, but also is changed by, the way that humans purposefully transform nature—not by their ideas about the world. In short, Marx thought that all of history could be understood by examining the ways in which people perform economic activities such as work, management, or the selling and purchasing of goods and services. The dialectical portion of dialectical materialism is the integration of Hegel's philosophy of the nature of change—that conflicts and contractions clash, resulting in change. For Marx, the fundamental contradictions of a society in which ownership of the tools used in production is divorced from the people who perform that production result in constant struggles and conflicts, which in turn produce change. The outcome of this process is never predetermined; instead, it depends on the relative strengths and effectiveness of the strategies of the groups in conflict.

The analysis of capitalism comprises almost all of Marx's work. Despite common misperceptions, he rarely wrote about socialism or communism. He believed that capitalism drained people of their most creative energies, and that economic exploitation was unjustified, unfair, and inefficient. As part of his analysis of classes, Marx and his coauthor, Frederick Engels, argued that the conflict and inequality that are inherent in a class society lead to collective action on the part of classes—or class struggle. Their hope and political project was that the working class would triumph in its struggle to create a more equitable and humane society.

Modern political economy continues to draw from Marx its emphasis on the importance of economic classes and how these classes struggle and conflict in a capitalist society. Nonetheless, over a century of further work and attempts to create nonclass societies have revealed serious flaws with Marx's approach. As experience in the Soviet Union, the Eastern Bloc, and the People's Republic of China revealed during the 20th century, simply eliminating capitalist class distinctions is no guarantee that race and gender oppression will be eliminated, or that democracy will flourish. For these reasons as well as others, political economists strove to broaden their analysis in ways to which we now turn.

Including Institutions and Customs

In the late 19th and early 20th centuries, some political economists began looking at the roles of customs and socially constructed institutions in the economy. Inspired by late-19th-century anthropological accounts of the evolution of humans and of cultures, early institutionalists developed theories of economic activity that, like Marx's, were concerned with social relationships and human needs along with systematic inequality. This approach was based largely on an appreciation of the importance of culture in both explaining and changing social, political, and economic relations. Culture (e.g., a society's religious practices, treatment of children, rituals and celebrations, sexual division of labor, and consumption customs) provides norms for social (i.e., communicative) interaction. The person who most often is credited with establishing institutionalist thought is Thorstein Veblen, a U.S.-born, German-trained economist who taught in the political economy departments of several major U.S. universities in the late 1800s and early 1900s.

While neoclassical economists are most interested in the outcome of the exchange process (i.e., the price of the good as determined by the supply and demand), institutionalists like Veblen argued that the exchange process itself is of as much, if not more, interest in explaining economic phenomena. For example, where do people meet, and what important rules or customs are followed there (think about malls!)? What social and technical relations are necessary to produce the goods coming to market? What cultural and/or social relations exist in society that help to determine what kinds of goods people want to buy and how much they are willing to pay for them? Why do women perform most of the child-rearing work in society? In other words, institutional analysis is interested in the cultural, social, and political context in which economic activity occur.

Institutionalists analyze the status differentiation that is created by the cultural uses of economic behavior, such as Veblen's famous analysis of conspicuous consumption in *The Theory of the Leisure Class* (1973). Later, the institutionalist Gunnar Myrdal, who won the Nobel Prize, wrote a classic analysis of race relations entitled *An American Dilemma* (1944), which showed how discrimination was a vicious circle that resulted from and reinforced status distinctions between blacks and whites. Status distinctions also can explain the rigidity of wage patterns, job ladders, and other phenomena (see Chapter 7). Institutionalists have used concepts such as these to dismiss the neoclassical notion that each person's utility is independent of other people's utility. In their view, the interdependence that is expressed by culture and enshrined in institutional structure is most important for understanding economic behavior.

John Maynard Keynes

It was not until the 1930s, and particularly the publication of John Maynard Keynes' *The General Theory of Employment, Interest and Money* (1936), that "macroeconomics" emerged as a distinct field within economics. Keynes argued that the neoclassical interpretation of single markets being "added up," or aggregated, to explain the entire national economy was wrong. He believed that the market system as a whole was not self-regulating, and that it was possible for the economy to stagnate for long periods of time. Some economists, such as Paul Samuelson, argued that Keynes' theories were only modifications of the standard, equilibrium framework, which concluded that capitalism was efficient and equitable. However, others rejected this interpretation and pointed to Keynes' argument that profit is a return to the scarcity of capital that is available for investment, not a return to the productivity of capital.

An important component of Keynes' theory is the role of uncertainty in explaining economic decisions. Because no one knows the future, there is an inherent uncertainty to economic decision-making (especially investment) when an individual must predict future rates of return. Given this uncertainty, it is futile to try to understand economic systems in terms of adjustment to a stable equilibrium. Further, Keynes believed that the determination of national wealth had more to do with the behavior of groups than of individuals, and that individual and social interests rarely coincided. He showed that economic problems can become self-perpetuating and, in particular, that the market system may be unable to eliminate unemployment. So, while individual markets may work fine, there may be too many goods being produced such that individuals will not purchase them all and firms will lay off workers as a result, meaning that even fewer goods will be purchased and produced, and so forth. This process results in unused resources. Further, Keynes believed that once down, the economy would not be able to pick itself up again on its own. All of this suggested that capitalism cannot be efficient.

Joan Robinson, who worked with Keynes, described his impact when she stated that "Economics once more became Political Economy" (1962; 77). Keynes' contribution to political economy today is the concern that unfettered markets will be insufficient to create prosperity for all.

Expanding Rights: The Protest Movements in the 1950s to 1970s

The fourth major influence on the development of political economic thought is the integration of race and gender dynamics into economic models of conflict and change.

In the 1950s, the Civil Rights Movement called the nation's attention to the racial ordering of economic, social, and political institutions in this country. Jim Crow laws, which were established in the South after Reconstruction, sanctioned separate educational and public facilities. However, separate was anything but equal. Using the powerful arguments of democratic rights and opportunity, black men and women organized to confront white individuals and institutions that had legally and illegally excluded them from equal participation.

The economic implications of racial inequality always have been a focus of the civil rights and later black nationalist movements. The role of people of color since colonial times, allocation of physical and human capital, and access to publicly provided goods and services all have played crucial parts in the history of racial inequality in the United States.

Feminists also have focused on the importance of culture, politics, psychology, and the language of rights in understanding economic behavior. Their contribution has been to dissect the belief system that differentiates male and female, one which is largely situated in the home and not the firm per se, and to analyze the impact of patriarchy on the division of labor within the family and the firm. The concept of patriarchy—the system of male domination—sharply distinguishes this view from the neoclassical perspective that the sexual division of labor is efficient and gender differences in occupational attainment equitable. Feminist economists such as Heidi Hartmann (1979) argue that the free female labor that benefits men in the household has important implications for the relationship between men and women, both in the home and at work. As a result of this and other work, gender now is recognized to be as fundamental as race and class in the determination of economic outcomes (Folbre, 1982; Humphries, 1991).

The contributions of the civil rights and feminist movements to political economy emerged from the fact that these were political movements calling attention to problems of inequality and conflict by appealing to the importance of democratic participation in all realms of life. Because these movements highlighted the dynamic of power and conflict, many in them looked to political economy for help in explaining—and transforming—a system of racial and gender economic inequality. In doing so, political economy's vision was broadened to explain the inequality so clearly demarcated not just by class but by skin color, gender, and native language as well.

ENDNOTES

[1]The notion of sites and practices comes from Samuel Bowles and Herbert Gintis (1986).

[2]Marx's most famous work is Capital (1967), which was first published in 1867. Much of his work with Engels appears in Tucker (1978). Among many biographies, see David McLellan (1973).

[3]For a discussion of the various interpretations of economic classes, see Erik Olin Wright (1994).

[4]Of course, you may receive some money from ownership of stocks and bonds, as this is how many workers save for retirement. The key point is whether you have much choice about whether to seek employment.

[5] As the black scholar W.E.B. DuBois put it: "The Negro is exploited ... and that exploitation comes ... from the white capitalist and equally from the white proletariat." (From "Marxism and the Negro Problem," *The Crisis* 40(5), 1933: 104.

[6] Schumpeter was not a political economist, but his vision of competition is used by many political economists. See Schumpeter's *Capitalism, Socialism, and Democracy*, New York: Harper & Row, 1942.

[7] For Fortune 500 figures, see http://money.cnn.com, accessed July 18, 2013. For overall profits, see *The Economic Report of the President, 2013*, Table B-28. Washington, DC: Government Printing Office. Labor force figure from U.S. Bureau of Labor Statistics, "Labor Force Statistics from the Current Population Survey," accessed July 18, 2013. Number of corporations figure from U.S. Bureau of the Census, Statistics of U.S. Businesses, accessed July 18, 2013. Source for the odds of being struck by lighting is the National Oceanic and Atmospheric Administration: http://www.lightningsafety.noaa.gov/medical.htm, accessed July 18, 2013.

[8] See Rosemary Tong (1989) for a discussion of the various meanings of "alienation."

[9] See Amott and Matthaei (1996) for a more complete discussion of this idea.

[10] Quoted in Robert Heilbroner, ed., *The Essential Adam Smith*, New York: W.W. Norton, 1986; 195–196.

WORK AND WAGES IN THE POLITICAL ECONOMY APPROACH

INTRODUCTION: MORE THAN A PAYCHECK

The neoclassical analysis of labor markets outlined in Chapter 4 started with the fact that labor markets are different from other markets: people are hired in the labor market, and people often have different tastes and preferences. Additionally, those who hire labor do so because of the "derived demand" for labor services—people are hired for their productivity, not their looks or personality quirks. Political economists also highlight the fact that people, rather than things, are involved in labor markets. Beyond this commonality, the two approaches diverge.

In political economy, wages and the world of work are embedded in the social and political fabric of life, as well as in economic mechanisms. In many ways, looking at wages and labor markets is a perfect example of applying the Four C's discussed in Chapter 6. Working for a wage is a relatively new phenomenon in world history. It evolved with the rise of capitalism and therefore needs to be understood within this historical context. In the last chapter, we argued that workers are exploited in capitalism. Exploitation implies conflicting interests between workers and capitalists. In addition, wages are determined by an array of "extramarket" activities, including the ability of workers to be organized and demand higher wages. Workers' wages fluctuate with the business cycle and the relative strength of workers' organizations, but wage levels also are influenced by society's definition of a "fair wage for a fair day's work," particularly as this is written into minimum/maximum wage laws.

Political economists also argue that the labor market and wage levels are important beyond the exchange between workers on the one hand and firms on the other. Wages are the major source of income for families and are influential in shaping communities' economic well-being. Therefore, wages are an important component of an entire distribution mechanism that depends on the cultural organization of families and firms, race relations, and the role of government in providing income and services.

We begin our discussion of work and wages in political economy by examining the concept of the customary standard of living. Political economists argue that at the most abstract level, wages must be sufficient for people to survive. We approach wages from two angles. First, we look at the labor theory of value, and then we examine the role that customs and institutions play in wage determination. However, because the customary standard of living is influenced by the ways in which income is shared within families and by the level of goods and services that the government provides, we broaden the concept of wages to encompass the roles of families and government in wage determination. Then, we outline the political economy view of unemployment and business cycles, as these too exert a strong influence on wages. Later, our focus turns to two specific ways that firms are able to exploit workers over a long period of time: the cost of not having a job (i.e., the threat of unemployment) as a motivator, and management practices in controlling the labor process. We then look at labor market segmentation as a way in which political economists understand wage differences among workers, and how this has changed in recent years.

WAGE DETERMINATION

The factors that govern wages—and with it, wage inequality—are difficult to measure. Political economists believe there is little question that differences in productivity alone provide a very incomplete explanation for wage levels and differences in the economy. The assumption of competition that is required by the productivity explanation clearly is violated by labor market rigidities such as long-term contracts, minimum wages, worker immobility, and persistent unemployment.

If the touchstone for the neoclassical understanding of wages is supply and demand, the touchstone for political economists is the labor theory of value and the constraints of customs and institutions. The theory of political economy (outlined shortly) explains the prices that we expect to see in the economy, whether for cars, bubblegum, or in labor markets, and tells us how workers are exploited. The theory is modified substantially, however, by looking at work in the home and at government income supports, because these change the terms or context under which capitalists and workers struggle over wages. We take up these modifications after considering the labor theory of value and the role of customs and institutions.

The Labor Theory of Value

Early economists, such as Adam Smith, David Ricardo, and Karl Marx, believed that wages were set equal to the customary standard of living for workers. When these economists envisioned wages, they thought about the entire wage bill—the total amount going to all workers, not to a particular individual. In this case, the wage bill is the value of the total output that must go to all workers for them to avoid starvation.[1] Capitalists had to pay workers their subsistence wages and all other costs of production (e.g., rent, raw materials, depreciation of equipment): What was left over—the surplus—was profits.

Karl Marx, extending the arguments of Smith and Ricardo, developed a labor theory of value. He argued that the value of any good or service was the amount of labor time that it customarily takes to produce the product.

> ***Labor theory of value: Commodities are worth the total amount of labor that is required to produce them***

In Marxian economic theory, the value of anything is the amount of time it takes to make that thing within the technical, social, and cultural context of that society. The level of technology, skills, equipment, and work habits all influence the value of goods and services. Marx argued that every commodity exchanges at its value—equivalent for equivalent. So, for

BOX 7.1
LABOR FOR SALE?

If workers are exploited, why don't they just sell their work to capitalists? Piece rates, where individuals are paid for the number of "pieces" that are produced (or units sold, telephone calls completed, and so on), would seem to do exactly this. While some jobs—sales representatives, for example—are almost always associated with piece rates or commissions, capitalists prefer to pay either hourly wages or salaries. The latter systems allow managers to compete more effectively, because they can more easily control workers and increase output while reducing wages.

In Bolivar, Tennessee, Sidney Harman decided to let his workforce participate in managerial decisions, and they created a system much like piece rates called "Earned Idle Time." When the workgroup completed its assigned projects for the day (e.g., making rearview mirrors for automobiles), they could go home. This made it difficult for managers to increase output, because workers would demand more pay. It also made participation difficult, because workers wanted to leave (rather than manage) the plant when they had a chance. The program ended after Harman sold the plant.

At a small clothing operation in New England, the (female) stitchers operated under piece rates, but this created managerial difficulties. If allowed, the women would work very hard some, but not all, of the time, so when the manager needed an order completed quickly, the piece rate did more harm to the owner than good. Nor could he lower rates on existing work to improve his costs *vis-à-vis* his southern U.S. competitors. His solution? The women worked in rooms of 50 each, where the supervisor could see them at all times. Supervisors harassed workers who seemed to be idle, talking was prohibited, and for many years, workers could not even go to the bathroom without the supervisor's permission. In addition, whenever new work came in, the rate was reduced.

Sources: On Bolivar, see John Simmons and William Mares, *Working Together*, New York: Alfred Knopf, 1983, and Appelbaum and Batt (1994). On the clothing case, see Robert Drago, *Success and Failure in Quality of Work Life Programs*, unpublished PhD dissertation, University of Massachusetts–Amherst, 1983.

example, if it takes me three hours to make a vest using the current level of technology, and I have what is considered to be the average skill in the industry, then I should be able to trade that vest for a chair that takes the same amount of time to make.

If equivalent exchanges for equivalent, then how could workers be exploited? The first trick to answering this question is to ascertain what is actually exchanged in the labor market. The exchange is not as simple as it would be if the question referred to the apple market, for example. Apples can be owned and eaten by the buyer, and apples rarely complain in the process. Workers, however, are not exchanged in labor markets, because workers cannot be owned (this distinguishes capitalism from slavery). Nor are labor services the commodity that is bought and sold, because for most jobs, each and every specific task the worker must perform would be difficult, if not impossible, to specify (Box 7.1). Instead, workers offer their time—or more precisely, their potential to work within that time. In exchange, they receive a wage. Labor time is the actual commodity that is bought and sold in the labor market.

Next, put the idea of workers selling labor time together with the labor theory of value. Labor time must be worth the amount of time that it takes to "produce" a worker given the current context (i.e., the amount of time needed to support a worker and his or her family at the customary standard of living). The amount of time required to produce a worker is then a social and cultural relation, a matter of conflict over the customary standard of living. If the customary standard of living requires a DVD player (and, of course, the TV or computer attached to it!) and a car, then the wage bill will reflect that. The wage rate is not simply tied to productivity and the price of the good. The wage—or the amount of time that is devoted to producing workers—depends on context and will change over time. Now, we can get at the major source of conflicting interests between workers and capitalists.

Marx noted that the labor theory of value seemed to leave exploitation as a "mystery." How can a capitalist make money if everything exchanges at its value? Where do profits come from? The secret to this mystery lies in the special nature of labor time, because it is the only commodity that exchanges at its value but produces more than its value following the exchange. Stated differently, the capitalist pays for labor power (i.e., the cost to produce the worker), but the capitalist receives, or hopes to receive, labor (i.e., actual work that is worth more than the value of labor power).

Labor: Actual work that is performed
Labor power: The potential to work (i.e., labor time)

To understand how exploitation works, consider an example. Every worker (including managers) in a meat-packing factory works eight hours a day and produces an average of 32 pounds of packaged meat per day. Thus, each hour worked is equivalent to four pounds of meat. To buy all the raw materials and equipment used every day, the owner of the meat-packing firm pays the equivalent of four pounds of packaged meat per worker per day (or approximately one hour of an average day's work). The customary standard of living is equivalent to 24 pounds of packaged meat per day (or approximately six hours of an average day's work). The owners get whatever is left over—the surplus—the value of four pounds of packaged meat. Everything exchanges for its value, yet the owners end up with a profit. The secret of profit is that workers produce eight hours' worth of commodities but are only paid the value of their labor power—which is less than eight hours' worth of commodities. After the capitalist pays for all the raw materials and the depreciation, the rest is profit—or surplus labor. In other words, the capitalist purchases the potential for work (i.e., labor power), but then sets the employee to doing actual work (i.e., labor).

The labor theory of value implies that workers produce all commodities for exchange in a capitalist economy—but are only paid a portion of it. A portion must be preserved to purchase raw materials and account for depreciation of machinery (labor goes into these, too). What's left over is profit and belongs to the capitalist because she or he owns the means of production—not because he or she did any work. Remember, the capitalist puts up the money (she or he usually does not manage work) and then sits back and counts the profits.[2] Marx called the extraction of surplus labor (i.e., the labor time during which workers are generating profits) exploitation. Any level of profit-taking exploits workers.

The production of profit and exploitation of workers can be simply illustrated. Consider a work day broken into two time segments, A to B, and B to C:

A ——————————— B ————— C

The amount of time that is represented by the distance from A to B is the amount of time for workers to produce an amount equivalent to his or her day's wage. The amount of time that is between point B and C during the day is the surplus. Workers want the amount of wages they receive to increase and/or want to work less for the same amount (on the A-B-C time line, this would be represented by pushing B closer to C or pulling C and B closer to A). Workers can do this by organizing and demanding more pay or a shorter work day.

Capitalists, conversely, want to increase the B-C portion of the working day and/or reduce the A-B portion. This can be done by making the workers work harder or more efficiently, so that they produce a day's worth of work in a shorter period of time, or by increasing the standard length of the working day.

As argued in Chapter 6, political economists stress the notion of how collective action and change are generated by conflict. In other words, those who are oppressed do not take it lying down. They struggle against oppression and, in the process, change the economy. In terms of wages and exploitation, this argument implies that workers will strive both individually and collectively for higher wages. How do they do it? Going in as an individual and demanding a raise from the boss usually doesn't work—especially if there are a hundred more just like you dying for a job. If there is no one else out there with your training, however, you will have a much better shot at getting a raise. When unemployment is low and workers difficult to replace, wages tend to rise; when unemployment is high and workers are a dime a dozen, wages tend to fall. We return to this phenomenon when discussing the business cycle later in this chapter.

A much more forceful and sustained way to improve wages, however, is to get all your coworkers to go to the boss and ask for a raise at the same time. In other words, acting collectively—organizing workers into groups, demanding that everyone receive higher wages, and signing a contract to this effect—is an important way that workers improve their wages. Indeed, since the beginning of capitalist production in the early 19th century, workers have organized themselves in trade and craft unions as well as workers' associations. Workers were successful in reducing the length of the working day in advanced industrial countries and improving the standard of living for many. These changes often have come out of direct conflict and confrontation.

The reason that capitalists and workers maintain conflicting interests now should be apparent: those who do all the work only claim a portion of the bounty. Further, the higher the wages, the lower the profits. Class struggle, then, is a fight over the surplus, and class struggle is tied closely to wages.

The Role of Customs and Institutions

Nonmarxist political economists do not rely on the labor theory of value to explain how wages are determined, but they do rely on an argument about the customary standard of living. In this argument, wages are in large part determined by social, historical, and cultural influences. What people earn and what firms are willing to pay are determined by what people consider to be "fair" in a particular context.

The role that custom might play in wage determination is hard to model but very easy to understand. Economist Albert Rees, who taught neoclassical labor economics for 30 years, after which he served on several wage stabilization boards, as a corporate director, as a university provost, as a foundation president, and as trustee of a liberal arts college, found this out for himself. Here are Rees' conclusions from comparing his real-world experiences with the theory he had faithfully taught:

> In none of these roles did I find the theory I had been teaching for so long to be the slightest help. The factors involved in setting wages and salaries in the real world seemed to be very different than those specified in the neoclassical theory. The one factor that seemed to be of overwhelming importance in all these real world situations was fairness, and fairness always seemed to be judged by making some kind of wage

comparison: with another union, with another employer, or with another person … I cannot recall ever being involved in any dispute or controversy in which any party to the dispute questioned the criterion of fairness as the basis for settling the controversy. Even employers never argued that supply or demand conditions in the labor market should be taken into account. The question was always which wage or salary comparison was appropriate … and of course each party would always contend that the comparison favorable to its cause was by far the most relevant one.[3]

Wage determination is largely influenced by collective behavior, which makes us concerned about where we stand relative to others, while what is specifically considered to be fair at any point in time can be traced to the social context.

Rees goes on to argue that neoclassical theory is not so much wrong as incomplete: "The most it can do is set the stage for players such as personnel directors, union officers and individual workers. It cannot write their lines."[4] In other words, supply and demand may create loose limits on where wages can go, but within those limits, ideological and institutional factors must be invoked to explain the levels that actually are set. Beliefs about issues such as fairness and custom, as well as organizational characteristics such as internal labor markets and unions, work alongside the supply and demand considerations to determine wages. Consequently, productivity differentials cannot be the entire explanation for wage differentials.

Nobel Prize-winner Robert Solow also believes that ideological factors such as fairness are crucial to the understanding of wages and unemployment. The title of his 1990 book, *The Labor Market as a Social Institution*, reveals a marked similarity of perspective with that of political economy. Solow agrees that labor markets are unlike other markets, because labor time is unlike other commodities. Labor market behavior involves social interactions and perceptions as well as traditional economic motivations. Workers not only react to the price paid for their own services but also to the wages received by others. Consequently, unemployed workers may not be able to bid down the wage—even if they want to. Employers may refuse to lower the wage scale when they hire new workers, because they fear their existing workers will react negatively and destabilize production. Once wage patterns are in place, they tend to be perpetuated as workers strive to maintain their positions relative to one another. This helps to explain why wages (unlike other prices) tend to rise easily but tend to fall with great difficulty, why relative wage patterns tend to be maintained through time, why (as we will see shortly) involuntary unemployment rises in recessions, and why (as we shall see in the next chapter) inequality may be difficult to eradicate even when it cannot be justified by productivity differentials.

Wage levels will depend on what other workers are receiving. For example, when the United Automobile Workers receive a 5% wage increase, the United Steelworkers will be well aware of this increase and typically ask for the same. After all, it's only "fair." What is so visible in the presence of labor unions often occurs in nonunion settings as well. When considering wage increases, a bank, for example, might survey other banks in the area to see what they are paying. Indeed, some will go so far as to "peg" their wage at 80%, 100%, or 120% of whatever the average bank in the area pays. (Check with your bank teller, and see how it is done there.) It works the other way, too. When workers in one industry agree to wage concessions or forgo cost-of-living increases, it becomes harder for other workers to argue for higher wages.

Wage levels often are based on job evaluation. The institution of job evaluation is widespread in the United States. Some research suggests that over two-thirds of all employees have their pay affected by job evaluation, while over 80% of large organizations use the system.[5] A firm or governmental agency using a job evaluation system will hire a consultant to examine each job and assign points to various aspects of it, ranging from complexity to skill requirements to human relations to managerial responsibilities. The points for each job are then added and wages set accordingly. So, for example, if a job that is "worth" 150 points pays $300 per week, then a job "worth" 200 points will pay $400 per week.

Job evaluation: Systems that assign points to job characteristics to set relative wages within an organization

Job evaluation makes wage-setting appear to be objective, but it is not. Instead, it is rooted in cultural and historical notions of what certain kinds of work and workers are worth. Economist Marlene Kim has shown how gender bias was built into the California Civil Service pay system in 1930, when it was decided to pay "somewhat higher for those occupations filled predominantly by men."[6] This allowed the state to pay a higher wage to men without explicitly paying women less than men for the same job. Partly as a result, women in the service were paid 73.9% as much as men in 1937. Once these differences were locked in place, they proved difficult to remove. As recently as 1975, the wage-setting body for the California Civil Service admitted that maintaining existing relative wages (i.e., men's jobs paying more than women's) was "more important than responding to short-term changes in prevailing rates" (Kim; 47). The term prevailing rates, of course, means supply and demand as measured by wage surveys of other organizations, so it is not surprising that by 1986, women in the system earned only 74.9% as much as men.

This case demonstrates that historical context matters. It also demonstrates conflict between groups or collective behavior, because the only reason we know these facts is Kim's involvement in a comparable worth lawsuit that was filed by women against the California Civil Service. The suit was ultimately lost, but this does not mean that conflict or change was contained. Similar lawsuits in Minnesota and Washington State have been successfully pursued.

Looking more closely, sociologist Ronnie Steinberg (1990) has undertaken detailed studies of job evaluation systems. Steinberg finds that gender bias often is hidden in seemingly objective evaluation criteria. For example, in the Massachusetts state job evaluation system, potential employees for four male job areas (labor, skilled labor, carpenter, painter) were each required to have the "ability" to lift heavy objects, stand for a long time, climb, and so on, and they were given separate points for their "willingness" to do the exact same tasks. In female jobs, points were given for "ability" to deal tactfully with others, establish and maintain harmonious relations, exercise discretion, and so on, but their "willingness" was not mentioned and, thus, presumably did not count![7]

If you look at the most common job evaluation system, developed by the Hay group, you will see that it does *not* tie wages to performance.[8] Instead, it includes elements such as knowledge, responsibility, accountability. In other words, points are assigned using criteria related to "labor power" and not the actual performance of "labor." Further, once points are assigned to a job, the overall wage must still be set, presumably in light of the market, but also in the context of the customary standard of living and the relative strength of the specific employer and group of employees. The forces of supply and demand may still be there, but they have moved far into the background. Instead, we see an emphasis on traditions, collective action, social custom, and notions of fairness.

Home Production and the Family Wage

Wages are paid to the individuals who work in a firm, but any individual's wage may have to support more than one person. For example, suppose there is only one person who earns a wage in a family. He or she has to bring home enough money to support all family members. If this worker can't find a job that pays enough to cover monthly housing expenses, buy enough food, provide child care when kids are not at school and he or she is at work, pay for health insurance and clothing, then this worker and family are in trouble. The family may have to rely on extended family members or friends to help out—or even on public assistance to help assure they have the basic necessities. If many families are supported by one parent and there are not enough jobs that pay living wages for many of those adults, then society as a whole is in trouble. Jobs and wages just do not match family needs.

Now, imagine if our single working parent lives with another adult (perhaps a husband) and he stays home and takes care of the kids, cooks, shops, sews, and cleans house. Because there is another adult in house, the woman's paycheck will need to buy more food, clothing, and health care. But, because there is another adult, he also can take care of the children, do chores around the house, and cook meals. If he is "cost-effective" (i.e., the new needs he brings to the household cost less than the money saved by having him work at home), then her family's standard of living has significantly improved. If he also goes to work for part of the day when the children are at school, she now can actually "afford" to take a job that pays less or requires fewer hours.

As this situation illustrates, wages are the outcome of how workers and capitalists meet in the labor market, but they also are an important distribution mechanism for family members who don't have access to wages. This means that the customary standard of living depends not only on the wage but also on work at the site of the home, the typical family structure, and as will be argued shortly, government supports.

More formally, the value of labor time includes the time and energy that it takes to get wage workers to work, which includes important—although often unpaid—work done by family members and communities, such as raising children and providing volunteer time to neighborhoods, schools, churches, and temples not only to improve the quality of our lives but to make sure family members are taken care of and get the moral, ethical, and spiritual support to grow up and become workers themselves.

An implication of this argument is that if all workers are to experience similar customary standards of living, then a worker with no dependents should receive lower wages than a worker who is financially supporting children. The lone worker is not helping to "produce" future workers, so he or she is worth less (although not worthless). If you accept this logic as fair, you might, for example, support a subminimum wage for teenagers, because they need less money to achieve a given standard of living. As a firm, you might provide health benefits that cover workers' dependents so that workers with dependents actually receive more health benefits.

Historically, this logic was tied to the domination of women by men through the notion of the family wage. The idea of the family wage is itself gender-neutral: an individual worker should be able to earn enough money at a full-time job to support an average-sized family. The idea was used concretely, however, as the basis for explaining why women should earn less than men. Women worked for "pin" money, while men had to earn enough to support entire families. As historian Alice Kessler-Harris documents, this notion has been prevalent since the beginnings of wage labor in the United States in the early 1800s. For example, in 1912, a New York State Factory Investigating Commission set out to make a case for increasing the minimum wage applying to women, so it surveyed several thousand employers on the wage that was "required to support in health and efficiency" people in the following categories: women who are teenagers, men who are teenagers, adult women living alone, adult men living alone, and one man supporting a wife and three children (Kessler-Harris, 1982; 42). The ideal of the family wage—and its restriction

BOX 7.2
THE STRUCTURE OF FAMILIES IN THE UNITED STATES: A HISTORICAL PERSPECTIVE

Before wide-scale industrial capitalism in the United States, many people lived in extended families on farms. Surviving grandparents, parents, and children often shared the same quarters, and all were typically engaged in production. While there was a fairly strict division of labor by age and gender, all members worked. Older family members, women, and young children typically produced goods for home production (e.g., clothes, candles, soap, etc.), while men and older male children were primarily responsible for goods produced for market (e.g., livestock, wool, food, etc.). Taking care of children was the responsibility of women and older members, but all other economic activity happened at the household level. Land ownership provided the primary source of income (Matthaei, 1982). Only white men were allowed to own land, which gave them considerable power over women and anyone who wasn't white.

With the advent of widespread wage labor in the mid-1800s, both the work done in households and family structure changed dramatically. Earned wages—not land ownership—became the primary source of income for most families. Also, while custom dictated that women did most of the child care, capitalism reshaped women's inferior status. The development of the family wage came with the influx of immigrants and the movement of rural families into cities to seek employment at the newly developed factories. Men went to work; women stayed home with children. Young men who were not in line to inherit their livelihood through land transfer often left their families as soon as they were able to earn enough to support themselves. Young women usually left only on marriage and to set up their own household. By the 1900s, the typical family was no longer extended but nuclear: a married couple and their children. Further, married women tended not to work outside the home.

Certainly not all families were nuclear, nor did all men earn enough to support their families. In low-income families, especially those that faced racial and ethnic discrimination, wives and children often had to find some form of employment or income-producing activity. Still, the emerging capitalist job structure developed with a particular type of family, and a very set notion of who the main breadwinner in that family was. The sexual division of paid labor and the corresponding wages reflected this notion of family structure.

It is not only job structure that reflects a certain family structure. Many of the most important governmental wage support systems were created in the 1930s with the nuclear family dependent on one male breadwinner in mind. The social security benefit system, unemployment insurance, and Aid to Families with Dependent Children (all originating in the 1935 Social Security Act) were established to replace the wages of male breadwinners.

Now consider the radical change in family structure that has occurred over the last half-century. In 1955, only 30% of married women worked for wages. By 2008, 62% did. Indeed, the fastest-growing household type is one with a person who lives alone or with other unrelated people. Between 1970 and 2010, the number of women who lived alone increased by nearly 150% (from 7.3 million to 17.3 million). In the same period the number of men who lived alone rose by 297% (from 3.5 million to 14 million). Currently, men living alone account for about 12% of all households, and women living alone for about 14% of all households. In 1970, about 72% of all people over 18 years of age were married. By 2008, that figure had dropped to 56%.

Perhaps more important, however, an increasing number of women—especially women with children—are working for pay. It is no longer an oddity to see women of child-bearing age at work. Women have entered the labor force for many reasons: some because they want to and, like men, get an important sense of themselves from work, and some because they must make ends meet. Therefore, it now is virtually expected that women will work regardless of whether or not they have children.

Sources: U.S. Department of Commerce, *Marital Status and Living Arrangements, 1993.* Washington, D.C.: Government Printing Office, 1994, and *Households and Families: 2010*, 2010 Census Briefs, April 2012, www.census.gov (accessed July 18, 2013).

to male heads of households and breadwinners—was clear. Economists Deborah Figart, Ellen Mutari and Marilyn Power trace the early 20th century debates over minimum wages just for women workers in specific industries that were implemented in ten states. The debates uncover several assumptions about women and their wages that were common at the time. For one, it was argued that legislation was needed because women were too timid to defend their own interests. A second argument was that very low wages for women were more likely to drive single women into prostitution. Third, it was argued that women's wage needs were different from men's—they were not presumed to be supporting families and did not need a family wage—but did need a minimum amount to survive.

> ### Family wage: The amount that a single wage earner requires to financially support an entire family

This notion that good jobs with good wages should be reserved for men supporting families was linked to the historical exclusion of women, and particularly white married women, from the labor force. As noted in Chapter 5, the starkest evidence of this phenomenon is found in the marriage bars holding in professions like teaching and nursing from the 1900s through the 1960s in the United States. By cutting off opportunities for women in the labor market, many women may have escaped direct exploitation. The general domination of women by men was reinforced, however, and opportunities for indirect exploitation, like those outlined earlier, were enhanced.

While the family wage was intended to "free" wives from the burden of paid employment, many capitalists took it as a signal to intensify the demands on workers receiving a family wage. To see why, consider a simple story. A husband goes to work in a firm while his wife stays at home and takes care of their children. Suppose the husband buys a sandwich at lunchtime for $5.00. One day, the boss says, "Look, your wife could make those same sandwiches at home for $3.00, so I'll cut your pay by $2.00 a day, your wife can make sandwiches, and your customary standard of living won't change." The wife now has more work to do at home for her husband, and her husband is receiving a lower wage. In this case, the family is getting less income but the husband's standard of living has not fallen, because the lost income is being made up by more of the wife's time being spent serving her husband. The wife now is being "exploited" partially by the firm and partially by her husband!

Economists Randy Albelda and Chris Tilly (1997) call the set of jobs that pay family wages but also assume the worker does not have to spend time taking care of others "jobs with wives." These are jobs where the main breadwinner (usually the husband) is freed from obligations to deal with household duties, particularly child care. He often is expected to work long hours and not be interrupted during the day with family matters. To succeed in his job, he may even be expected to have his wife entertain his work colleagues at their home. At the turn of the 20th century, the working class dream was to have a wife who didn't work. Until the 1950s, jobs with wives were mainly for white managerial male workers, but with large-scale unionization in many manufacturing industries during the 1950s, many blue-collar skilled and semiskilled jobs also became "jobs with wives."

> ### Jobs with wives: When a family wage is paid and the job makes extensive demands on a nonwaged spouse

No one has calculated the number of men who received a family wage historically. What we do know is that the family wage has been eroding in the United States since the 1960s. As the numbers presented in Chapter 2 show, men's wages have been declining since that time, implying that fewer men receive a family wage. Related to this is that many of the blue-collar jobs that historically have paid a family wage have disappeared. Additionally, the exclusion of women from the family wage has been illegal since passage of the Equal Pay Act: women must receive the same wage for the same work. Finally, a key condition that made the family wage viable for male, married managers—jobs with wives—has evaporated as women have entered the professional ranks and the number of nonemployed wives has dwindled (Box 7.2).

The context for firms paying a family wage—the declining possibilities for jobs with wives—has changed, but firms may be behind the times in recognizing this shift. As Ellen Bravo, the executive director of 9 to 5, National Association of Working Women, notes, only 8% of households have a husband working for pay and a wife at home full-time, but the remaining 92% have precious little say over corporate policies. Of those who do set such policies (i.e., managers), a full 91% are men with a wife who is home full-time (Bravo, 1995; 4–5).

Even if corporations are moving only slowly, the shifting context for the family wage has changed the implications of supporting this idea. Employers paying a family wage find it increasingly difficult to demand that the wives of male employees provide work with no remuneration from the firm. In other words, with some important exceptions (like president of the United States or a corporate manager), the link between "family wages" and "jobs with wives" is being broken. In turn, this means that family wages can be made available to anyone, whether male or female, married or single.

Income Supports and the Social Wage

In 1935, sweeping wage-support legislation was passed by the federal government—the Social Security Act. In this watershed law, the government established itself as supplementing families with income when the main breadwinner could not find work. The Old Age, Survivor, and Disability Insurance system (what we commonly refer to as Social Security), Unemployment Insurance, and Aid to Dependent Children (the precursor to Aid to Families with Dependent Children [AFDC], which was replaced by Temporary Assistance to Needy Families [TANF] in 1996) all were established under this act. The notion was that not everyone in a market-based system can, or is able to, find work; hence, they might not have a wage or live with someone who has a wage. Retired persons, the unemployed, and single mothers fell into this category. In each case, the idea was to supplement or replace a male breadwinner's wages.

This legislation suggests another important underlying component of the value of labor power and of the wage—the degree to which necessities are provided by communities or government rather than purchased with wages. If families must spend time and money to educate their children and provide health care to their families, then the value of labor power must rise as well, because the amount of time and money that it takes to care for children and other dependents is higher. The larger the social wage—the value of necessary goods and services that are provided by pooling resources in communities and through government—the lower an individual's wage can be. Think about it this way. If the U.S. government provided low-cost or free child care to children aged three to five years (as in France), then one huge expense to workers with children would be reduced, and parents of young children might be willing to take jobs at a lower wage than if they had to pay for all child-care costs themselves. An even more immediate example is the cost of health insurance. If all people in the United States had health-care coverage, workers might be willing to work at jobs with lower wages if, in effect, they would have more take-home pay.

Social wage: That part of the customary standard of living that is provided by government

Of course, community-based and government-provided goods and services typically are paid for through fees, tithing, or taxes. If taxes on working people are higher than the benefits they receive, they indeed might require higher wages to make ends meet. The relationship of the social wage to the actual wage rate will depend on the structure of taxes. Since World War II, the United States traditionally has had a much lower social wage than other industrialized countries. Most countries offer health care, child care, K–12 education, and pensions for the elderly. The United States only offers the last two universally.

Various political economists have calculated the social wage, and their results vary. Samuel Bowles, David Gordon, and Thomas Weisskopf (1983) find that the social wage rose from the 1950s through the 1970s as workers struggled to improve their standard of living. This is the same period that large, state university systems were mainly built, the interstate highway system was put into place, and both Medicare and Medicaid were created. They argue that workers successfully increased their standard of living at the expense of profits.

However, economist John Miller found a falling social wage during this period—workers were paying more in taxes than they received in government services. Basically, Miller argues that the government was mainly taxing workers (not capitalists) to fund not only social benefits for workers but also the military. Miller goes on to show that the Reagan years made the social wage fall even further, as military expenditures rose and taxes on capitalists fell.

What we do know for certain is that the social wage in the United States declined severely in recent decades. Social welfare expenditures, including Social Security, Medicare, Medicaid, Food Stamps, and so forth, amounted to just over 5% of GDP in 1980, but declined to just over 4% by 2002 (a 20% drop). We also know that the Social Security Administration stopped its practice of publishing annual data on social welfare expenditures after 2002, presumably because the expenditures continued to fall. The stimulus package enacted in 2009 under the Obama administration may have helped to reverse these long-term trends.[9]

The important point here is not so much that political economists agree on the exact size of the social wage or the amount of unpaid work that is performed in the home. Rather, the point is that for political economists, "wages" need to be looked at in the social context, and work in the home as well as government taxing and spending policies are part of that context. Further, wages are more than just another market transaction. Wages are the primary source of income for families and, therefore, also an important component of income distribution and equity in capitalist economic systems.

MACROECONOMICS: THE ROLE OF UNEMPLOYMENT

Another ingredient in the political economy view of wages is unemployment. In Chapter 4, we saw that neoclassical economists view unemployment as being subject to negative feedback: if something bad happens (e.g., unemployment), it will be stamped out (e.g., wages will fall and labor markets will clear). Keynesian economists believe in positive feedback: some unemployment will create more, unless the government steps in.

Political economists are closer to the Keynesian view in believing that free markets will not stamp out unemployment. They go farther, however, by arguing that capitalism may require unemployment. Here, Keynes' optimism in government intervention takes a pessimistic turn.

Again, we look back to the work of Karl Marx, who believed that involuntary unemployment is both generated and required by capitalist economies. On the one hand, each individual capitalist has an incentive to improve productivity and individual work effort and, hence, to use fewer and fewer workers while producing more and more products using the cheapest labor available. A dramatic example occurred in agriculture, and is still occurring in manufacturing. Such cost reductions force more people into the labor market as families discover they cannot make it on a single income. Thus, capitalism creates unemployment as part of the normal processes of competition and growth. At the same time, capitalism requires the government to permit and facilitate unemployment to keep the cost of losing a job high. If unemployment disappeared, then workers would slack off, demand higher wages, and be more likely to act collectively against capitalists. So, Marx interpreted unemployment as a necessary byproduct of market competition and the conflicting interests of capitalists and workers. Any government trying to eliminate unemployment does so at its own peril, because a stronger working class would undermine capitalist exploitation and control.

Nonetheless, Marx saw unemployment as contradictory. While capitalists profit from the high levels of work effort and low wages that extensive unemployment permits, unemployment also means there are fewer consumers with money to make purchases. Only workers form a large enough block of consumers to purchase the mass of products that capitalism creates, and if workers are unemployed or their wages fall, they do not buy very much. Therefore, capitalists are caught between their need to shed labor and reduce wages to compete and their collective need to sell products to those same workers.

Marx's understanding of unemployment is used by modern political economists in three ways. First, unemployment is central to the "cost of job loss" (discussed later), because without unemployment, profits are likely to fall. For the same reason, welfare spending and other measures that mitigate the pain of unemployment for workers are generally opposed by the business sector (Cloward and Piven, 1982). The relative strength of capitalists during the Bush administration of 2001 to 2008 motivated the government to cut social welfare spending, partly to help fund the wars in Afghanistan and Iraq, but also to pull the social safety net out from under workers so they would work hard for capitalists—and for less money.

Second, political economists focus on the ideology of unemployment. If workers collectively understand unemployment as a strategy to reduce their wages and make them work harder, then workers are likely to support full-employment policies. In a democratic system such as ours, workers could always win through votes if the will was there, but of course, profits would then fall. So, capitalists have an incentive to peddle to workers the neoclassical belief that unemployment is an individual event and responsibility. To the extent capitalists can sell this idea successfully, workers will see unemployment as something they as individuals can avoid through hard work and initiative.

Evidence from a plant closing at RCA provides a glimpse at how successful capitalists have been in convincing workers that unemployment is an individual responsibility.[10] In a sample of comparable workers who were continuously employed as opposed to workers experiencing job loss through the shutdown of the RCA plant, it was found that the individual's sense of mastery over his or her environment was significantly higher for the continuously employed. The lack of any sense of mastery among those experiencing the plant closing was related to their also giving up on the ideology that capitalism rewards hard work, with around two-thirds disagreeing with the statement: "There is a good job waiting for me if I just look harder."

More generally, this "blame the victim" mentality regarding unemployment affects the unemployed themselves; it sets the context for their beliefs about themselves. Although the federal government has known how to control unemployment for over half a century, studies nonetheless find that a one-percentage-point increase in unemployment (e.g., from 6% to 7%) increases the incidence of suicides by 4.1%, homicides by 5.7%, and admissions to mental hospitals by 4.3% for men and 2.3% for women.[11]

Third, modern political economists draw from Marx the view that business cycles are inherent to the capitalist economy (Boddy and Crotty, 1975). In a business cycle of four to six years, we find unemployment first rising and then falling. Government policy makers have been unable to eliminate the business cycle (although Keynesian economists attempted to do so during the 1960s). The problem political economists see as driving the business cycle is that not merely high but rising unemployment is periodically required to reduce workers' wage demands and keep their efforts high. After all, if the same people were unemployed year after year, that would hardly act to motivate workers who hold jobs. Therefore, when times are "too good"—when unemployment is low and sales for firms are high—investors become fearful of workers working less hard and demanding higher wages. Investment slacks off, leading to higher unemployment. Unemployment alone would not bother investors, however, except that there also is a positive feedback effect as newly unemployed workers (or those fearing unemployment) decrease their purchases, thereby creating even more unemployment. When workers are sufficiently cowed, investors will slowly move back into the market, thereby reducing unemployment and improving sales.

The business cycle has particular implications for women and minorities, as they are often are the last hired when the economy improves and the first fired when it deteriorates. When the white male unemployment rate increases a little, the rate for blacks and women increases a lot (Reich, 1981; Bernstein 2005). Further, wage inequality between blacks and whites and between men and women increases as well. Both of these issues receive further discussion in Chapter 8.

LABOR MARKETS IN CAPITALISM: MOTIVATION AND THE LABOR PROCESS

As stated earlier, labor markets do not operate like other markets. When a firm purchases a worker's labor time (i.e., labor power), it is the performance of actual work (i.e., labor) that the firm really wants. The employer faces the problem of transforming labor power into actual labor; this also is known as the problem of capitalist management.[12]

Now, we ask how capitalists get workers to perform. As we saw, part of the answer lies in the fact that capitalists have the money to buy capital equipment and to hire workers, while workers can afford to do neither. However, this is not the entire story. We now consider two additional avenues for capitalists to extract surplus labor and keep wages down in the bargain: the cost of job loss, and the labor process.

The Cost of Job Loss: Unemployment Is No Picnic

Think about what happens if you get up in the morning and say to yourself, "This job stinks. I'm doing all the work and the guy that owns the joint goes to the bank every day. I think I'll just stay home." Go ahead, stay home—but you'll be out of a job. Then what? Unless you are independently wealthy or find someone (like a wife/husband or the government) who is willing to support you, you had better hit the lottery or hit the pavement and start looking for work. And this may be a problem. With over 12 million people unemployed on any given day in the United States (when there is technically no longer a recession), it may not be so easy to find a new job. So, in the end, you get up and go to work. You may not like being exploited, but considering your options, you'll take it.

Surprisingly, this story implies that capitalists are actually paying workers "too much," or providing a positive cost of job loss to make people work hard.[13] As economists Herbert Gintis (1976) and Samuel Bowles (1985) tell the story, suppose that capitalists pay workers the market-clearing, competitive equilibrium wage where there is assumed to be little or no unemployment (see Chapter 4). Workers then have no reason to work beyond the absolute minimum level of work. If workers get tired of dealing with an irate customer on the phone, they'll hang up. If workers are worried about the quality or safety aspects of what they are producing, they may slow down and force the firm to miss an important deadline. If workers want to sing, dance, or listen to poetry, there is nothing the capitalist can do. Fire them, and they all walk across the street and get another job at the same wage. If capitalists raise workers' wages, then some people will be unemployed (by the law of demand), but those who are lucky enough to still have a job will work much harder as they worry about losing their jobs, homes, cars, and source of family support. They worry about the "cost of job loss."

Cost of job loss: The difference between your income at your job and your income if you lose or leave your job (e.g., from unemployment insurance)

The basic argument here is that as the cost of job loss rises, workers work harder, and conversely, when the cost of job loss falls, workers reduce their efforts. The capitalist can, of course, simply raise wages to increase the amount of labor being extracted from workers, but the cost-of-job-loss logic suggests several other devices to get more work out of workers: supervision, home production, and the social wage.

If the capitalist threatens workers with job loss but does not monitor them closely, they will commit acts of sabotage, steal from the firm, and generally goof off. After all, why help someone who has just threatened you? In response, capitalists hire supervisors to make sure these things don't happen. Supervisors don't produce anything, but they do help to extract work from workers.

The capitalist has to spend money to increase the cost of job loss by raising wages or hiring supervisors, so other ways of increasing the cost of job loss may be considered. Among them is the notion of "jobs with wives" (discussed earlier). Suppose that an employer is choosing between two job candidates, one of whom has an employed spouse and the other a spouse who works in the home without wages. Which should the employer pick? With the notion of the cost of job loss in hand, the answer is obvious: pick the applicant whose spouse does not receive any wage income, because this employee has more to lose—the entire family income—following job loss. Better yet is a worker with a financially dependent spouse and children; that person is even more likely to worry about the cost of job loss. Of course, it may be illegal for an employer to ask job candidates about their family status. In many cases, however, the legality won't much matter, because the employee is likely to volunteer the information anyway. This is just one more aspect of the employer's power over prospective and actual employees.

Finally, capitalists can generate a high cost of job loss by asking the government to limit—or cut off—unemployment benefits or other income supports that are received by potential employees who are out of work. As mentioned in the last section, Bowles, Gordon, and Weisskopf argued that the social wage rose during the 1950s and 1960s. Further, they argue that this increase in the social wage reduced the cost of job loss, led workers to reduce their efforts, and reduced profits as a result. The capitalist response was the Reagan and later Bush years, which involved cut-backs in the social wage so that by the turn of the new century, workers again were "properly" fearful of losing their jobs. The social safety net was pulled out from under them.

However, it is worth noting that the cost of job loss is complicated. For example, as economist William Tabb notes, per capita GDP has increased by over two-thirds since 1980, while the real (inflation-adjusted) wages of the average worker have actually declined (Tabb, 2007). The lower wages were good for the profits of capitalists, but also meant that the cost of job loss was *falling* over this period. Of course, the dramatic rise in unemployment, beginning early in 2008, served to raise the cost of job loss by scaring workers with the threat of losing their livelihoods.

The Labor Process: Simplify and Control

Having people who are motivated to work is not enough for the capitalist to turn a profit. In addition, the capitalist must make investment decisions and hire managers to figure out how the work is to be performed. In a worker-owned firm, this is not a problem, because it is in the interests of workers to find the best ways to get the job done. In a capitalist firm, however, workers might work very hard, but in general, they have little or no interest in letting managers know how the work can best be performed. Therefore, an important component for understanding labor markets, and with it wage rates, is how capitalists deal with the labor process itself (Braverman, 1974; Edwards, 1979).

Labor process: Methods by which work and workers are controlled

Much of the history of the development of the capitalist firm—and with it, labor markets—deals with how the workplace is structured to assure that workers indeed work, and in a productive fashion. Management develops in part to face the task of controlling workers and choosing technology, with the explicit goal of eliciting the desired work behavior. Managers are also workers, but unlike nonsupervisory workers, they have authority and a vested interest in making other workers work hard. Control can be exercised by increasing the cost of job loss, as discussed earlier, but technology and managerial strategies play a role as well.

Because capitalists (and their hired managers) have the right to design and run the labor process, they do so in a manner that facilitates the extraction of labor from labor time. As economist Harry Braverman (1974) argued, one way to improve the extraction process is to simplify jobs. Jobs can be divided into components that require little training or skill and are easy to supervise. For example, typing used to be a highly skilled task, because the result had to be perfect the first time or else unsightly "white-out" had to be applied. With most writing now done on computers with word processors mistakes are not only easy to correct, you do not even need to know how to spell! Braverman argued that if you look over the long sweep of history—the switch from skilled individual mechanics to assembly line production of bicycles, the switch from grocery checkers being skilled with arithmetic to needing only to punch in the right numbers, the switch from architects needing a steady hand to using a computer "mouse"—the pattern is one of jobs being simplified, and the reason is that simplification makes sense in firms where workers do not share in the rewards for their efforts.[14]

In addition to labor processes being simplified, they may be systematized depending on the product the firm produces, the technology it employs, and the market situation it is in. There are three types of control systems used by different types of firms (or sometimes mixed within a single firm): simple, technical, and bureaucratic control (Box 7.3).

All firms rely on some system of control—and sometimes on more than one. For example, think of the last job that you held (or ask a friend who has worked for pay). Were you watched closely by a supervisor? If so, you probably were subject to simple control. Was there equipment that either checked how much work you did or kept the

BOX 7.3
THREE FORMS OF LABOR CONTROL

In his 1979 book *Contested Terrain*, Richard Edwards traces the development of three distinct forms of control that capitalists use in the workplace to extract labor from workers. The first type is *simple control*. It is most commonly used by the small firms that most closely correspond to the competitive model of neoclassical economics. Such firms typically exist in wholesale and retail trade or the service sector. Wage and skill levels are generally low, and job ladders (i.e., promotion opportunities) are nonexistent. Incentives are therefore minimal. Instead, the employer (or the manager) directly supervises workers and evaluates their work. Workers who please the boss may be given small incentives, such as better working hours, but the primary means of exercising control is the threat of unemployment. Workers in these firms are easy to replace, so management has no hesitation about firing those who it feels are not working hard enough. Managers use the personal exercise of authority to control the pace of work and elicit the desired behavior from workers. If you've ever worked at McDonald's or Walmart, this should sound very familiar.

In contrast, *technical control* relies on machinery to set the pace of work. This system of control is most often found in large or very large firms in manufacturing and mining industries. These firms are frequently unionized, and the personal authority of managers is limited by grievance procedures and seniority rights. Nonetheless, supervisors are still needed to ensure that workers keep up with the assembly line. Workers tend to be more highly skilled and paid, and management has more of a stake in reducing turnover to stabilize production and minimize the costs of on-the-job training. The classic example of technical control is the assembly line, which regulates both the type and pace of work. However, technical control can also be associated with low wages, especially in nonunionized, light manufacturing, and in some service industries. For example, computers now allow managers to easily and quickly know how many telephone calls an operator answers, or how many groceries a checker handles. Because the design and implementation of technology is in the hands of management, the labor process will be organized in a way that maximizes output and profits, and minimizes wages.

Bureaucratic control is the third method of eliciting desired work behavior from workers. This system relies on pay and promotional incentives and, frequently, on internalization of the norms of the firm. The worker wants to succeed because she or he believes in doing the best job possible to scale the job ladder. There tend to be high returns to seniority and education, and credentials are important as a means to job placement and advancement. This is most common among professional, technical, and administrative workers in large corporations where work cannot be standardized by technology or supervised in a one-on-one fashion.

work moving? If so, we have technical control. Were you trusted to "do the right thing"? If so, then bureaucratic control may have been present.

What the capitalist would like—but cannot often get—is loyalty. Given the conflicting interests between capitalists and workers, this is difficult, expensive, and takes time. The one system discussed earlier that can generate loyalty—bureaucratic control—requires high wages, real promotion opportunities, and fair rules to function adequately. In this case, it looks like conflicting interests disappear, but they have not. As soon as the capitalist finds another way to make more money, the interests of workers will be sacrificed.

To make the point more strongly, certain combinations of control strategies and historical context have, at times, given groups of workers shared interests with capitalists. In fast-growing industries and those with powerful worker organizations (usually unions), workers and capitalists can see eye-to-eye on sharing the gains from growth, so when profits go up, so do workers' wages. Historically, there have been times in the United States when workers and capitalists have seen their interests as shared and agreed with statements like "What's good for GM is good for America."

During the 20 years following World War II, industrial unions and corporations in automobiles, steel, rubber, and coal all struck agreements that tied wage increases to gains in productivity. Workers in those industries saw their wages rise with profits. However, as is all too painfully obvious to those who live in Midwestern cities that housed these industries, this compact was short-lived. International competition facilitated a massive downsizing that decimated employment (and with it, union membership) in those industries and reduced wages.

There are three major qualifications to our discussion of the labor process. First, workers exert some control over the labor process through collective and individual behavior. Second, there is nothing "natural" about having capitalists control the labor process. Third, there is nothing "unnatural" about working hard (when it is in your interest to do so). Let's take these in order.

Are workers powerless in the face of capitalist control over the labor process? Hardly. Indeed, much of the historical evolution of the systems for control has been a response to worker resistance (Gordon, Edwards, and Reich, 1982; Jacoby, 1985). Seniority systems, wage ladders, grievance procedures, and other aspects of technical and bureaucratic control in many ways emerged as a concession to workers. Unions and the labor movement were influential in the attitude of class compromise, which was consolidated after World War II—only to see this compromise evaporate since the late 1970s as unions have grown weaker and weaker. The systems of control thus serve the interests of management, but they do so in a way that responds to the demands and struggles of working people. Conflicting interests do not disappear even with the most effective managerial control.

Employers have a legal right to design the labor process, but this does not have to be the case. We can imagine a system where workers make the decisions about work organization, work rules, pay and promotion, technological choice, and so on. This would require a very different type of economic system than ours is at present. In capitalism, the owner of capital is vested with control over all aspects of the labor process as a result of property rights—the legal rights that are imbued in capital ownership. Capitalists have the right to make these decisions, because the government has granted them the legal right to do so, not because there is some economic necessity in their being the decision makers. To us, it may seem inevitable simply because it is all that most of us have ever observed, but in fact, it is nothing more than a legal arrangement—albeit one with substantial consequences.

Finally, note that this conflict does not mean work is inherently disagreeable. Most of us gain more from work than our paycheck. Much of our identity and self-respect comes from work. This, however, does not mean that our primary objective at work is to maximize the firm's profits. Of course, the more stake that workers have, the harder they will work. Studies have shown that productivity rises when workers can exercise their judgment, express themselves, and/or directly benefit from the work process or product (Appelbaum and Batt, 1994). Unfortunately, few of these conditions apply to most work situations. Most workers have little or no say in what is produced, how it is produced, where investment should take place, or what the firm's priorities should be regarding its workers and community. Work is designed to benefit the capitalist; workers are only a means to an end.

EXPLAINING WAGE DIFFERENTIALS

We now turn to the ways in which political economists explain wage differences among workers. Political economists have two ways of explaining these differences. The first, labor segmentation, refers to a hierarchy of jobs that have developed in capitalism over time. We have already alluded to a hierarchy of workers by discussing the role of managers in shaping the work process. The second explanation of wage differences has to do with tradition (i.e., customary levels of wages for different jobs, but more importantly for different workers). This second explanation largely relies on understanding how discrimination works in labor markets.

Labor Segmentation: Divide and Conquer Everywhere

So far, we have seen that managers try to motivate workers through threats of job loss and to govern them with various control strategies. However, there also are larger patterns in the economy that help the firm to extract labor at low cost. These patterns concern the fact that distinct types of workers are hired for particular types of jobs by certain types of firms, so firm, job, and worker types are connected. The theory that makes this connection and explains wage differences between workers is called labor segmentation theory (Gordon, Edwards, and Reich, 1982).[15]

> *Segmentation: A bundling of firm, job, and worker characteristics that limits worker opportunities and divides the work force*

Segmentation means that the labor market is split into distinct portions, which diverge in terms of the organization of work, employment and wage-setting processes, and labor market outcomes. Table 7.1 summarizes the characteristics of labor segments. There are two main labor segments (or sectors): the primary and the secondary.

> *Primary independent sector: High-wage, white-collar, professional jobs with employer-sponsored benefits and career ladders*

The primary sector contains jobs that pay living wages, provide a range of employer-sponsored benefits, have opportunities for promotion or regular wage increases, and in which education and experience pay off. The primary sector is divided into two subsectors: the primary independent and the primary subordinate. The primary independent sector contains white-collar, high-paying jobs in which entry largely is a function of educational credentials. The primary subordinate sector contains blue-collar, high-paying jobs. The jobs often are unionized, and pay increases come with seniority and experience. Primary subordinate jobs require specific skills, but these often are obtained on the job. Social networks and family connections are important factors in getting these jobs.

> *Primary subordinate sector: Medium-wage, blue-collar, skilled and semiskilled jobs with job security*

The secondary sector contains jobs that pay poorly, offer little or nothing in the way of job benefits, and typically are dead-end. Many of us have held these jobs at some point in our lives, but chances are that if you are reading this book, you are trying to get the necessary skills or credentials to never have to work at a job in this sector again.

Secondary sector: low-wage, blue- or pink-collar, jobs in which skills do not pay off and which offer little job security

Mobility between the segments is restricted, so the competitive assumptions of neoclassical economics have only limited applicability. In addition to the forces of supply and demand, labor markets depend on social and institutional factors, such as the control system in the labor process, the race and gender of the workforce, and the size and structure of the firm—but this is jumping ahead of the game. We return to the role of race and gender in labor segments in the next chapter.

According to the theory of labor segmentation, distinct types of labor control strategies will be linked to different types of labor markets (Edwards, 1979). Workers in simple control systems are found in the secondary sector of the labor market, workers in technical control systems the primary subordinate sector of the labor market, and workers in bureaucratic control systems the primary independent sector of the labor market. Each sector has distinct wage and employment setting processes and, consequently, distinct sets of labor market outcomes.

Wage- and employment-setting processes vary from one control system and segment to another. This assertion received confirmation in an influential study by economists William Dickens and Kevin Lang, who found that wages are set in the economy in different ways, with some people (primary subordinate and primary independent sector) receiving higher wage returns to education than others (secondary sector).[16] This means that supply and demand provide only a partial explanation for how wages are decided. Let's take a closer look at how wages are set in the three sectors.

The secondary sector is the low-wage portion of the labor market. Employment growth is sensitive to the business cycle, because these firms usually subsist on cash flow, making their employment highly responsive to current sales. With few returns on experience or education, turnover tends to be high. As a result, unionization is difficult. Jobs in this sector are more likely to be part-time and/or part-year jobs. This gives employers maximum flexibility. People with less than full-time labor market commitments (e.g., full-time students, people with young or several children) often have to take these types of jobs—even when they have considerable experience or education—because they need jobs that require less than a 40-hour-per-week commitment. These are not desirable jobs (see Box 7.4).

With people regularly flowing in and out of secondary sector jobs, you might think that the laws of supply and demand would apply more strongly here than in either of the primary sectors. This is basically correct, but there are two important reasons why, even in the secondary sector, supply and demand do not rule alone. First, the government sets minimum wage levels, so even secondary sector jobs may be hard to get. For example, anthropologists Katherine

TABLE 7.1
CHARACTERISTICS OF LABOR SEGMENTS

Type of segments	Type of control	Job conditions	Wages	Examples
Primary independent	Bureaucratic or simple	Job security & job ladders	High	Managers, engineers
Primary subordinate	Technical bureaucratic	Job security	High to medium	Auto workers
Secondary	Simple or technical	No job security	Low	Sales clerk

---

BOX 7.4

NICKEL AND DIMED: LIFE IN THE SECONDARY LABOR SEGMENT

Barbara Ehrenreich, in doing her own personal research on the assertion by policymakers and others that poor single mothers didn't need welfare because they could get a job, placed herself in their shoes and went looking for jobs that most low-income mothers would find—jobs in the secondary labor segment. She held jobs as a waitress, motel "chambermaid," a dietary aide in a nursing home, a housecleaner, and a retail clerk in a hardware store and at Walmart. She chronicles her experiences in her 2002 book *Nickel and Dimed: On (Not) Getting by in America*.

Here's what she finds. In all these jobs, the wages were low. Indeed, in most of the jobs she had she was barely paid enough to pay her rent and buy food, even though she was only supporting herself, not any children. She talks frequently of overbearing managers (mostly men) who personally supervised her work and those of her co-workers. However, unlike the way many people describe this work (including academics), doing each of these jobs required a host of new skills that Ehrenreich did not have (even though she has a doctorate in biology). All of the jobs required an inordinate amount of physical stamina and finely honed social skills to deal with clients and managers.

It is hard to miss the sexual and racial composition of labor in the secondary labor segment. Most of Ehrenreich's co-workers (doing the same work as she was) were female. She also found that she had to move to the whitest states she could find (Maine and Minnesota) in order to get hired in any of these jobs, since she found employers in Florida much preferred African-American, Latina, and immigrant women.

Source: Barbara Ehrenreich. 2001. *Nickel and Dimed: On (Not) Getting by in America.* New York: Metropolitan Books.

Newman and Chauncy Lennon (1995) document the extreme difficulty that people have in getting even minimum wage jobs in Harlem. Second, because secondary sector jobs provide no job security or career ladders, the firm may have to pay enough so that the cost of job loss is positive; it's the only way to get workers to perform in such jobs.[17]

Firms that are characterized by technical control set wages and employment by different means. Wages and benefits are set by negotiations with unions and depend on bargaining strength as well as supply and demand. These firms are capital intensive, which means that disruptions to production (e.g., strikes) are expensive. Therefore, they tend to pay higher wages, offer decent benefit packages, and limit managerial discretion with seniority rules and grievance procedures. Returns on education are low, but returns on experience are high. Employment traditionally is stable, because on-the-job training is costly, encouraging firms to "hoard" labor during economic downturns. However, unemployment can become severe during periods of economic turmoil, such as in the 1980s.

In firms or labor processes that are characterized by bureaucratic control, professional, technical, and administrative functions are dominant. These positions generally are non-unionized but highly paid, with high returns on both education and experience. Wages and benefits usually are determined by internal labor markets (Doeringer and Piore, 1971), where people are paid according to their job title and rewards take the form of promotions to job titles with higher pay. Internal labor markets are separated from the forces of supply and demand, because wages and promotion opportunities are set by administrative rules. Incentives are created by well-developed promotional ladders offering opportunities for mobility within the firm. On-the-job training is extensive and supplemented by high average levels of education among the workforce. Therefore, employment tends to be stable as the costs of turnover are high for both the employee and the firm. Further, employers expect workers to be fully committed to their jobs and available for overtime or to take work home if necessary. Here is where the firm requires loyalty and often creates "jobs with wives," leaving workers precious little flexibility or time for activities such as caring for children or older relatives.

Internal labor markets: Where firms create job ladders and promote workers from within

In sum, supply and demand play a strong role under simple control in determining wages, but this is tempered by government minimum wage requirements and the need to set wages high enough to produce a positive cost of job loss. Under technical control, the game of bargaining between organized workers and employers will work alongside supply and demand to determine wages. Under bureaucratic control, wages are attached to positions on job ladders and set internally by management, with only a minimal role for supply and demand.

Now, we need to bring divide and conquer into the picture. We introduced this notion in Chapter 6 when discussing ways for firms to profit by setting subcontractors or employees into competition with each other (see Box 6.2). Political economists such as David Gordon, Richard Edwards, and Michael Reich (1982) argue that labor segmentation exists because it divides workers and, in the process, conquers them, such that the firm can make money.

Divide and conquer: Capitalist attempts to profit by splitting workers into groups that compete against each other

Divide and conquer fits into labor segmentation in several ways. First, consider the problem of management. To produce, capitalist firms create a natural group that has an interest in collective behavior—the firm's employees. However, if the employees act collectively against the firm, profits will fall. Segmentation solves this problem partly by dividing workers into the employed and the unemployed. Employed workers may believe they are being exploited and so band together, but if the cost of job loss is positive, the firm can always threaten to replace every last worker who makes so much as a move to join a union or band together in other ways. The firm can simply leave for sunnier shores with lower wages.

Second, in the case of bureaucratic control, workers are divided by promotion opportunities. Workers are told to "keep your nose clean" and you'll get promoted; joining a union in such circumstances is a pretty sure way to damage your career.

Third, workers are divided by education and occupation, such that those who have good jobs will believe they have little in common with those who do not. Limits on mobility between the segments are partly responsible for this division, but the lack of "good" jobs and their being given only to highly educated workers also contributes. This division has become even more severe in the last decade. Jobs in the primary subordinate sector have been severely cut by deindustrialization as manufacturing firms closed their doors in the United States and reopened them in Taiwan or Singapore. Jobs in the primary independent sector have grown, but much more slowly than jobs in the secondary sector have. Most job growth over the 1980s went to low-wage jobs, many of them part-time or contingent (Harrison and Bluestone, 1988). Thus, the ability of workers to transit between the secondary sector and the primary sector has become even more limited. This restriction also has led to "credential inflation," because employers increasingly can demand higher and higher levels of schooling from applicants seeking primary sector jobs. It also has meant that many workers, including many white males, have found that their probability of downward mobility has been much greater than their probability of upward mobility. In addition, by the logic of divide and conquer, capitalists will strive to convince white male workers who are threatened with losing their primary sector jobs that it is not the fault of the firm but instead of affirmative action, immigrants, or government interference that caused the problem.

Along with providing a theory of wage differentials, labor segmentation (like the cost of job loss and labor control strategies) represents another capitalist response to the problem of conflicting interests with workers. Workers have a material interest in collective behavior, but the context of labor segmentation inhibits them from acting in their interests. Labor segmentation implies that the link between productivity and wages is tenuous at best (Box 7.5).

The New Labor Segmentation

The model of labor segmentation described above is a less accurate picture of the labor market today than it was in the early 1980s. Deindustrialization (discussed in Chapter 2) has meant that primary subordinate jobs in manufacturing have been disappearing for decades. Global production and increased competition has also meant that the job security enjoyed by both primary subordinate and primary independent jobholders has also largely vanished (Capelli 1999). Job security was a key ingredient in the functioning of internal labor markets, so the implicit promise to many workers that if they worked hard the corporation would take care of them has been broken. Further, even where job ladders continued to exist, the absence of job security made the rungs on the ladders increasingly slippery. Finally, with wages falling for the average male, the possibilities for "jobs with wives" became increasingly rare, and women entered the workforce in droves, denying employers and employees the guarantee of uninterrupted and unpaid work in the home. So, if the old form of segmentation has disappeared, what has taken its place?

Recent research by economist Kenneth Hudson (2007) suggests that the importance of race and gender in filling secondary sector jobs has declined, while nonstandard work arrangements (like part-time, temporary, or work from home) and immigrant status have become more important for filling jobs at the bottom of the labor market. At the top of the economy, a norm developed around a growing group of "ideal workers," as described by Joan Williams (1999).

> *Ideal workers: highly educated managers and professionals who receive high wages and benefits in exchange for long work hours over periods of years or even decades*

Robert Drago (2007) has traced the emergence of ideal workers, defining them as employees holding at least a bachelor's degree and working at least 45 hours per week. In 1977, ideal workers represented only 7% of employees, while by 2002 they encompassed over 17% of the workforce. Looking at the 2002 data, he compared the ideal workers to others, and found that ideal workers are more likely to be managers and professionals (79.4% compared to 23.6% for others), to be salaried (80.3% to 24.7%), and to have family health insurance (96.6% to 74.6%). But they are also more likely to be interrupted by the job while at home (84.9% to 55.1%).

Most students reading this will already have a good idea of what the ideal worker norm entails, because you probably expect to be one. And if you have thought about it much, you may have already figured out that most good jobs now involve working 50 to 60 hours per week, with lots of work on weeknights and weekends, and few vacations.

At the other end of the economy, we find an expansion of low-wage work, and of employer flexibility, along with the "motherization of poverty." Drago defines low-wage workers as those earning less than $8.50 per hour in 2002 dollars (this was the real value of the minimum wage at its height in 1968). In 1977, the low-wage group accounted for 11% of all employees, but the proportion almost doubled to 20% by 2002. Employers increasingly seized power over those workers in the weakest position in the economy by lowering their wages.

Employers were not only able to force the wages of the poorest workers down, they were also increasingly able to force these employees to work a mishmash of hours to suit the firm's needs, a phenomenon known as *employer flexibility*. Walmart, the largest employer in the United States (outside of the federal government), decided to take advantage of this flexibility in 2006.

BOX 7.5
MARGINAL PRODUCTIVITY AND WAGES?

Productivity differentials may be more of a consequence than a cause of wage differentials. If they expect to receive different returns, women and minorities may make different investment decisions in their human capital than white men. High quit rates may be the result of low wages, rather than the other way around, as is frequently asserted. People might earn low wages not because they lack intelligence and creativity, but because they lack the opportunity to exercise their intelligence and creativity. Low wages may reduce incentives and, therefore, output and productivity. Although neoclassical economists believe that causality runs from productivity to wages, it is easy to think of likely ways in which causality runs the other way around. The same association between wages and productivity exists in both cases, but the direction of causality—and hence, the interpretation of inequality—is reversed.

The suspicion with which political economists view the wage–productivity relation is understandable in light of the extreme difficulties that are attached to measuring productivity. No one has ever measured marginal productivity for anyone other than special groups, such as baseball players. For most workers, an increase in hiring corresponds to an increased use of capital, so it is impossible to isolate the pure effect of a change in labor input on output. It is equally difficult to prove that the productivity of capital determines profits, because there is no agreement on how to define or measure the contribution of the capitalist to production. Furthermore, the belief that pay rises with skill is more difficult to prove than you might think. Skills are multidimensional and cannot be summed into a single measurement. Some skills, such as child-rearing, go almost completely unrewarded despite being at least as complex as, and probably more important than, other types of highly rewarded skills, such as financial management. It also is worth noting that in some historical periods (e.g., the 1950s and 1960s), wage and productivity growth both were closely tied together, while in other periods (such as the early 1990s), wage growth has lagged behind productivity growth. The belief that productivity determines incomes is frequently used to justify the inequalities created by capitalism, but there simply is no clear-cut evidence that this linkage holds true.

If you ask around, you will find at least a few people who have taken a job and begun working *without even finding out how much they will be paid*! Usually, this can be traced to the job applicant's fear that "if I ask, I might not get the job." Political economy explains this phenomenon by the fact that many workers have few viable alternatives to working for capitalists, so they will take a job almost regardless of the wage. For political economists, wage determination is complicated, as the employer in this case would likely take the context into consideration (for instance, how much other employees are earning, how much the employee expects to earn, what other firms are paying, etc.) as well as the revenues the job will generate.

Walmart had been employing a mixture of 20% part-time and 80% full-time employees, and realized that part-timers were cheaper (because the subsidy for health insurance is so low that many part-timers simply skip health insurance through Walmart). The corporation set about doubling the proportion of part-timers to 40%. Wall Street analysts loved the strategy, and they loved it even more when Walmart simultaneously set a policy requiring *all* employees to be on-call, twenty-four hours and seven days a week, to better meet the needs of customers. Of course, what that really meant was that Walmart wanted to move employees to "family times" like nights and weekends, when customers have more time to shop, but at the expense of family time for Walmart employees.[18]

The motherization of poverty occurred at the precise moment when women were making the greatest strides in terms of entry into higher education and managerial and professional jobs. At the high end, women only represented a little under a quarter of ideal workers in 1977, but came close to *half* by 2002. But the story for women in general misses what happened to mothers. Mothers represented 5% of ideal workers in 1977, and that figure only rose to 7% by 2002. So where were the moms?

They were increasingly represented among low-wage workers. The proportion of women who were low-wage workers actually shrank from 1977 to 2002 (from around 73% to just over 60%), in part because a substantial proportion of men lost their good factory jobs over the period. But the proportion of mothers rose from around 34% to 42%. So a lot of the Walmart employees who are now on call *also* have children at home.

Mothers were also increasingly prevalent among Americans living in poverty. As of 2004, data from the Current Population Survey found that adult men and women who were married with no children experienced a poverty rate of 3.4%. That rate more than doubled, to 7% if the couple had a child. For single *fathers*, the rate more than doubles again, to 18.2%, but for single *mothers*, the rate again more than quadruples, to 37.7%.

So the new model of labor segmentation appears to involve a cleaner dividing line between the primary sector where highly educated "haves" work, with long hours and high wages, and a secondary sector where the "have-nots" receive low wages, often live in poverty, and are forced to adapt to bosses who enjoy lots of flexibility. We also know that mothers appear frequently at the bottom. What about the other groups of concern here?

Traditions: Faces Filling Places

As it turns out, workers are divided under labor segmentation by race and gender. Jobs in each sector are not shared proportionately. The upper echelons of the primary sector are disproportionately white and what is left of the primary dependent sector is disproportionately male. Women and people of color have the lion's share of secondary sector jobs. However, segmentation theory per se does not tell us why certain groups find themselves in the secondary or the primary sectors, only that those divisions exist.[19] In short, certain faces end up filling certain places, and this is not an arbitrary process.

One way to understand why women and blacks predominate in the secondary sector is to argue that those are the jobs that women and blacks have always held. Traditional gender and race roles in the labor market get reproduced over time. Although this is true, scratching the surface and asking why the tradition exists requires thinking more seriously about labor market discrimination. Political economists have much to say on this topic, and it is the subject of the next chapter.

SUMMARY

The political economy view of wage-setting starts with the notion of conflicting interests: capitalists seek to exploit workers, and workers try to stop exploitation. The labor theory of value helps to explain why exploitation continues, because wages are set at the customary standard of living while workers produce more than is needed to maintain that standard. We then looked more closely at the role of tradition and institutions (as opposed to supply and demand) in influencing wages. Neoclassical economists who have been involved in actual wage-setting procedures admit that supply and demand play only a limited role, while political economists who delve more deeply into wage-setting institutions find that historical gender bias tends to survive in apparently "objective" rules.

The standard of living depends on more than take-home pay, however, because work in the home and the social wage also influence the standard of living. Considerations of home and the government dictate that we broaden our context for understanding wages and provide additional avenues for conflict and change over such ideas as the "family wage" or "jobs with wives."

We also considered unemployment, because this affects wage levels as well. In the political economy view, capitalist economies require unemployment and periodic increases in unemployment through business cycles to keep wages down and the cost of losing a job up. Unemployment is contradictory, however, because it reduces sales and may lead to collective action on the part of workers. One implication is that capitalists must constantly strive to convince workers that only individual hard work for low wages will "save" them from unemployment.

In their battle to extract work from workers, capitalists have various tools. Most important is lack of a viable alternative to employment for most people. Additionally, capitalists may create a positive cost of job loss so that workers worry about losing their jobs and work hard in response. Capitalists also may use various labor control strategies, such as simple, technical, or bureaucratic control, and the way that wages are set will depend on the control strategy that is applied to each group of workers.

Finally, we considered how political economists explain differences in wages among workers. Labor segmentation argues that different types of jobs carry different types of wages. Because there are different labor segments, there will be different wages. The two sectors that exist today are the primary and secondary sectors. The labor segments also help to explain wage differences and to create divisions between workers that are so effective that workers will be loyal to the firm and, possibly, even have shared interests with the firm's owners.

While labor segments describe why wages differ by jobs, they do not explain why women and blacks tend to get the worst jobs. Political economists turn to theories of discrimination for that, which are discussed in the next chapter.

DISCUSSION QUESTIONS

1. If you wanted to, could you start your own business and make as much money as you would with a career-type job?

2. Can you think of examples from your own experience where one person provided unpaid labor to the firm where a spouse was employed?

3. Is there some form of governmental support that, if removed, would reduce your standard of living? If there is, would you be willing to give up that support if your taxes were reduced accordingly?

4. Have you ever worked at a job you worried about losing because of lost wages? If so, could you calculate the approximate "cost of job loss" for that job?

5. Can you identify further examples of jobs with simple control, technical control, and bureaucratic control?

6. What has happened to someone you know who used to work in the "primary" sector and lost a job during the recession starting in 2008? Did the person find another primary sector job or instead move into the "secondary" sector?

7. Thinking of a job that you or someone you know has held, do you believe the wages were set by supply and demand, so that people performing similar jobs at different workplaces received the same wage? Do you think considerations of fairness entered in? Were job evaluations used? Did the wages set by the organization lead to women earning less than men or blacks less than whites?

8. If you know someone who recently lost his or her job, do you think it was that person's fault? Does the person who lost the job believe that it was his or her fault? What happened to that person's standard of living and lifestyle after losing the job?

SUGGESTED READINGS

Albelda, Randy and Chris Tilly. 1997. *Glass Ceilings and Bottomless Pits: Women Work, Women's Poverty.* Boston, MA: South End Press.

Appelbaum, Eileen and Rosemary Batt. 1994. *The New American Workplace.* Ithaca, NY: ILR Press.

Bernstein, Jared. 2005. "Snapshot: African Americans in the Current Recovery." Washington, DC: Economic Policy Institute. Retrieved October 2009, http://www.epi.org/economic_snapshots/entry/webfeatures_snapshots_20050406/.

Boddy, Radford and James Crotty. 1975. "Class Conflict and Macro-Policy: The Political Business Cycle." *Review of Radical Political Economics* 7, Spring.

Bowles, Samuel. 1985. "The Production Process in a Competitive Economy." *American Economic Review* 77(1), March.

Bowles, Samuel, David M. Gordon, and Thomas E. Weisskopf. 1983. *Beyond the Waste Land: A Democratic Alternative to Economic Decline.* New York: Anchor/Doubleday.

Braverman, Harry. 1974. *Labor and Monopoly Capital.* New York: Monthly Review Press.

Bravo, Ellen. 1995. *The Job/Family Challenge: Not for Women Only.* New York: John Wiley & Sons.

Cappelli, Peter. 1999. "Career Jobs Are Dead." *California Management Review* 42.

Cloward, Richard A. and Frances Fox Piven. 1982. *The New Class War: Reagan's Attack on the Welfare State and Its Consequences.* New York: Pantheon Books.

Doeringer, Peter and Michael Piore. 1971. *Internal Labor Markets and Manpower Analysis.* Lexington, MA: Lexington Books.

Drago, Robert. 2007. *Striking a Balance: Work, Family, Life.* Boston: Dollars & Sense.

Dunlop, John T. 1979. "Wage Contours." In *Unemployment and Inflation.* Michael J. Piore, ed. White Plains, NY: M.E. Sharpe Inc.

Edwards, Richard. 1979. *Contested Terrain.* New York: Basic Books.

Figart, Deborah, Ellen Mutari and Marilyn Power. 2002. *Living Wages, Equal Wages: Gender and Labor Market Policies in the United States.* London and New York: Routledge.

Gintis, Herbert. 1976. "The Nature of Labor Exchange and the Theory of Capitalist Production." *Review of Radical Political Economics* 8, Summer.

Gordon, David M., Richard Edwards, and Michael Reich. 1982. *Segmented Work, Divided*

Workers. Cambridge: Cambridge University Press.

Harrison, Bennett and Barry Bluestone. 1988. *The Great U-Turn: Corporate Restructuring and the Polarizing of America.* New York: Basic Books.

Hudson, Kenneth. 2007. "The New Labor Market Segmentation," *Social Science Research* 36(1).

Jacoby, Sanford. 1985. *Employing Bureaucracy.* New York: Columbia University Press.

Kessler-Harris, Alice. 1982. *Out to Work: A History of Wage-Earning Women in the United States.* New York: Oxford University Press.

Keynes, John Maynard. 1936. *The General Theory of Employment, Interest, and Money.* New York: Harcourt, Brace and Co.

Kim, Marlene. 1989. "Gender Bias in Compensation Structures: A Case Study of Its Historical Basis and Persistence." *Journal of Social Issues* 45(4).

Matthaei, Julie. 1982. *An Economic History of Women in America: Women's Work, the Sexual Division of Labor, and the Development of Capitalism.* New York: Schocken Books.

Miller, John. 1992. "A Negative Social Wage and the Reproduction Crisis of the 1980's." In *International Perspectives on Profitability and Accumulation.* Fred Mosley and Edward N. Wolff, eds. Aldershot, England: Edward Elgar.

Newman, Katherine and Chauncy Lennon. 1995. "Finding Work in the Inner City: How Hard Is It Now? How Hard Will It Be for AFDC Recipients?" Mimeo. Department of Anthropology, Columbia University.

Reich, Michael. 1981. *Racial Inequality: A Political-Economic Analysis.* Princeton, NJ: Princeton University Press.

Solow, Robert. 1990. *The Labor Market as a Social Institution.* Cambridge, MA: Basil Blackwell.

Shulman, Steven. 1990. "Racial Inequality and White Employment: An Interpretation and Test of the Bargaining Power Hypothesis." *Review of Black Political Economy* 18(3), Winter.

Steinberg, Ronnie. 1990. "Social Construction of Skill: Gender, Power, and Comparable Worth." *Work and Occupations* 17(4), November.

Tabb, William. 2007. "Wage Stagnation, Growing Insecurity, and the Future of the U.S. Working Class," *Monthly Review* 59(2).

Williams, Joan. 1999. *Unbending Gender: Why Work and Family Conflict and What to Do About It.* New York: Oxford University Press.

ENDNOTES

[1] Historically, economics was known as the "dismal science," because early economists like Thomas Malthus were convinced that population would grow faster than the food supply, resulting in mass starvation—pretty dismal.

[2] "Clipping coupons" refers to the way in which bondholders used to be paid for lending money. Each bond had a set of coupons attached that, periodically, bondholders would clip and redeem for money.

[3] Albert Rees, "The Role of Fairness in Wage Determination," *Journal of Labor Economics* 11(1), 1993.

[4] Ibid., pp. 251–252.

[5] Figures from Ronnie Steinberg, "The Debate on Comparable Worth," *New Politics* 1 (Spring 1986), p. 114. See also The Hay Group, "Hay Job Evaluation" (2005) at www.haygroup.com/downloads/ww/wp-Job_Evaluation.pdf.

[6] Marlene Kim, "Gender Bias in Compensation Structures: A Case Study of Its Historical Basis and Persistence." *Journal of Social Issues* 45(4), 1989; p. 42.

[7]This example is from Ronnie Steinberg and Lois Haignere, "Equitable Compensation: Methodological Criteria for Comparable Worth," in *Ingredients in Women's Employment Policies*. Christine Bose and Glenna Spitze, eds. Albany, NY: SUNY Press, 1986; p. 167.

[8]For example, see www.bbk.ac.uk.jobevaluation/evaluation.

[9]For social expenditure figures, see www.libraryindex.com/pages/72/How-Much-Does-Nation-Spend-on-Welfare.html]. The last publication by the Social Security Administration on social welfare expenditures can be found at http://www.socialsecurity.gov/policy/docs/statcomps/supplements/2002/3a.pdf.

[10]The evidence here is from Carolyn C. Perrucci, Robert Perrucci, Dena B. Targ, and Harry R. Targ, *Plant Closings, International Context and Social Costs*, New York: Aldine De Gruyter, 1988.

[11]See D.W. Riegle, Jr., "The Psychological and Social Effects of Unemployment," *American Psychologist* 37, October 1982.

[12]"Manage" originally meant "to train (a horse) in his paces." Now, it means "to get (a person) to do what one wishes, especially by skill, tact, flattery, etc.; to make docile or submissive to control." Source: *Webster's New Twentieth Century Dictionary*, Unabridged, 2nd ed., New York: Simon & Schuster, 1979, p. 1093.

[13]There also are various neoclassical versions of this argument. See George Akerlof and Janet Yellen, eds., *Efficiency Wage Models of the Labor Market*, New York: Cambridge University Press, 1986.

[14]For example, a superior technological alternative to numerical machine tools (which can, supposedly, be operated by unskilled workers) was abandoned for this reason. See David Noble, *Forces of Production*, Oxford: Oxford University Press, 1986.

[15]The term labor market segmentation originally was used to capture the idea that one group of workers—inner-city black men—were locked out of labor markets for good jobs. In recent political economy discussions, the simpler term labor segmentation is used, because segmentation applies to jobs within firms and types of firms as well as in markets.

[16]See William T. Dickens and Kevin Lang, "A Test of Dual Labor Market Theory," *American Economic Review* 75(4), September 1985.

[17]Economist James Rebitzer finds evidence that secondary sector employers set wages high enough so that a positive cost of job loss exists. See James Rebitzer, "Unemployment, Long-Term Employment Relations and Productivity Growth," *Review of Economics and Statistics* 69(4), November 1987.

[18]Steven Greenhouse and Michael Barbaro, "Wal-Mart to Add Wage Caps and Part-timers," *New York Times*, Oct. 2, 2006.

[19]The segments define jobs, not the people who fill them. See Randy Albelda and Chris Tilly, "Towards a Broader Vision: Race, Gender, and Labor Market Segmentation in the Social Structure of Accumulation Framework," in *Social Structures of Accumulation*, David M. Kotz, Terrence McDonough, and Michael Reich, eds., Cambridge: Cambridge University Press, 1994.

8

THE POLITICAL ECONOMY MODEL
OF DISCRIMINATION

INTRODUCTION: EXPLOITATION, DOMINATION, AND EXCLUSION AGAIN

In the last chapter, you learned how political economists view labor markets and the workplace. This chapter builds on that analysis to highlight race and gender inequality. In other words, we now put "faces" into the "places" outlined in Chapter 7. Those places are defined by inequality—between capitalists and workers, the employed and the unemployed, workers in the primary and in secondary sectors, and those who are expected to work for pay and those who are not. This chapter develops a theory of discrimination to understand who ends up in these respective positions.

For political economists, discrimination is primarily perceived to be "institutional," in that it is embedded in the customs and rules that govern the behaviors of institutions (e.g., the family), organizations (e.g., the firm), and markets (e.g., the job market). In this view, one concern is that institutional discrimination may persist even if the ideas and motives of individuals change. On the other hand, institutions, organizations, and markets also can change, so discrimination need not last forever. Collective action can reduce race and gender inequality through its impact on social attitudes, market dynamics, organizational behavior, and government policies.

The emphasis on institutional discrimination does not mean that political economists are indifferent to racial and sexual prejudices and attitudes among individuals. Political economists are well aware that the conflicts between counterpart groups can encourage people to stereotype, objectify, and sometimes even hate each other. Discrimination can provide "psychic benefits" if the damage inflicted on one group builds the self-esteem of another.[1] Indeed, it is exactly because discrimination creates social divisions that allow one group to gain economic, political, or social power by oppressing a clearly defined "other" that attitudes and beliefs can become so entrenched. In this sense, these divisions can be viewed as the consequence of discrimination rather than the cause.

In this chapter we argue there are three keys to distinguishing the neoclassical and political economy views of discrimination. First, neoclassical economists believe that the discriminator often pays for discrimination, while political economists believe the discriminator often benefits. Second, neoclassical economists view discrimination as an individual phenomenon, while political economists view it as being related to oppression and counterpart groups. Third, neoclassical economists believe that discrimination will have a short shelf-life in a competitive economy, while political economists believe discrimination will persist unless there is collective action to oppose it.

This chapter looks at the ways in which political economists understand discrimination: who are the winners and losers, why it persists, and how it changes over the business cycle—as well as over long periods of U.S. history. It explains why political economists view discrimination as being a function of group behavior and interests rather than individual tastes, which is in turn closely linked to exploitation, exclusion, and domination. In this view, discrimination is not simply inefficient, but rather it helps one group to hold power over (or make money from) another group.

DISCRIMINATION IN CONTEXT: WHAT YOU DON'T KNOW CAN HURT YOU

Political economists tackle the analysis of discrimination by applying the "Four Cs" of political economy: context, collective behavior, conflicting interests, and change. Political economists think about discrimination in a way that connects our collective past with our collective present. Genocide, slavery, disenfranchisement, violence, poverty, segregation, and ghettoization are the backdrops for contemporary discrimination. At the same time, the Civil Rights movement, the women's movement, and other social and political changes have had an enormous impact on race and gender relations and fundamentally altered the way in which discrimination works. When political economists analyze discrimination, they seek to show not only how the present reflects the past, but also how it is different from it, and can be different still, in the future.

Because political economists see discrimination as part of a historical process, it is easy to see why they consider discrimination to be an important component of a system of racial and gender oppression. By paying women less than men, or blacks less than whites, capitalists not only exploit workers but also help to maintain systems of oppression that exist outside of the firm and the labor market. If women or blacks are not paid enough to be self-supporting, their economic options are limited, and with limited economic options, it is difficult to escape other forms of oppression. Eliminating discrimination in labor markets is difficult, in part because it serves an important role in upholding long-standing and firmly held notions of the racial and gender pecking order.

Judging and harming people based on their skin color, country of origin, gender, or sexual orientation—discrimination—occurs today and has occurred for a long, long time. The political economist usually does not take it as his or her task to discover the original source of people's desires to discriminate, but rather seeks to understand how discrimination is translated into system-wide mechanisms that result in unequal outcomes. Why some people feel that women are best suited to stay at home to raise children is of less interest than understanding how that notion translates into a generally accepted assumption that women should earn less than men. The issue of individual productivity, which is so central to the neoclassical analysis of discrimination, drops into the background here, because productivity is associated with jobs rather than individuals and is only loosely connected to wages (as we saw in Chapter 7).

Discrimination cannot always be directly observed or measured. You might "know discrimination when you see it," but then again, you might not. Few people in this day and age admit to actively practicing discrimination, and even fewer will tell a member of a counterpart group "Yes, I am discriminating against you" by not hiring you, not giving you a promotion, or not giving you a raise. Indeed, although numerous court cases have resulted in findings of discrimination, these cases frequently use statistical evidence that is unavailable when people apply for jobs. Similarly, studies in which equally qualified black and white candidates apply for the same jobs consistently indicate racial discrimination in the labor market. Other studies involving equally qualified male and female job applicants show evidence of discrimination against mothers (Box 8.1). These studies demonstrate that those who experience discrimination often will not know it unless a test is performed. On the other side of the fence, people who discriminate might not know they are doing it.

BOX 8.1
DIRECT TESTS FOR DISCRIMINATION

In 1961, John Griffin's book *Black Like Me* was released. Griffin, a white man, decided to see what it was like to be black in America. He convincingly transformed his appearance and experienced racial discrimination firsthand. His book describes how despite being exactly the same person, the white John Griffin was treated very differently than the black John Griffin. Griffin felt what few whites in our society have—the power of the color line in the United States.

Griffin's "experiment" led researchers to think about direct tests for discrimination that would allow us to pull out more than just a wage residual which may or may not be linked to discrimination.

Basically, two types of tests are used to check for hiring discrimination. In the first, called a "correspondence" test, researchers scour want ads in newspapers or on the Internet for jobs where the employer asks that a resume be faxed or mailed in prior to any actual interview. Researchers then send employers resumes that are otherwise identical except some of the fictitious applicants have a racially identified name (e.g., Lakisha for a black woman) or signal difference by including information about membership in a racially identified organization such as the NAACP. Each prospective employer receives only one application to make sure the employers cannot figure out that a test is involved. On average, whites are asked for further information or an interview around 50% more often than blacks. Of course, only certain types of jobs, typically administrative, clerical, or white collar, use a hiring procedure with an initial request for a resume, so we cannot know if this result applies to all or even to most jobs.

A related procedure is known as an "audit," where testers are trained to behave identically in job interviews, are given identical resumes, but differ by race. These studies reveal that white applicants are more likely to receive a positive response than black applicants by a factor of *between 50 and 500%!*

And even highly educated white students, who say they are not racially biased, often exhibit unconscious bias. In a simulation involving applications for a teaching fellowship, the students gave approval more often to whites than blacks. No surprise there. The surprise: film of the exercise found the whites *smiling* more often at white applicants as well.

And discrimination is hardly limited to race. A correspondence study found that mothers were less than half as likely as non-mother women to receive a positive response to a job application. But fathers received around twice as many positive responses as men who were not fathers.

Sources: Devah Pager, "The Use of Field Experiments for Studies of Employment Discrimination: Contributions, Critiques, and Directions for the Future," *Annals of the American Academy of Political and Social Sciences*, Vol. 609, January 2007. E.J. Vanman, J.L. Saltz, L.R. Nathan, and J.A. Warren, "Racial Discrimination by Low-Prejudiced Whites: Facial Movements as Implicit Measures of Attitudes Related to Behavior," *Psychological Science*, Vol. 15, 2007. Shelley Correll, Stephen Benard, and In Paik, "Getting a Job: Is There a Motherhood Penalty?" *American Journal of Sociology*, Vol. 112, March 2007.

The neoclassical understanding of discrimination presented in Chapter 5 presumes that workers can be unambiguously ranked in terms of their qualifications, and that wages generally reflect productivity. More often than not, however, qualifications vary in subtle ways between job applicants, because the characteristics of actual people come in "bundles." Someone may have a slight edge on interpersonal skills, another may be a better word processor, another a better leader, and another better organized. This bundling of characteristics opens the door to subjective interpretations about which job applicant is the most qualified. Employers often must rely on hunches and first impressions when comparing job candidates who look objectively more or less comparable. Employers may honestly and truthfully deny that they have discriminated—even when their decision-making consistently leads them to prefer white men. Is it still discrimination if there is no conscious intent to discriminate?

Political economists answer "yes." Discrimination can, and often does, result from unconscious behaviors and attitudes in individuals. It can stem from a social context that is built into the rules and structures of organizations and markets. This view contrasts sharply with the neoclassical perspective, in which discrimination is interpreted as a conscious choice made by individuals. The contrast is telling, and it is worth spending a moment to explore in some detail.

For political economists, discrimination involves more than individual choice. Of course, individuals can choose to discriminate, but discrimination also may occur even when individuals believe they are not discriminating. For example, if a firm recruits job applicants by using referrals from existing workers (the way that many job openings are filled), it may wind up with an all-white applicant pool because of residential and social segregation. Nobody at the firm is necessarily *trying* to discriminate, but the result is that nonwhites are systematically excluded from applying for job openings. It also may be the case that a male employer is more comfortable with, and sympathetic to, male applicants for a managerial position. Again, he may not be trying to discriminate, but he will tend to prefer the male applicants and genuinely believe that they are "more qualified" or "less risky" hires than the female applicants. In addition, a seniority system may result in a last-hired/first-fired pattern among minorities, who can never accumulate enough seniority to avoid layoffs. In all these cases—and in others that we discuss in this chapter—the rules of the game systematically put women and minorities at a disadvantage.

These examples illustrate the notion of institutional discrimination, which contrasts with the neoclassical emphasis on individual discrimination. Individual discrimination is carried out as a conscious decision by individuals and results from their particular prejudices. For this reason, individual discrimination corresponds to Gary Becker's concept of a "taste for discrimination." Institutional discrimination, however, is created by the rules and incentives of organizations such as firms, markets, and the government. It can be overt (e.g., segregation laws in the Jim Crow South) or covert (e.g., irrelevant employment tests that systematically exclude minorities), conscious (e.g., redlining minority neighborhoods by banks) or unconscious (e.g., difficulties in socializing or communicating with people who are "different"), rational (e.g., white unions minimize job competition by excluding blacks) or irrational (e.g., unions refuse to organize female workers). In all cases, however, the issue has less to do with the decisions of individuals than with the rules and incentives that govern the behavior of economic institutions and alter people's preferences, and in so doing, disadvantage women and minorities.

Institutional discrimination: Adverse treatment of women and minorities because of the explicit and implicit rules that regulate society or institutions

For an example of how institutional and individual discrimination differ, consider the situation facing a woman on a university faculty. To hold the job for more than seven years, she must be granted tenure, and to get tenure, she needs to work long hours (50, 60, or even 70 hours per week). If she has children, there is likely to be a serious time conflict, which ultimately may cost her the job. Few people would be surprised at this outcome given the sexual division of labor that is typical of most families. Yet, if we had been discussing a man going up for tenure, the issue of children would rarely even be mentioned, because the unwritten rules of family life work to benefit men—just as they work to disadvantage women. Nonetheless, it is doubtful that tenure rules were written with the *purpose* of discriminating. Nobody may bear any ill will toward female professors. The rules of the tenure game are applied equally, but their interactions with other rules make the game less fair.

A different face of institutional discrimination appears in the towns of Naperville and Aurora, Illinois, home of the Indian Prairie School District. These towns turned down proposals for single-family houses in the $65,000 to $75,000 range in favor of houses on large lots in the $300,000 range along with townhouses and apartments with one or two bedrooms. The purpose was to increase the tax base while keeping the number of primary and secondary public school students down. The intent was clearly discriminatory in terms of families with children, but the effects were undoubtedly larger as single mothers and black families, both of whom tend to have lower incomes than two-adult and white families, also were effectively excluded (as well as many of the "Indians" for whom the school district is named). The "rules" were applied equally, but the inequality of results was virtually foreordained.[2]

Neoclassical economists focus on individual discrimination, as it is consistent with their emphasis on individual choice and free markets. As discussed in Chapter 6, however, political economists place more emphasis on collective behavior and conflicting interests. Political economists therefore are more interested in institutional discrimination. They disagree with the neoclassical belief that capitalism tends to erode racism and sexism, and they believe that the notion of institutional discrimination can help us to understand the economic problems faced by women and minorities.

GROUNDS FOR DISCRIMINATION: ECONOMIC INCENTIVES AND ORGANIZATIONAL ADAPTATION

Political economists have two main ways of explaining why discrimination exists in labor markets. The first is that some people directly benefit from discrimination. In other words, there are strong economic incentives to discriminate, and both capitalists and white males may have a direct financial stake in discrimination within the firm. The second reason has to do with mirroring inside the firm the relations of oppression that exist outside of the firm. We refer to this phenomenon as organizational adaptation. It speaks to the ways in which traditional social beliefs and practices are transported into the firm so that it does not "rock the boat," even if in the abstract it is not always the most profitable solution. We discuss each argument in turn.

Economic Incentives

The neoclassical possibility that individuals "pay" to discriminate (as they would to indulge any other taste or prejudice) is turned on its head in the political economy framework. Here, much discrimination is perceived to be in the interests of those who practice it, and it is exactly for this reason that the political economy theory of discrimination does not depend on personal prejudice. Instead, discrimination is held to be self-sustaining because it generates rewards for those who are willing to discriminate (or at least unwilling to act against discrimination). Indeed, the forces of competition in such circumstances can actually work to perpetuate discrimination, as we shall argue in the following section. For now, however, we need to understand how discrimination can confer benefits and how these benefits can influence behavior.

Economic incentives—the potential monetary gains from behaving in a certain way—provide an economic explanation for discriminating based on group identity and conflict. Of course, historical, emotional, and political reasons for group identity and conflict are important, but there also are powerful economic forces that encourage and reward individuals for identifying with groups and, as groups, for engaging in collective conflict with other groups.

Benefits can be classified in terms of who receives them. The two broad groups that interact in the workplace are employers (including management) and employees. The political economy analysis of discrimination focuses on the potential benefits received by members of each group.

As argued by economist Michael Reich in his work *Racial Inequality* and by economist Robert Cherry in *Discrimination*, discrimination can benefit employers as a result of class struggle effects. Class struggle refers to the conflict between employers and employees over the distribution of income and the organization of work. Employers want to keep wages as low as possible and to maximize their control over the labor process. These goals are difficult to achieve when workers remain unified as a group. If workers recognize that they have common class interests and act together (by organizing a union, for example) to increase wages and establish their rights in the workplace, then management will face higher costs and lower profits. If workers fail to recognize their common interests, however, and therefore are unable to cooperate to achieve these goals, then management can retain the upper hand. Thus, management has a strong incentive to "divide-and-conquer" its workforce (as we discussed in Chapters 6 and 7).

Class struggle effects: The use of discrimination as a tool to increase profits by reducing the solidarity and bargaining power of workers

Given that class struggle is an inherent feature of all firms (except those that are employee owned), employers may systematically discriminate to keep workers physically and socially separate and stratified. In essence, this is an attempt to make it harder for workers to perceive and act on their common interests. The differences between white males, women, and minorities in society at large become mirrored in the workplace. Management may assign white male workers to the "best" jobs to reduce the chances that they will feel a need to cooperate with women and minority workers, who have the most to gain from a wage hike or improvement in conditions. Women and minorities may blame white male workers as much as management for their problems. If workers fight each other based on race or gender, they will find it much more difficult to unite as workers to achieve their common goals. As a result, wages for all workers (including white males) are kept down, and managerial control is enhanced.

In Reich's 1981 study, cities with greater income inequality between blacks and whites were found to be those in which firms made the highest profits, and the majority of white workers suffered corresponding wage losses. Reich took this to mean that capitalists have an incentive to create racial inequality (i.e., to discriminate) to weaken the bargaining power of workers. The conclusion of class struggle logic is that workers have the same fundamental interests, and that racism (and, by implication, sexism) results from "false consciousness."[3] The solution is for workers to "unite and fight" management for higher wages, better working conditions, and other demands. This is a simple and appealing strategy, and it often works.

Consider the following example. As Reich documents, the Congress of Industrial Organizations (CIO) was able to sweep by the old-line American Federation of Labor in the 1930s to win major gains for workers in terms of rights, job security, and wages, for many reasons. Among those was the CIO's explicit antiracism policy. Without such a "unite-and-fight" policy, it would have been much harder, if not impossible, for the United Auto Workers (part of the CIO) to organize the massive Ford River Rouge plant, since 13% of the workers there were black.

Unfortunately, this is not the entire story. The historical examples of unity between white and black workers, and between male and female workers, are so rare that "false consciousness" is unlikely to be the entire explanation for racial and gender divisions. Other studies fail to confirm Reich's conclusion that class struggle effects account for continuing racial (or gender) divisions in the United States. For example, economist Steven Shulman found that discrimination against black workers may improve the job prospects of whites. Therefore, the reason that whites and men have yet to unite with women and people of color may have less to do with their failure to see through capitalist attempts to divide and conquer than with the fact that they may benefit from discrimination.[4]

White male workers can benefit from discrimination as a result of job competition effects. The logic here is that if women and minorities are excluded from the "best" jobs, then white males will face less competition for them. This will improve their chances to earn higher wages, get promoted, and enjoy job security. Further, a reduction in job competition for white males means that they will be better positioned to find jobs for their (white male) relatives and friends. They also will be more likely to work among people like themselves, with whom they are comfortable and able to communicate. Job competition effects therefore benefit white males in five ways: higher wages, better promotional possibilities, enhanced job security, nepotism, and social comfort.

Job competition effects: The use of occupational exclusion of women and minorities to increase the wages and job security of white males

Job competition effects depend on the exclusion of women and minorities from consideration for certain jobs. Exclusion can result from direct or indirect intervention. Direct intervention (for example, a strike in protest of the hiring of black workers) was more common in the early part of the century. Today, indirect intervention by white male employees is the common method of exclusion. Instead of boldly presenting their demands, white males exert pressure in a more covert fashion: women coworkers may be sexually harassed, and black coworkers may be ostracized, ignored, or subtly informed that they got their new job through quotas rather than qualifications.

Management in general is therefore understandably hesitant to introduce women and minorities into previously all-white-male workgroups. Even if conflict does not arise, the fear of it is always present. Of course, management is not necessarily loathe to discriminate. Aside from benefitting from class struggle effects, management also may feel that it can maintain a positive relationship with its white male workers by encouraging them to feel that they have exclusive rights to certain jobs. This set of shared values and interests between management and workers (in this case, white male workers) is called hegemony. It is one means by which management maintains control over the labor process.

Although women and minorities are always hurt by discrimination, class struggle and job competition effects have a variety of effects on employers and white male employees. Class struggle effects benefit employers and hurt white male employees. Job competition effects benefit white male employees. The consequences of job competition effects for employers are more complicated. On the one hand, employers may benefit from the hegemonic control over white male workers that discrimination facilitates. On the other hand, job competition effects may reduce the ability of employers to make the best use of their human resources or to minimize their wage costs. It also may strengthen labor solidarity among white male workers, which can inhibit managerial control over those workers (see Chapter 7).[5]

BOX 8.2
BIG MONEY FROM DISCRIMINATING IN MILWAUKEE

While no one knows for certain how much capitalists or white males gain from discrimination, econometricians (i.e., economists specializing in statistical techniques) have devised methods that allow us to calculate the approximate gains under the extreme assumption that either job competition or class struggle effects, but not both, exist.

In both cases, we control for differences in experience, education, and other factors that could influence individual productivity (although for political economists, many of these differences may themselves be traced to discrimination).*

Given these assumptions, we can estimate the wages that white males would receive if they were rewarded for their productive characteristics at the same rate as everyone else. The difference between what white male workers do make and what they would make if they were treated like women and minorities (holding the total wage bill constant) can be interpreted as an outer-bound estimate of gains from job-competition effects. Making these calculations using 2007 American Community Survey (ACS) data for the metropolitan area of Milwaukee, Wisconsin, it is estimated that white males receive a wage premium of $2 per hour. That is well under the overall difference of $6.02 per hour between white males and all other employees (i.e., women and minorities), with the remainder explained by differences in productivity. Nonetheless, the discriminatory differential adds up to a gain of $4,018 per year for each white man, or $1.48 billion per year for all white men in the area.

If instead it is capitalists who benefit from discrimination due to class-struggle effects, then the issue is not the gains of white male workers, but rather the losses of female and minority workers. This loss can be estimated by comparing the earnings that women and minorities do make with the amount that they would make if they were rewarded at the same rate as white males. In this case, women and minorities are estimated to have lost $3.69 per hour or just under $6,300 each per year, with capitalists pocketing an extra $3.3 billion per year in profits due to discrimination.

Fast forward to the 2011 ACS data for metropolitan Milwaukee, after the Great Recession. Total employment among white men had shrunk by 17%, while employment shrank by only 5.5% for women and minorities. Even though things worsened for white men in terms of employment, discriminatory differentials actually rose. In the job-competition case, the hourly gain for white males increased to an estimated $2.22, or $4,412 per year. In the class-struggle case, women and minorities lost $4.13 per hour or $7,000 per year (an additional $700 each!), with $3.5 billion per year in capitalist profits flowing from discrimination.

*Figures here control for years of schooling, high school or college diploma, years of experience, part-time employment, number of dependents, marital status, citizenship, language skills, school enrollment, public sector employment, military veteran status, location of job and housing, as well as occupation and industry.

Sources: Robert Drago, "The Effects of Job and Housing Location on Race/Gender Wage Differentials in Milwaukee," mimeo, University of Wisconsin-Milwaukee, March 1994; Data: Steven Ruggles, J. Trent Alexander, Katie Genadek, Ronald Goeken, Matthew B. Schroeder, and Matthew Sobek. Integrated Public Use Microdata Series: Version 5.0 [Machine-readable database]. Minneapolis: University of Minnesota, 2010.

In reality, both class struggle and job competition effects can occur simultaneously. This complicates the distributional effects of discrimination. White workers may gain from job competition effects and lose from class struggle effects, while the opposite may be the case for capitalists (Box 8.2). The net results may not be apparent to either workers or capitalists. For this reason, it is unlikely that discriminatory behavior is based solely on incentives in any simple or direct fashion.

Organizational Adaptation: Don't Rock the Boat

Just as exploitation is only one form of oppression, monetary incentives are only part of the political economy explanation for discrimination. We now turn to a second component of institutional discrimination: how practices inside the firm mirror practices external to the firm. In other words, we need to look at how discrimination gets "integrated" into the firm.

The basic logic here is if you want to "get along," you "go along." Firms do this by adapting to whatever divisions—by race, gender, sexual orientation, age, etc.—already exist in a given society. Organizational adaptation refers to the tendency of firms to adopt social customs and practices from outside of the firm or to transport practices from other sites into the firm.

Organizational adaptation: The tendency of firms to adopt the social conventions prevalent in society

The transportation of practices may sound abstract, but the logic is simple: people do not leave the rest of their lives at the factory gate or the office door when they go to work, so the attitudes and customs that reign outside the firm are brought inside regardless of the firm's wishes. Somewhat differently, the firm has good reasons to avoid offending the government, their suppliers, their neighbors, and their customers. If these groups expect to see certain social relations in the firms, the firm will tend to adapt to their expectations.

To understand organizational adaptation in a practical sense, we have to look at oppressive relations outside of the firm and how these are brought inside. For example, if a husband benefits from the sexual division of labor in the home but the family needs a dual income, the husband will have an interest in the wife obtaining a job that pays less than his. If she earns as much or more than he does, then her dependence—and his control—will be reduced. The husband then may generalize his need for his wife to earn less than he does into a belief that *all* women should earn less than men, and then act on that belief in his role as an employer or employee.

The process of organizational adaptation may also express domination pure and simple, as when a male manager expects his female secretary to get coffee and wait on him in other ways—because this is how he expects women to act in general. Similarly, having blacks and Latinos do all the clean-up work at the firm—as home health aides, orderlies, janitors, cafeteria workers, or dishwashers—serves to demonstrate and reinforce the subordinate stereotypes of people of color.

In addition, organizational adaptation may show signs of exclusionary practices outside the firm. As Rosabeth Moss Kanter shows, the division of labor in the home, which typically excludes women from authority and decision-making power concerning major issues (e.g., where the family lives, where they vacation, the cars and homes they purchase, etc.), is mimicked inside the firm. This process will result in occupational segregation where the jobs with power and authority are defined as "male." Similarly, occupational segregation may reduce the opportunities for black workers and managers, as their exclusion from white communities is mirrored inside white-majority firms.

Organizational adaptation implies that firms that attempt to buck social trends will find such actions costly. If a major corporation finds that the most qualified candidate for Chief Executive Officer is a black woman, it may avoid appointing her because of potential repercussions. Perhaps the business press would make a big deal of this and accuse the firm of engaging in "reverse discrimination" at the expense of shareholders. The board of directors might wonder how she will fare, and if she will be taken seriously, in a big meeting with bankers trying to arrange corporate financing. They might be concerned about how other senior managers will respond to her when they are used to giving orders to, rather than taking them from, a black woman. And, they might ask, how will she do, and where will her sympathies lie, if she winds up in a smoke-filled room with a bunch of male union leaders? Organizational adaptation means that the firm is much less likely to take such a chance, and qualifications are not the issue.

Psychologist Jan Yoder documented the effects of organizational adaptation in her research on "tokens." These are women (or men) who are introduced into a job and work setting where women (or men) were historically rare. Yoder argues that if men dominate women throughout society, then those relations of oppression will be mirrored inside the firm, regardless of whether there are many or few women in a particular type of job. Supporting this argument, Yoder finds that while token women in male-dominated professions such as firefighting and the military typically are isolated, receive little support, and often are harassed, these adverse effects stem mainly from women entering men's jobs. Yet when men enter a female occupation or workplace as tokens, Yoder found that they experience few of the adverse effects that women experience when entering a male occupation. The domination of men over women in the home is transported into the workplace even when men are in the minority.

Ultimately, organizational adaptation implies that jobs and wages are socially determined. What matters is not just the productivity of an individual or a job, nor just any immediate economic gains from discrimination. What goes on outside the firm is just as important to understanding both wages and discrimination. For example, in a comparable worth case during the mid-1970s, the judges agreed that according to objective standards, it was difficult to justify paying tree trimmers more than registered nurses. Nonetheless, the judges ruled against pay equity in this case, because they saw it as "pregnant with the possibility of disrupting the entire economic system of the United States."[6] While it is conceivable that the judges simply were trying to protect male wages, the fear expressed here reflects the logic of organizational adaptation: in other words "don't rock the boat."

Gender and race divisions across jobs used to be almost universal. Over time, however, change has occurred. Social conventions have weakened, and it has become more likely to see female administrators or managers, as well as male nurses and clerical workers. Minorities also are more likely to be managers, administrators, and professionals of various types. The process of organizational adaptation can respond to changes in the external environment, as the occupational mobility of women and minorities after the Civil Rights Act of 1964 attests.

Nonetheless, once a firm establishes a division of labor, it tends to become entrenched and difficult to change. According to sociologist James Baron, "The evidence suggests that social forces and discriminatory cultural beliefs prevalent when a job or organization is founded condition the way that positions are defined, priced and staffed, becoming institutionalized within the formal structure and informal traditions of the enterprise."[7] Jobs become socially identified as male or female, white or black, and although change is possible, it usually is slow, costly, and difficult. New forms of segregation may emerge. For example, new job titles may be created for white men to shield them from integration with women and minorities who hold similar qualifications. Women and minorities may be less likely to wield supervisory authority than white men despite being qualified to do so. Organizational structure thus maintains the hierarchy of race and gender even as it responds to external political pressures for change.

Obviously, it is possible for organizational adaptation to operate in reverse, with changes inside the firm causing changes in the home and community. For example, economists William Darity Jr. and Samuel Myers argue that, for a variety of reasons, corporations no longer need the labor of black men—and particularly young black men. The availability of low-wage women, whether black or white, as well as of low-wage production in other countries, has meant that black men largely are "unwanted" by the firm. Darity and Myers believe that society at large is adapting to this shift by further excluding black men, building prisons, reintroducing capital punishment in numerous states, and permitting—and even facilitating—often deadly violence among young black men.

THE DYNAMICS OF DISCRIMINATION

If people with power have an interest in discrimination and firms adapt to oppressive relations elsewhere in society, we would expect the capitalist firm to continue discriminating in the face of changing conditions and challenges to discrimination. The firm may integrate its managerial structure if necessary but, in the process, shuffle female and minority managers off to human resources and public relations—areas with small budgets and little real decision-making power. Workgroups may be integrated on the shop floor, but a new division of labor may emerge that maintains the subordination of women and minorities. And, one way or another, firms will strive to keep the wages, benefits, and promotional opportunities of all their workers— especially their female and minority workers—as minimal as possible.

This means that discrimination tends to be dynamic: it can change in response to political and economic pressures, yet tends to do so in ways that are self-perpetuating. Any theory of discrimination must be able to explain its variations in intensity and form. Political economists believe that, unlike the neoclassical approach, their theory is able to do exactly that.

The dynamics of discrimination are both short-run and long-run. The short-run refers to fluctuations in discrimination over the business cycle; the long-run refers to the response of discrimination to changes in its broad social and political context. In both cases, we use the political economy approach which shows that within any historical context, conflicts, and collective actions that are taken in response to those conflicts, bring about change, which those in power will attempt to shape in their favor.

Discrimination in the Short Run

Political economists acknowledge that firms face costs from discrimination that can arise from either market pressures or the government. A refusal to hire qualified blacks and women can result in higher search costs, higher wage costs in the effort to find qualified white males, or both. It can create inefficiencies in the use of human resources. It also can result in government sanctions if the firm is subject to antidiscrimination laws. This part of the argument is similar to that made by neoclassical economists; however, the political economy model goes one step further by noting that it also may be costly to eliminate discrimination. If it is costly to both continue and cease discriminating, then the firm's behavior cannot be predicted beforehand. Instead, it will depend on the concrete circumstances that make one alternative less costly (or, equivalently, more beneficial) than the other.

From the discussion in the preceding sections, we can identify four reasons why ending or reducing discrimination can be costly:[8]

1. A decline in discrimination can disrupt traditional patterns of association and authority. In other words, it can undermine organizational adaptation. Realigning social patterns is a risky and time-consuming proposition that may threaten the firm's internal and external stability. Placing minorities and women on a par with white males can raise costs, because it can potentially undermine the notions of entitlement on which white male morale and productivity depend.

2. Ending the practice of discrimination can raise wage costs and reduce managerial control because of class struggle effects and the reduction of hegemony.

3. Reducing discrimination can increase training costs—a crucial component of labor costs and productivity—if white male workers refuse to train or work cooperatively with their female and minority coworkers.

4. A decline in discrimination can reduce team efficiency by reducing social homogeneity. Much work in the modern workplace or firm takes place in groups where output depends on the ability of members to work in a cooperative fashion. Trust, communication, and work-sharing are easier to achieve within groups that are composed of socially similar people. It may be irrational for the cost-minimizing firm to introduce women and minorities into previously all-white-male working environments if the result is to impair the group process and reduce team productivity.

Discriminatory practices therefore can be costly and risky to change because of the impact on employers, white male employees, and organizational structure. If it also is the case that discrimination increases costs, then the firm faces a set of contradictory pressures. The direction that it is prone to take in the face of this contradiction is determined, in the short run, by the strength of the economy (i.e., the business cycle).

For example, imagine that the economy is moving into a recession. As unemployment rises, more white male workers become available to fill vacancies. As a result, it is easier to find qualified white male applicants at the going wage if the firm chooses to discriminate against female and minority applicants. The costs of discrimination thereby fall.

At the same time, the costs of ceasing to discriminate rise. In weak labor markets, workers place a premium on job security. The ability to protect one's job and to maintain some influence over the hiring process becomes increasingly important to white male workers as their occupational alternatives diminish. The significance of informal job distribution channels (i.e., inside information) grows as the availability of jobs declines. White male workers therefore face increasing incentives to discriminate as unemployment rises. Management may be willing to accommodate them because the costs of continuing discrimination have declined. Management has an incentive to do so because wage growth will be dampened as a result of class struggle effects.[9] Management is able to meet short-term goals (e.g., stability during a downturn) as well as long-term goals (e.g., hegemonic control) by allowing the interests of white male workers to supersede those of other workers.

In short, in bad economic times, the costs of continuing to discriminate will fall while the costs of ceasing to discriminate will rise. This means that the incentives to discriminate will increase in a recession and, conversely, decrease in an expansion. High levels of unemployment are bad for all workers—but far worse for blacks.[10] The political economy model of discrimination therefore predicts that the intensity of employment discrimination should rise during bad times and fall during good times.

The Long-Run Dynamics of Discrimination

The ups and downs of the economy in general and the labor market in particular help to shape patterns of institutional discrimination, but discrimination is also influenced by other contextual factors. Laws, customs, and traditions all change, particularly as people struggle collectively to reduce various forms of oppression in the firm, home, and community. These struggles can raise the costs of discrimination and alter the process of organizational adaptation with the result that discrimination enters a long-run period of decline. Many scholars—including some political economists[11]—have argued that economic and political forces worked against discrimination beginning with the Civil Rights movement, but eventually switched course in the wake of the "Reagan Revolution" of the 1980s.

Once again we simply admit that opposing forces exist. This contradiction gives us hope that the forces working against discrimination will cumulatively and progressively force it to decline over time, but it also means that the forces working to perpetuate discrimination can set in motion a chain of events that are very difficult to stop.

The initial focus of this section is on the latter set of dynamics. We look at positive feedback mechanisms that can sustain discrimination even in the face of pressures to eradicate it before turning to more complex forces. These initial mechanisms can be divided into four types: perception, socialization, choice, and market interactions.

In his famous 1972 study of race relations, *An American Dilemma*, Gunnar Myrdal argued that white perceptions of blacks are reinforced by black life conditions.[12] Black poverty, and the problems that both follow from and surround it, reinforces negative white perceptions, which in turn reinforce discrimination by whites against blacks and, therefore, perpetuate black poverty. In other words, perceptions make discrimination self-reinforcing, so prejudice becomes a self-fulfilling prophecy. For example, white employers may believe that blacks are more likely to be criminals, so they are less likely to hire blacks, and then blacks become more likely to commit crimes as they have no other means of supporting themselves.

Perceptual feedback: Events due to discrimination that reinforce discriminatory stereotypes.

Perceptual feedback can be compared to the neoclassical model of statistical discrimination. In that model, individuals get treated based on their group's characteristics (as we saw in Chapter 5). That type of discrimination is not self-sustaining, however, because competition should push employers to use tests and other means of learning about individuals to make the best use of their human resources. In other words, the statistical discrimination model predicts that discrimination should not persist because of the convergence of expectations with reality (Darity, 1989). Feedback from perceptions, in contrast, leads to a convergence of reality with expectations. Discrimination creates conditions that reinforce bigotry and, therefore, create more discrimination.

As an example of the feedback created by perceptions, assume for a moment that you are a young black man living in New York City. Projections for the city in late 2012 do not address your situation specifically, but we know that men and women are about equally likely to be unemployed (9.6% to 9.7%), blacks are far more likely to be unemployed than whites (14.4% to 6.9%), and people 18-24 years old are far more likely to be unemployed than those 25-44 (17.0% to about 10%).[13] Those figures do not account for the possibility that you have simply given up the hope of finding a job—factoring that in could double your odds of being unemployed. Furthermore, nationally, one-quarter of black males between the ages of 20 and 29 are either in prison, on probation, or on parole. If you are in jail you do not get counted as unemployed, and the odds of getting a job while on parole or probation are bleak. So, overall, your "real" odds of being unemployed are probably well over 50%. If you happen to conceive a child with a woman, you will therefore have little to contribute financially to a family, so unless you are really good at cooking, doing laundry, and childcare, the mom will have few material reasons to keep you around. And now you can be stereotyped as a deadbeat dad. You also have a "cool pose," as described by Richard Majors in his 1992 book *Cool Pose: The Dilemmas of Black Manhood in America*, to hide your anger and appear calm and ready for anything. But that mask, while allowing you to function, may get you stereotyped as dangerous, making it even harder to get a job.[14]

Socialization is another source of feedback. Discrimination may change the conditions in which children develop into adults, and in doing so perpetuate itself. For example, residential segregation isolates many blacks in the inner cities where they can grow up with few or no interactions with whites or people from outside the inner city.[15] As a result, their cultural milieu is different from the mainstream—their speech patterns, appearance, and daily habits may make them stand out and appear to be inappropriate for mainstream work settings. Interviews with over 300 managers in four large cities conducted by economists Chris Tilly and Phillip Moss confirm this. They found employers' perceptions of skills and desirability of hiring from certain neighborhoods literally colored their decisions. In particular, managers told Tilly and Moss that the lack of "soft skills" (such as speech, appearance, and ways of interacting socially) affected their perceptions of inner-city black workers, and they feared how they might interact with customers. It is not surprising then that young black men have problems both finding and holding jobs, and are therefore more likely to stay trapped in the inner city.

Socialization effects: The training of members of counterpart groups to behave in ways that perpetuate discrimination.

Economists Mary Corcoran and Paul Courant argue that labor market discrimination against women discourages parents from raising girls to specialize in wage work. When girls grow into women, their standard of living will depend more on their husband's job than on their own, in part because discrimination lowers female wages relative to male wages. Consequently, parents will raise girls to specialize more in finding a suitable husband than in finding a suitable job. As a result, women will exhibit different work behaviors than men (e.g., higher turnover rates), and employers will be encouraged to maintain occupational segregation.

The third avenue by which feedback occurs is through choice. Political economists are especially interested in the ways in which people respond to the availability—or unavailability—of opportunities. Consider the argument made earlier that capitalists, whites, and males may have economic incentives to discriminate. Those who are victimized by discrimination in turn experience incentives to behave differently than those who do not. For example, if job discrimination reduces the payoff from acquiring education, then blacks and women may choose to get less education (or a different type of education) than white men. Are their lower incomes then a result of their educational choices or of job discrimination?

Choice effects: Rational behavior in the face of oppression and desperation that supports discrimination because it is either illegal or contrary to social norms.

In a related vein, economist Elaine McCrate argues that black teenagers are more likely than white teenagers to get pregnant, because future job opportunities (before pregnancy) are more limited. Consequently, the monetary losses from bearing and raising children during the teenage years are lower for blacks than for whites. Black teenage girls therefore may make the "rational" decision that getting pregnant is not such a disaster after all—but by doing so, reinforce their lack of opportunity. These are examples of the ways in which people make choices in response to circumstances and, in doing so, reinforce those circumstances. Again, inequality becomes self-perpetuating.

For many members of groups experiencing discrimination, the ultimate "choice" question is whether to seek community with other group members or instead to strike out and seek acceptance as an individual in our society. Economist Patrick Mason has addressed this question, and notes that in the 2000 Census, when individuals were allowed to identify with multiple race/ethnicity categories, over 95% of African-American respondents self-identified as "black" alone, while less than 5% self-identified as being black in tandem with other categories (including "white"). Why do so few African-Americans not seek to "pass" as at least partially white? His answer is that the benefits of community support, whether from church, family, and friends, outweigh the benefits of attempting to pass, even if passing might help to raise one's income somewhat.[16]

Finally, feedback can occur as a result of interactions between the job market and other markets, especially the housing market. For example, residential segregation may reduce job prospects for blacks if they are physically or socially isolated from vacancies. If jobs move from the cities to the suburbs and blacks are locked into the inner cities as a result of housing discrimination, then they will be in an unequal position compared with whites in the competition for jobs. Or, black workers may lack access to information about job openings, or job vacancies may be traditionally filled by the recommendations of existing employees. In situations such as these, blacks and whites may find themselves on an unequal footing in the labor market because of discrimination elsewhere in society.

Institutional interaction effects: Privilege creating more privilege due to linkages across systems of exploitation, exclusion, and domination.

Two studies provide telling evidence about the impact of segregation on racial gaps in education and employment. Douglas Massey and Nancy Denton's 1993 book *American Apartheid: Segregation and the Making of the Underclass* analyzes the extent, causes, and consequences of ghettoization and housing discrimination. They show that segregation largely results from discrimination by banks, realtors, the government, and the white population as a whole. Residential location largely determines access to jobs and public resources such as schooling and transportation. Therefore, if residential choices are restricted by discrimination, inequality will be reinforced in other arenas. Here is one example:

> For blacks … high incomes do not buy entree to residential circumstances that can serve as springboards for future socioeconomic mobility; in particular, blacks are unable to achieve a school environment conducive to later academic success. In Philadelphia, children from an affluent black family are likely to attend a public school where the percentage of low-achieving students is three times greater than the percentage in schools attended by affluent white children. Small wonder, then, that controlling for income in no way erases the large racial gap in SAT scores. Because of segregation, the same income buys black and white families educational environments that are of vastly different quality.[17]

A similar argument is made by Gary Orfield and Carole Ashkinaze in *The Closing Door: Conservative Policy and Black Opportunity*. They show that strong economic growth and local black political leadership were unable to reduce racial inequality or black poverty over the 1980s in Atlanta. Job growth primarily occurred in white suburbs. As a result of housing segregation, economic opportunity bypassed blacks who were trapped in the inner city. The high schools were unable to provide equal educational opportunity in the context of the stratification of their student populations, so black access to colleges declined. The result was a vicious circle that sustained racial inequality despite the presence of political and economic circumstances that many conservatives (and liberals) believe are sufficient to create equal opportunity.[18]

Perception, socialization, choice, and institutional interactions all help us to understand how difficult it may be to escape traditional biases and stereotypes (Box 8.3).

Good intentions may not be enough to create equal opportunity. For this reason, when political economists advocate activist government policies to reduce discrimination or alleviate its effects, they consider the ways in which such policies can improve conditions yet also sustain the existing power relations—and discrimination—in practice.

Finally, there are at least two long-run dynamics that have complex effects on discrimination. These forces include globalization and communications technologies.

The creation of a truly world economy is a fairly recent event. In 1970, exports and other income from foreign sources accounted for only 6.3% of total U.S. economic production, a figure that rose to 11.7% by 1980, 11.5% in 1990, 13.4% in 2000, and climbed to 17.5% in 2012.[19] Capitalists who pursued foreign trade were often seeking low wages overseas, including those available from sweatshops, These efforts were tied to class struggle effects playing on discriminatory attitudes in the United States, with capitalists reducing wages here by appealing

---

BOX 8.3
WANT TO BE A MANAGER?

In modern America, women (like minorities) are heavily stereotyped. Studies have shown that both men and women expect women to be "easily influenced, submissive, sneaky, tactful, very aware of others' feelings, passive, lacking in self-confidence, dependent, unlikely to act as a leader, unaggressive, and uncomfortable about being aggressive." These behaviors might be fine for baking cookies and raising children, but they won't help you get ahead as, for example, a manager for a major corporation. The males in charge might rationally view such a person as having poor management skills.

What's a woman to do? You could try acting "more like men," who are stereotyped as "assertive, defends own beliefs, independent, strong personality, forceful, has leadership abilities, willing to take risks, self-sufficient, and willing to take a stand." With the help of willing consultants and management trainers, many women have tried to do exactly this through "assertiveness training."

There is, however, a problem with this approach. Discrimination against women is dynamic enough to generate a new stereotype: the "aggressive woman." Indeed, studies show that women who do act assertively are consistently evaluated less positively than men for the same behavior.

The core of the problem—patriarchy—remains untouched in either case. Is there reason to think that abandoning patriarchy would improve the workplace, that men should behave more like women? Yes, because studies also suggest that if we wish communication to exist in the firm that results in positive consequences for all parties, women are superior to men. Women do score higher on tests of verbal ability.

Maybe women aren't the problem after all.

Source: Amy Herstein Gervasio and Mary Crawford, "Social Evaluations of Assertiveness," *Psychology of Women Quarterly*, Vol. 13, March 1989, pp. 1-25.

to nationalist (and racist) sentiments. These efforts were symbolized in recent years by former CNN news analyst Lou Dobbs, who regularly criticized Hispanic immigrants as stealing jobs from (presumably white) Americans.

Economist Rhonda Williams argues that progressives should use at least two strategies in response to these class struggle effects weakening the power of workers in the United States. First, she believes the United States needs an explicit conversation and negotiation on the legacy and continuation of racism. But she also believes that we need to work *within* our communities to organize and help to advance economic development. This argument is complex, but it makes sense of a simple fact—no matter how much globalization occurs, we each still need to live somewhere, and that means we will be part of a neighborhood, and that community will always be important.

But globalization is not all bad. First, to manage a global economy requires a large group that is capable of working across cultures—that understands and can work successfully in diverse environments. As a result, the rewards for overcoming and abandoning discriminatory sentiments are large for managers, professionals, and government officials working across international borders. Universities have increasingly recognized this need, and have introduced diversity initiatives designed to prepare students for participation in the global economy. Second, globalization has also generated protest groups inside of the United States, such as United Students Against Sweatshops, a group that has successfully forced many universities to police and monitor the corporations who produce athletic apparel with their logo on it.[20]

Added to globalization are the world-flattening effects of telecommunications and particularly the internet. These technologies permit capitalists to operate on a world scale, and they have allowed small groups of racists and those associated with religious extremism and violence to organize as well. However, the technology also allows workers, women, and people of color to organize across borders, from the inner city to the suburbs, from urban to rural areas, to gain knowledge of diverse cultures, and to break down the barriers of exploitation, domination and exclusion. For example, in 2000, a shipping firm tried to switch to non-union workers to load and unload cargo in Charleston, South Carolina. The union that represented the workers, International Longshore and Warehouse Local 1422, contacted workers in a small Spanish port who accepted one shipment that had been loaded by the non-union workers. The Spanish workers announced that in the future that they would refuse future deliveries if the shipping firm did not return the work immediately to Local 1422 members. The shipping firm caved, but only the fast communications technology available today permitted this victory to occur.[21]

WHAT TO DO?

The political economy theory of discrimination is both pessimistic and optimistic. On the one hand, it predicts that discrimination can adapt to and survive in a changing environment. On the other hand, it predicts that the individual and collective struggles of women, minorities, and their white male allies can result in meaningful steps toward race and gender justice. The result depends on the strength and success of these struggles.

Capitalism tends to reproduce race and gender hierarchies unless the pressure for reform is great enough to create changes in the policies and behaviors of firms and government. So, as collective struggles wear on, they must result in institutional changes if they are to have long-lasting effects, but what is done can eventually be undone. Movements for progressive change come and go while capitalism remains. For this reason, some political economists, such as Robert Cherry, believe that race and gender justice will never be fully achieved until capitalism is replaced by a different economic system, called socialism.

Socialism is a system in which workers rather than capitalists wield economic and political power. The versions of political economy that are rooted in the work of Karl Marx are sympathetic to this vision. They believe that capitalism is fundamentally based on domination and exploitation. If this is true, then the effort to reform capitalism will never succeed in more than a superficial and a transient fashion. The system itself must be replaced by one in which human needs are more important than profits.

Other political economists are not so sure. They point to the existence of race and gender hierarchies in socialist societies such as China and Cuba. While it is debatable whether these societies should be called "socialist," it is clear that the elimination of capitalism is no guarantee that race and gender justice will be automatically achieved. Further, it is not clear how capitalism can be transformed into socialism, or even what socialism would mean in practice. For these reasons, many political economists now focus more on achieving race and gender justice within capitalism rather than advocating the establishment of socialism.

How can capitalism be reformed to achieve race and gender justice? Justice is not a state that can be achieved once and for all—rather, it is a process that tends to go forward or backward depending on the balance of forces. These forces include the dominant ideology, which in America can be characterized in terms of democracy, individualism, and opportunity. As Gunnar Myrdal noted over a half-century ago, this ideology is incompatible with race (and, by extension, gender) exclusion and discrimination.

We have seen the good that ideology can do with the creation of diversity efforts at many of our colleges and universities. The premise of much of this work is that if students can be integrated in settings where they will come to know and share ideas with individuals who are different, then the students will become more tolerant, more inclusive, and more likely to engage in collective action to help eliminate race and gender inequalities. In this case, the idea is to set into place perpetual feedback mechanisms that work to reduce or eradicate discrimination.

Two careful studies performed at the University of Michigan support these claims. In one study, a diverse group of students who enrolled in a freshman diversity course were matched with similar students who did not take the course. The researchers checked back with the same students four years later and found that students who took the course were more likely to enjoy learning about the experiences of other groups, perceived more common values with other groups, had more positive evaluations of conflict and negotiations, had a greater interest in politics, and reported that they were more likely to work in their communities and to promote racial and ethnic understanding following graduation. Further, most of these differences held even after controlling for initial student attitudes.[22]

Ideology is not powerful enough to singlehandedly create a momentum for justice, however.[23] After all, Jim Crow was ended by a civil rights movement, not just a civil rights ideology.

The process of race and gender justice depends most fundamentally on the balance of power. In this view, race and gender oppression result from the concentration of resources and power among majority males, particularly capitalists. Equity and justice depend on the transfer of power—and the resources on which power depends—toward women and minorities. Political economists thus advocate policies with a view toward their ability to redistribute resources and power in a more equitable and democratic fashion.

Remember, however, that attempts to redistribute resources and power can always be contested. Those with power usually are loathe to give it up. A transfer of power may appear to be unfair or unjust to those whose worldview depends on the power they have traditionally held. As Susan Faludi noted, a backlash frequently follows on efforts to transfer resources and power to women, minorities, or workers. In fact, we can even think of domination-resistance-reforms-backlash-domination as a typical cycle of the distribution and redistribution of power.

Ideology and power came together in the presidential elections of 2008 and 2012, when a broad coalition of the young, women, people of color, and those with higher education elected and reelected the nation's first African-American president. Further, Obama had campaigned in support of many of the issues discussed above, and his first act as president was to sign the Lilly Ledbetter Act, legislation which strengthened the ability of women and people of color to sue employers for pay discrimination. Will there be a backlash? William Darity provides a theory predicting that there will, and that even with an African-American president, discrimination on the basis of race will not only continue, but may become worse. He argues that in many societies, including ours, discrimination in the provision of education and other credentials is often used to keep the less privileged out of good jobs and without wealth. Once some individuals break through these barriers, however, they will be explicitly attacked as incompetent or worse in an effort by those in power to maintain privilege. Importantly, he argues that all of this occurs in a context where those in power deny that discrimination is involved. This is precisely what happened to President Obama, who has been vilified by some whites and the conservative media, including Rush Limbaugh and Glenn Beck, on charges ranging from being a socialist or communist or Nazi, to not being a native-born citizen. None of these individuals will admit to attacking the president due to his race, but in the political economy view, discrimination is the most plausible explanation, as Darity suggests. By this same logic, had Hillary Clinton won the Democratic primary in 2008 and been elected president, she too would have faced attacks, this time due to her gender.

A Work and Family Bill of Rights

Political economists recognize the decline in both individual and institutional discrimination over the last 50 years. The popular TV series "Mad Men," which depicts life in the early 1960s as it revolves around workers in a Madison Avenue advertising firm, is a stark reminder of the way it was—cigarette-smoking white men hold all the managerial and professional positions (except for the one female copy-editor character who is reluctantly promoted to be with the "boys" but is often denigrated for being a woman), white female unmarried secretaries, unhappy suburban white housewives, black male elevator operators, and black female maids. The show's producers, however, remind its viewers that change is coming by background and radio and TV programs that feature speeches by Martin Luther King Jr. But political economists also recognize that despite these changes, women and minorities continue to face structural discrimination and on occasion individual discrimination. Political economists understand these structures to be built into our economic system, and do not think that they will merely go away on their own. Instead, change comes because political actors, through collective action, demand it. There are a host of policies that political economists promote to reduce wage inequality generally and especially for women and minorities. We highlight only one set here.

The Work and Family Bill of Rights outlined in Box 8.4, developed by political economists and advocates, responds to a large number of persistent problems of inequality, poverty, and discrimination that can and do occur across lines of gender, race, ethnicity, age, place of birth, religion, sexual orientation, marital, family, or disability status. On the one hand, those with power benefit from discrimination across each and all of these lines. On the other hand, the solidarity needed to successfully fight discrimination means recognizing that a wide variety of groups—encompassing the vast majority of society—are and should be involved and empowered.

BOX 8.4
THE WORK AND FAMILY BILL OF RIGHTS

Families face a shortfall of time and money for care. A majority of America's children have no one at home full-time to care for them, while others, including the elderly and people with disabilities, increasingly need care. Jobs divide employees into those with high pay, benefits, but long hours and little time for family or leisure, and those with low wages, few benefits, and insufficient flexibility and financial resources to care for their families. We can and should do better. Working families have fundamental rights to financially sustain and to care for themselves and their families. These rights include:

1. The right to annual paid family, medical and personal leave for full- and part-time employees. Minimum standards for leave are:
   a. two weeks of employer-funded paid personal leave for all employees to be taken at the time of their choosing.
   b. seven days of employer-funded sick time for personal or family illness
   c. twelve weeks of paid leave for parents of newborn, adoptive and foster children, and for serious illness of the employee, a child, a parent or other relative, spouse or partner.
   d. sixteen hours of employer-funded leave to be taken in small increments for doctor's appointments, parent-teacher meetings, and other small necessities.
2. The right to negotiated flexibility over work hours and place:
   a. the ability to shift between full-time and reduced hours as family and personal circumstances change.
   b. equal pay rates and at least pro-rated benefits for reduced hours employees.
   c. no mandatory overtime.
   d. flexible schedules and place of work, mutually agreed upon by employees and employers.
3. The right to quality, affordable child and elder care.
4. The right to a minimum wage set at a living wage level and indexed to inflation.
5. The right to adequate health insurance for all.

These rights shall apply to all regardless of gender, race, ethnicity, age, place of birth, religion, sexual orientation, or marital, family or disability status.

From the Take Care Net, www.takecarenet.org/WorkFamilyBOR.aspx.

How Does the Work and Family Bill of Rights Involve and Empower Groups?

Let us take the points in order.

1. The right to paid leave for one's own illness, for personal time (or vacation), for the illness of another family member, the arrival of a new child, and for appointments with doctors, dentists, or for parent-teacher conferences (also known as "small necessities" leave).

Virtually everyone gets sick at some point, and if you are at the bottom end of the labor market, that can mean losing your job. More importantly, being disadvantaged means you are more likely to get sick and need leave: you have a lesser ability to buy high-quality food, have safe housing, a safe job, or health insurance. The health dangers of being oppressed show up in the numbers of workers reporting that they need leave under the Family and Medical Leave Act (FMLA, providing twelve weeks of unpaid leave to about half of all private sector workers): only 16.3% of men but 24.6% of women reported needing a family or medical leave in the last year; only 18.7% of white employees, but 26.9% of black employees needed leave; only 19.7% of employees in families with incomes above $30,000 per year needed leave, while 23.9% of poorer employees did. However, the employees who actually took leave showed a reversal in the expected direction—towards privileged employees. Of those needing leave, 84.2% of whites but only 76.0% of blacks took leave; 84.0% of employees in families with incomes above $30,000 per year who needed it actually took leave while only 81.4% of poorer employees did so.[24] The story for gender is different, with 85.7% of women and only 80.0% of men who needed leave taking it.

As the matrix of oppression leads us to expect, the connections between gender and race and class are important. A recent analysis of leave-taking under the FMLA reveals that, yes, women are more likely to take leave than men—particularly for childbirth and infants—but it is *white* men who are the main culprits: black and Latino men are as likely as women to take leave.[25]

The major beneficiaries of new policies making paid family leave universal are the precise groups that political economists see as disempowered: women, people of color, and the poor.

2. The right to negotiated flexibility over working time and place, with no mandatory overtime.

In the political economy view, this seemingly innocuous component of the Work and Family Bill of Rights turns out to be important because it helps to provide a voice in the workplace to employees who have historically had little say in how the workplace operates. The Working Families Flexibility Act (WFFA), introduced by the late Senator Ted Kennedy and Representative Carolyn Maloney in 2008, would provide this right without employers even needing to prove that they had reasonable grounds for rejecting requests for flexibility.

It is telling that employers are not exactly jumping on the bandwagon for the WFFA. They claim that they already provide flexibility, so the bill is unnecessary,[26] but if this is true, then why would they object? The underlying reason, in the political economy view, is that employers do not want employees to be heard in the workplace, even if there are no penalties for employers who choose not to provide flexibility.

And which employees are not being heard? Economist Lonnie Golden has studied the question of who wants and gets flexible work hours. Women want more flexibility, but get less than men, while nonwhites get less flexibility than white, and employees with a high school diploma or less also get less flexibility. At present, employers are handing out flexibility as special incentives—but mostly to employees who happen to be white, male, and have a college degree.

So would the sky fall if the Working Families Flexibility Act were passed? Economist Arianne Hegewisch and sociologist Janet Gornick looked at 21 nations, including the United States, and found 17 *already* having a right to negotiated flexibility. They found a major upside to legislated flexibility: in the U.K., with one of the most successful laws, around 80% of all requests for flexibility are approved—even though employers are not penalized for rejecting requests. But in that same nation, mothers of young children were around three times as likely as fathers of young children to request flexibility. This is bad news in terms of gender equity—mothers are typically requesting part-time or reduced hours, with the result that they are spending less time at the workplace and more time on housework. Nonetheless, Hegewisch and Gornick found that when flexibility can be requested for purposes other than young children (e.g., for phased retirement or to care for ailing elders), men are just as likely as women to ask for flexibility. As with other facets of the Work and Family Bill of Rights, the importance of inclusion resurfaces.

3. The right to quality, affordable child and elder care.

Many employed parents of young children and employees with aging or ill parents face extreme difficulties in locating and paying for high quality child or elder care. Indeed, studies show that 80% of child care centers and 90% of nursing homes for the elderly are of poor quality—and often dangerous.

Political economists focus not just on the needs of the consumers—parents and young children, and the elderly who need care—but also on the workforce.

Parents who live in poverty are likely to be single mothers and particularly black, single mothers. And while we as a society promote work among poor, single mothers through government programs that provide cash assistance like the block grant Temporary Assistance to Needy Families, childcare remains of low quality and expensive. A program in Milwaukee, Wisconsin called "New Hope" tried to counter these poor conditions and offered poor single mothers income supplements, low-cost health insurance, and subsidies for childcare. A full eight years later, the children who had been supported were doing better on a variety of levels—they were less likely to have repeated a grade in school, received higher grades in school, and were less likely to need special education.[27] As economist Nancy Folbre argues in *The Invisible Heart*, we should view our children as an investment in the future of our society, which is precisely what the New Hope project did.

A major component of this investment view of political economists involves valuing those who provide care, whether paid or unpaid. At present we do not. The childcare industry has the highest concentration of workers earning poverty-level wages—according to economist Mary Tuominen, less than one-third of childcare centers provide health insurance to their employees and 96% of childcare workers are women. And while women of color represent only 13% of all employees nationwide, they account for one-third of childcare workers. According to a recent study by the Paraprofessional Healthcare Institute, those who provide direct care for the elderly (for example nursing assistants and aides, home health aides, and personal aides) do not fare any better. Over half of this workforce is minority and 88% are female. Just over one-quarter (27%) are uninsured by employers or through Medicaid (the government-sponsored health insurance program for low-income people and families). With median annual wages of $17,000 in 2007, it is not surprising that 15% of these direct care workers are in poverty.

The state of childcare and eldercare lays bare the intersection of race, gender and class in our society. Women, and disproportionately women of color, care for our children and our elders, yet they often live in poverty as a result. By improving the conditions of childcare and eldercare workers, a goal of the National Domestic Workers Alliance in recent years, we would not only help some of the most disempowered workers in the nation but also improve our economy in the future and honor our past.

Childcare and eldercare also highlights some ways in which the Work and Family Bill of Rights fits these issues together. If childcare and eldercare workers received a living wage and had health insurance (see below), these would go a long ways towards improving conditions in the childcare, eldercare, and healthcare industries, not to mention improving our own lives and that of our children, our elders, and others who need medical care. We can and, in the political economy view, should do better.

4. The right to a minimum wage set to a living wage level and indexed to inflation.

While neoclassical economics views raising the minimum wage to a living wage level as a "job killer," the evidence demonstrates otherwise. Economist Lianna Fox has shown that increases in the minimum wage result in minimal or no job losses. Given that most adults living in poverty are already employed, a living wage would help many of the poorest Americans. According to the U.S. Department of Labor, in 2008 (just before the minimum wage was increased from $6.55/hour to $7.25), 3% of all hourly workers earned the minimum wage or less. Furthermore, those working for the minimum wage tend to be women and people of color. But minimum wages, including the president's proposed $9 per hour figure, are not a living wage. Working a full-time job all year at the current minimum wage translates to $14,500 or $1,208 a month. In many areas of the country that is not enough to pay for housing, food and transportation for a single person, let alone a family. Raising the minimum wage to a living wage level would cut across lines of race, gender, and class to give those with the least power in our society a greater share of the economic pie.

5.   The right to adequate health insurance for all.

In the political economy view, our current health care system is rigged. Health insurance companies spend only around 80% of their revenues on actual health care (they call the 80% a "medical loss"), pocketing the rest in profits and executive salaries in the tens of millions of dollars, while 47 million Americans have no health insurance, and an estimated 90 million Americans went without health insurance for some portion of either 2007 or 2008.[28] By the time "Obamacare" became law in 2010, the health-insurance industry had been successful in staving off a single-payer system, which we could have had by extending Medicare coverage to all Americans. The American public would have benefitted by getting rid of the middle-man in health insurance—since insurance companies are a costly and unnecessary expense, and employers in other industries could have made their products more competitive both at home and abroad by reducing health care costs.

Who would benefit from a single-payer system? The answer is a little surprising. The U.S. Centers for Disease Control found that even among married men, the group under age 65 most likely to have insurance, the rate of private health insurance coverage declined from 85% in 1984, to just 78% in 2006. Health coverage rates were less than 60% for single women, 51% for African Americans, 40% for Hispanics, and under 33% for Americans living at less than 150% of the poverty line.[29] Obamacare will extent coverage due to an individual mandate, but it will not be universal.

Even whites and married men have found private health insurance less often available from their employers in recent decades, so many in these groups have an interest in a single-payer system. Nonetheless, the main beneficiaries would be single women (particularly mothers), people of color, and the poor. Again, this part of the Work and Family Bill of Rights would help to level the economic playing field across lines of race, gender and class.

Making Change

Although the Work and Family Bill of Rights has not been adopted nationally, parts of it have been implemented either locally or on a statewide basis. Massachusetts has near-universal health insurance. Georgia provides pre-kindergarten programs for all four-year-olds. The cities of Milwaukee, San Francisco and Washington, DC all require employers to provide paid sick days, and New Jersey and California both have paid family leave, providing some wage replacement for employees using the Family and Medical Leave Act.

How did they do it? The Labor Project for Working Families at the University of California at Berkeley studied the creation of paid family leave in California, which was signed into law on September 23, 2002. The process began in 1999, with the formation of a statewide Work and Family Coalition, involving the Labor Project, the California Labor Federation (part of the

AFL-CIO), and the Legal Aid Society. The groups found ways to educate individuals or groups about the possible law, made strong connections with the Democratic legislators who eventually passed the law, developed media materials and relevant research on the costs and benefits of the legislation, and drew in even more groups. By the time the bill landed on the governor's desk, it was backed by a steady stream of post-cards, calls, and emails from over 700 organizations and and thousands of individuals. The governor, facing a close election, signed the bill.

In the political economy view, there are many routes to progressive change in addition to or beyond legislation around the Work and Family Bill of Rights. For example, starting in the 1990s, many employees who were part of the Lesbian, Gay, Bisexual and Transgender (LGBT) community began forming support groups within their corporations, using email and other forms of social networking to connect, share information, and advocate for equal rights within their corporations. The success has been phenomenal. The Human Rights Campaign has rated major corporations since 2002, giving a 100% rating to firms that not only provide partner benefits (e.g., health insurance and pensions) to gay and lesbian couples, but also support transgender employees, and provide anti-discrimination training on LGBT issues. As of 2002, only thirteen corporations received a 100% rating, but by 2013, 252 businesses had received the rating. The publicity around the rating system serves as a reward for corporations such as General Motors, Citigroup, AT&T, and IBM (all firms that have a 100% rating), but it is the work of the LGBT community *within* these firms that typically drove change.

Further, there are examples of progressive legislation beyond the Work and Family Bill of Rights. In 2009, the Human Rights Campaign was part of a large coalition that helped pass the Hate Crimes Prevention Act, signed into law by President Obama in October of that year. The law gives the U.S. Justice Department the power to investigate and prosecute hate crimes where the victim was selected because of the sexual orientation or gender identity. The law is inclusive because it also covers hate crimes on the basis of race, color, religion, national origin, gender and disability.

LGBT rights have expanded in other ways, and quickly, in recent years: as of 2013, same-sex marriage was legal in thirteen states and the District of Columbia, the military had ended its discriminatory policy of "Don't Ask, Don't Tell" with regard to gay and lesbian members, and this shift towards equality seems likely to continue.

Other groups have targeted specific forms of oppression in various ways and with varying degrees of success. Some examples include the United Students Against Sweatshops, Moveon. org, Momsrising.org, CommonCause.org, 9to5, the American Civil Liberties Union, the NAACP, Take Back Your Time, the American Association of People with Disabilities, the Stonewall Democrats, the Log Cabin Republicans, Greenpeace, and Economists for Peace and Security. Each of these groups fights for equality and justice and, in the political economy view, offers great hope for a better future.

Finally, even if you do not become involved in political movements, how you live your personal life is also important according to political economists. When you choose your friends, lovers, where you live, and where you work, you are also choosing whether to be inclusive of those who differ from you according to income, education, race, gender, ethnicity, sexual orientation, and religion. When whites, men, or heterosexuals choose exclusion, whether by having friends who look and act like themselves, or by living in a segregated community or working in segregated workplaces, they are reinforcing existing inequalities. By the same token, reaching across these dividing lines in your personal life can help to break down barriers, to uncover our own hidden biases and discriminatory customs, to humanize those who are different, and to help fight oppression.

CONCLUSIONS

Political economists argue that because it may be profitable, labor market discrimination can be perpetuated by competition. Discrimination not only means lower wages for black and female workers, it also may mean lower wages for white male workers (i.e., class struggle effects). It also is possible for discrimination to benefit white male workers by improving their job security and wages (i.e., job competition effects). In addition, discrimination in the larger society may be transported into the firm as it attempts to stabilize its relations with its external environment (i.e., organizational adaptation). These incentives to discriminate offset the costs of discrimination that are emphasized by neoclassical economists. The balance between these opposing pressures is determined by the strength of the labor market so that discrimination will tend to increase in recessions and fall in expansions. The cyclical changes in discrimination occur in the context of feedback effects that can perpetuate discrimination over the long-run, such as perception, socialization, choice, and market interactions.

Connecting these reasons to discriminate back to the Four Cs of political economy—context, collective behavior, conflict, and change—leads to the conclusion that discrimination can adapt to changes in its environment. On the one hand, groups suffering from discrimination respond by engaging in collective conflict, which often results in change for the better. The Civil Rights Movement, women's movement, and entry of women into the labor market, as well as political changes such as the Equal Pay Act, all have yielded positive results through such struggles. Such struggles are limited, however, both by backlash from those who directly benefit from discrimination and by a historical context in which our day-to-day ways of acting and understanding others tend to perpetuate discrimination.

In the political economy view, the end of discrimination will require collective action to expose unintended acts of discrimination, to make those who benefit from discrimination recognize the high political and ethical costs, to change practices in the home and community that favor discrimination, and to change the rules of the social game. This is a very tall order, but as we saw in the last section, change and resistance to change are ever-present possibilities.

On the policy front, we finished with political economy arguments in support of the Work and Family Bill of Rights, with a discussion of targeted efforts against discrimination, including efforts within the LGBT community, with information regarding a host of groups fighting for progressive social change, and with ways in which our personal decisions influence the future of our society. Any or all of these efforts can help to level the economic playing field across lines of race, gender and class. They could help to bring a voice to those with less power in our society, whether that is due to gender, race, disability, religious intolerance, or sexual orientation. More importantly, they would put American workers and families in a stronger position in relation to employers. By providing a real economic safety net and legal and cultural supports for disempowered Americans, there would be less reason for intolerance and violence.

For political economists, there is a tension between universalistic and identity politics in both the policies we recommend and across groups fighting for progressive change. This is a logical outcome of the political economy view of people: we are all people and share many universal needs (health care and shelter, for example), but we are also members of multiple counterpart groups, such as women, Native Americans, or bisexuals. The purpose of supporting both universal and identity groups and politics is to both celebrate our differences and reduce unequal power relations.

There are those who will say we are dreaming, and that political economists are utopians. Fortunately, we can respond that much of what we seek can either be found in communities in the United States or in other developed nations. It will take work and organization to make our economy more humane, but it can be done.

DISCUSSION QUESTIONS

1. Identify one written or unwritten rule at your school or workplace that functions in a discriminatory fashion. Explain why the rule is discriminatory, and if possible, explain how it came into being and who benefits by it.

2. Discuss any instances of unintended discrimination where once the act was pointed out to whoever those involved (perhaps even to you), the behavior was changed.

3. How could passage of a balanced budget amendment to the U.S. Constitution be discriminatory? Discuss how this interpretation can help to explain who might support or oppose and benefit or lose from such an initiative.

4. In general, do you think that male or white workers benefit from the low wages paid to women and blacks? Explain why or why not, and use your own work experiences to illustrate your opinion.

5. In general, do you think employers often pit whites against blacks or men against women in the workplace? Again, explain why or why not, and use your own work experiences to illustrate your opinion.

6. Can you think of instances in a workplace setting (whether you worked there or not) where people "expected" women or minorities to perform certain tasks that were not expected of males or whites? If so, use the concept of organizational adaptation to explain the phenomenon. Do males or whites benefit in terms of money or power from the practice? Explain.

7. Discuss some ways in which the long-term decline of white male wages has affected their discriminatory attitudes. Do such attitudes benefit or harm employers? Do they influence the collective behavior of white males? Use your own work experiences to provide examples that illustrate your answers.

8. Suppose you decided to help support a national law supporting paid family leave. Where would you start and what would you do?

SUGGESTED READINGS

Armenia, Amy and Naomi Gerstel. 2006. "Family Leaves, the FMLA and Gender Neutrality: The Intersection of Race and Gender." *Social Science Research* 35(4).

Baron, James. 1991. "Organizational Evidence of Ascription in Labor Markets." In *New Approaches to Economic and Social Analyses of Discrimination*. Richard Cornwall and Phanindra Wunnava, eds. New York: Praeger.

Cherry, Robert D. 1989. *Discrimination: Its Economic Impact on Blacks, Women, and Jews*. Lexington, MA: Lexington Books.

Corcoran, Mary and Paul Courant. 1986. "Sex-Role Socialization, Screening by Sex, and Women's Work: A Reformulation of Neoclassical and Structural Models of Wage Discrimination and Job Segregation." Mimeo. Ann Arbor, MI: University of Michigan.

Darity, William A., Jr. 1989. "What's Left of the Economic Theory of Discrimination?" In *The Question of Discrimination: Racial Inequality in the U.S. Labor Market*. Steven Shulman and William A. Darity, Jr., eds. Middletown, CT: Wesleyan University Press.

Darity, William A., Jr. 2001. "The Functionality of Market-Based Discrimination." *International Journal of Social Economics* 28(10/11/12).

Darity, William A., Jr., Patrick L. Mason, and James B. Stewart. 2005. "The Economics of Identity: The Origin and Persistence of Racial Identity Norms." *Journal of Economic Behavior and Organization* 60(3).

Darity, William A., Jr. and Samuel L. Myers, Jr. 1994. *The Black Underclass*. New York: Garland.

Drago, Robert. 2007. *Striking a Balance: Work, Family, Life*. Boston: Dollars & Sense.

Faludi, Susan. 1991. *Backlash: The Undeclared War against American Women*. New York: Crown.

Folbre, Nancy. 2001. *The Invisible Heart: Economics and Family Values*. New York: New Press.

Fox, Liana. 2006. "Minimum Wage Trends." *Briefing Paper* #178. Washington DC: Economic Policy Institute.

Gerstel, Naomi and Katherine McGonagle. 1999. "Job Leaves and the Limits of the Family and Medical Leave Act." *Work and Occupations* 26(4).

Golden, Lonnie. 2001. "Flexible Work Schedules: What Are We Trading Off to Get Them?" *Monthly Labor Review* 124(3).

Hegewisch, Arianne and Janet Gornick. 2008. *Statutory Routes to Workplace Flexibility: A Cross-National Perspective*. Washington DC: Institute for Women's Policy Research.

Human Rights Campaign. 2009. *Corporate Equality Index, 2010*. Washington DC: HRC. Available at: www.hrc.org.

Kanter, Rosabeth Moss. 1977. *Men and Women of the Corporation*. New York: Basic Books.

Labor Project for Working Families. 2003. "Putting Families First: How California Won the Fight for Paid Family Leave." Berkeley CA: Labor Project. Available at www. paidfamilyleave.org.

Lewis, Gregory. 1986. "Race, Sex and Supervisory Authority in Federal White-Collar Employment." *Public Administration Review* 46(1).

Mason, Patrick. 2004. "NEA Presidential Address: Identity, Markets, and Persistent Racial Inequality," *Review of Black Political Economy* 32(1).

Massey, Douglas and Nancy Denton. 1993. *American Apartheid: Segregation and the Making of the Underclass*. Cambridge, MA: Harvard University Press.

McCrate, Elaine. 1987. "Trade, Merger and Employment: Economic Theory on Marriage." *Review of Radical Political Economy* 19(1).

Myrdal, Gunnar. 1972 (first published in 1944). *An American Dilemma: The Negro Problem and Modern Democracy*. New York: Random House.

Nembhard, Jessica Gordon, and Rhonda M. Williams. 1998. "How Race Matters: Global Perspectives on Ethnicity and Economic Inequality." Concept paper and funding proposal, cited in Gary Dymski and Jessica Gordon Nembhard. 2001.

Orfield, Gary and Carole Ashkinaze. 1991. *The Closing Door: Conservative Policy and Black Opportunity*. Chicago: University of Chicago Press.

Paraprofessional Health Institute. 2008. "Direct-Care Workers at a Glance." *Workforce Facts*, retrieved November 2009 at phinational.org/policy/about-the-workforce/at-a-glance/.

Reich, Michael. 1981. Racial *Inequality: A Political-Economic Analysis*. Princeton, NJ: Princeton University Press.

Shulman, Steven. 1984. "Competition and Racial Discrimination: The Employment Effects of Reagan's Labor Market Policies." Review *of Radical Political Economics* 16(4).

Shulman, Steven. 1987. "Discrimination, Human Capital and Black-White Unemployment: Evidence from Cities." *Journal of Human Resources* 22(3).

Shulman, Steven. 1989. "Racism and the Making of the American Working Class." *International Journal of Politics, Culture and Society* 2(3).

Steinberg, Ronnie. 1990. "Social Construction of Skill: Gender, Power, and Comparable Worth." *Work and Occupations* 17(4).

Steinberg, Ronnie. 1995. "Advocacy Research for Feminist Policy Objectives: Experiences with

Comparable Worth." In *Bridging Theory and Practice*. Heidi Gottfried, ed. Urbana, IL: University of Illinois Press.

Tilly, Chris and Philip Moss. 2001. *Stories Employers Tell: Race, Skill and Hiring In America*. New York: Russell Sage Foundation.

Tuominen, Mary. 2002. "Where Teachers Can Make a Livable Wage." In *Child Care and Inequality*. Francesca Cancian, Demie Kurz, Andrew London, Rebecca Reviera and Mary Tuominen, eds. New York: Routledge.

US Department of Labor, Bureau of Labor Statistics. 2009. "Characteristics of Minimum Wage Workers: 2008." Retrieved November 2009 from www.bls.gov/cps/minwage2008.pdf.

Wilson, William. 1980. *The Declining Significance of Race: Blacks and Changing American Institutions*. Chicago: University of Chicago Press.

Yoder, Jan. 1991. "Rethinking Tokenism: Looking Beyond Numbers." *Gender and Society* 5(2).

ENDNOTES

[1] For example, poor whites have often been described as more racist than wealthier whites because of their frustrated need for social status. Over a half-century ago, Gunnar Myrdal (1972:104) commented that "The white upper class person might feel a greater biological distance from the average Negro, but he has not the same need to emphasize the race dogma, since the social distance is so great and secure.… The lower classes of whites seem to be much more careful to keep the race dogma straight…"

[2] From Philip Langdon, A *Better Place to Live: Reshaping the American Suburb*. Amherst MA: University of Massachusetts Press, 1994.

[3] The concept of "false consciousness" is rejected by many political economists who believe that it explains beliefs in terms of ideals rather than reality (Shulman, 1989). Nonetheless, it provides an interesting contrast to the neoclassical view that beliefs are always rational.

[4] More complicated distributional patterns exist as well. For example, white women may benefit from race discrimination, and black men may benefit from gender discrimination. Other groups as a whole may experience discrimination but still thrive economically (e.g., Japanese-Americans and Jewish-Americans). For the sake of simplicity, we focus here solely on white men and capitalists as the potential beneficiaries of discrimination.

[5] In other words, job competition effects can offset class struggle effects if the solidarity that is lost between black and white and between male and female workers is offset by solidarity that is gained among white male workers.

[6] Steinberg, Ronnie. 1995. "Advocacy Research for Feminist Policy Objectives: Experiences with Comparable Worth." In *Bridging Theory and Practice*. Heidi Gottfried, ed. Urbana, IL: University of Illinois Press, 468.

[7] Baron, James. 1991. "Organizational Evidence of Ascription in Labor Markets." In *New Approaches to Economic and Social Analyses of Discrimination*. Richard Cornwall and Phanindra Wunnava, eds. New York: Praeger, 115.

[8] An early version of this argument can be found in Shulman (1984).

[9] This means that discrimination causes white male workers to trade off job security against wage growth. In a recession, they will tend to increase the weight they place on job security, because the difficulty of finding a new job increases.

[10] This model accurately predicts that black unemployment will rise more than white unemployment in recessions (and fall more in expansions). However, unlike blacks, women do not face higher unemployment rates or unemployment changes than their counterpart group. Instead, the male–female wage gap appears to rise in recessions, suggesting that wage discrimination against women (like employment discrimination against blacks) rises when the costs of discrimination fall

(Weinberger, 1993). More research on the relation between wage and employment discrimination—and between race and gender discrimination—is needed to clarify these contrasts.

[11]Perhaps the best-known scholar in this tradition is Wilson (1980).

[12]Gunnar Myrdal was the founder of the political economy view of discrimination. Both he and Gary Becker, the founder of the neoclassical view of discrimination, were winners of the Nobel Prize (see Chapter 1).

[13]Fiscal Policy Institute, *The State of Working New York 2012: Disappointingly Weak Recovery*. New York: FPI, September 2012.

[14] Source: Daniel Goleman, "Black Scientists Study the 'Pose' of the Inner City," *New York Times*, April 21, 1992.

[15]Massey, Douglas and Nancy Denton. 1993. *American Apartheid: Segregation and the Making of the Underclass*. Cambridge, MA: Harvard University Press.

[16]Mason has formalized this logic for racial identity formation in work with William Darity and James Stewart (see Darity, Mason and Stewart, 2005).

[17]Massey, Douglas and Nancy Denton. 1993. *American Apartheid: Segregation and the Making of the Underclass*. Cambridge, MA: Harvard University Press, pg 53

[18]We have just explained why political economists believe that economic growth should reduce the incentives to discriminate. The experience of Atlanta, however, shows that other factors (e.g., segregation) also must be taken into account before predictions can be made about the impact of growth on discrimination and inequality. In other words, context matters.

[19]Bureau of Economic Analysis (BEA), National Income and Product Accounts, Table 1.5. Gross Domestic Product; BEA, International Transactions, Table 1. U.S. International Transactions (bea.gov). Figures calculated by dividing the value of exports plus income receipts from foreign sources by the sum of Gross Domestic Product and income receipts from foreign sources.

[20]See www.studentsagainstsweatshops.org.

[21] Suzan Erem and Paul Durrenberger, *On the Global Waterfront: The Fight to Free the Charleston Five*. New York: Monthly Review Press, 2008.

[22] Patricia Gurin and Biren Nagda, "The Benefits of Diversity in Education for Democratic Citizenship." *Journal of Social Issues*, April 2004, Vol. 60, 17-34.

[23] Phrased more precisely, Myrdal's "American Creed" is neither a necessary nor a sufficient condition for race and gender justice.

[24]See Gerstel, Naomi and Katherine McGonagle. 1999. "Job Leaves and the Limits of the Family and Medical Leave Act." *Work and Occupations* 26(4).

[25]See Armenia, Amy and Naomi Gerstel. 2006. "Family Leaves, the FMLA and Gender Neutrality: The Intersection of Race and Gender." *Social Science Research* 35(4).

[26]For an example of employer opposition see Tim Gould, "'Mandatory Flexibility': Welcome to the Working Families Flexibility Act." Posted on BusinessBrief.com, August 20, 2009.

[27]See Cynthia Miller, Aletha Huston, Gerg Duncan, Vonnie McLoyd and Thomas Weisner, *New Hope for the Working Poor: Effects After Eight Years for Families and Children*. New York: MDRC, July 2008.

[28]Source for 80% figure is PriceWaterhouseCoopers Health Research Institute, "Medical Loss Ratio," accessed November 2, 2009 at www.pwc.com. Source for uninsured figures, National Coalition on Health Care, "Health Insurance Coverage," accessed November 2, 2009 at www.nchc.org.

[29]See U.S. Centers for Disease Control, Health, United States, 2008. Bethesda MD: CDC, 2008. Table 137. Available at www.cdc.gov.

INDEX